A TIME TO SPEAK
Diary of an NHS Whistleblower

Graham Pink

RCN Publishing Company Limited, The Heights,
59-65 Lowlands Road, Harrow-on-the-Hill, Middlesex HA1 3AW

First published 2013

British Library Cataloguing in Publication Data. A catalogue record
for this book is available from the British Library.

Disclaimer
The views expressed in this book are those of the author and not
necessarily those of the Royal College of Nursing or publisher. No part
should be reproduced without permission of the publisher.

ISBN: 978-0-9574308-6-0

Designed and typeset by Sujata Aurora
Printed by Cambrian Printers, Aberystwyth

ABOUT THE AUTHOR

Graham Pink was born in Manchester in 1929, the youngest of five children, and has lived in the area most of his life.

On leaving school in the late 1940s he was required, as were most young men at that time, to do two years' National Service and he found himself in the Sick Berth Branch of the Royal Navy where he began his nurse training. He finished his training at Withington Hospital in Manchester, qualifying as a state registered nurse in October 1951.

Three years working as a registered nurse followed, part of it spent in Toronto, Canada. Then in 1955 Mr Pink started teacher training and became a secondary school master for 24 years, the last ten as Head of English Studies.

After taking early retirement in 1981, Graham Pink returned to nursing, first as a student nurse tutor then as a night duty staff nurse in the regional acute burns and plastic surgery unit of Withington Hospital. In 1987 he became supervising charge nurse (nights) at the Stepping Hill Hospital, Stockport.

ACKNOWLEDGEMENTS

With thanks to Janet Snell, acting deputy editor of
Nursing Standard magazine, for her considerable help and advice
in the editing and publication of this book. I would also like to
acknowledge the support and encouragement I received from the
Royal College of Nursing.

Finally, my heartfelt thanks go to the thousands of people up and
down this land who wrote to me while the case was in the news
and who made the most generous and kind comments on
my stand for decent care. Your moving and overwhelmingly
supportive words sustained me during a most difficult period.

*To every thing is a season, and a time
to every purpose under the heaven:
a time to keep silence,
and a time to speak...*
— Ecclesiastes 3:1

FOREWARD

There are so many lessons to be learned from Graham Pink's story and his observations on how the health system dealt with him when he raised concerns about patient care. His determination and persistence helped to create the momentum for the Public Interest Disclosure Act 1998 and we should all salute his resolve and courage.

Yet, we have been confronted with many significant challenges around patient safety and care quality since Graham first wrote his account. The Francis Inquiry into Mid-Staffordshire NHS Trust, alongside other analyses of service failures, described indefensible harm to patients that has been damaging to the image of nursing and healthcare practice, and has led to suggestions that nurses lack compassion.

We know that when hospitals or community teams don't have enough nurses and allied staff, patients and patient care are put at risk. These incidents remind us of the need for us individually, and collectively, to take specific action to ensure that we are able to provide what Graham describes as 'decent care'.

Speaking up about these issues is critical and raises important questions for us as a profession and for the trade unions representing front line staff. Almost all of what happened at Stafford was avoidable and could have been prevented by staff at all levels in the organisation being enabled to question what they or others were doing and what was causing the quality of care for their patients to fall below acceptable standards.

Speaking up means being comfortable with challenging a colleague who you believe is not doing the best for a patient in a given situation as much as it means challenging a manager who tries to run a ward with insufficient staff.

So much of what goes wrong in health care is witnessed by someone else, and raising these concerns when we see them is the most important way of eliminating them.

It is not easy – as Graham's story demonstrated so starkly. The nursing community needs to overhaul everything we do to make sure that the confidence to raise concerns is second nature for nurses. The RCN has developed 'Raising concerns, raising standards' as a campaign and a process to make it easier for nurses to have the courage and support to report concerns about incidents that they observe in their day-to-day work.

In so doing we will all collectively challenge the suggestion that as nurses we lack compassion, and we will discredit the wholly false perceptions that poor care is the result of wilful neglect and that good care happens by accident. We know that neither is true.

It takes great ward and team leadership to create environments that design in safety for patients, and it takes huge commitment and skill on the part of nurses delivering care day after day to ensure that everything they do is delivered in ways that are perceived as compassionate. Both are underpinned by nurses having the courage to raise concerns when they see them – Graham's testimony illustrates just how important it is to intervene and take responsibility when we see something not working for a patient. The more we all follow his example, the easier it will be to change some of the cultures that made his pursuit of 'decent care' so difficult.

Tom Sandford
Director, RCN England

KEY PLAYERS

Mr Richards	Chairman, Stockport District Health Authority
Mr Milnes	District general manager/chief executive, Stockport District Health Authority
Mr Caldwell	General Manager, Stepping Hill Hospital
Mr Geraghty	Assistant general manager, Stepping Hill Hospital
Miss Fredericks	Chief nursing officer, Stepping Hill Hospital
Miss Carew	Night nurse manager
Miss O'Donnell	Assistant night nurse manager

CONTENTS

INTRODUCTION

'. . . one must not consent to oppression but resist it . . .'
— **Primo Levi**

When I was employed as the senior night duty charge nurse responsible for the care of the elderly wards in a large general NHS hospital some years ago, I became concerned at the inability of staff to properly nurse and protect our highly dependent and vulnerable patients. After being in post for some 16 months, I raised the issue at a meeting with the night nurse manager, pointing out the problems caused when too few nursing staff were on duty to carry out the work. Six months later, with no improvement in nurse cover and deteriorating care provision, I wrote at length to the health authority to officially report the situation and request urgent action.

This developed into a drawn out battle to bring to my superiors' attention the way the patients were being routinely and systematically neglected. Approaches to various officials within the authority and the health service, including MPs, throughout the winter of 1989/90 proved fruitless. Then, in the spring of 1990, the case came to the general public's attention when the *Guardian* newspaper printed extracts from the 50 letters I had by then written to 20 people, from nurse managers and consultants to administrators and politicians.

The publicity led to national interest at a time when the health service was being reorganised and made subject to cutbacks and commercial pressures, rather like it is today. The public interest surrounding my revelations seemed to reflect a deep-seated, countrywide concern, especially among healthcare staff, at what were generally seen as falling standards and a threat to the very existence of the highly regarded NHS.

My case raised a number of ethical and legal dilemmas surrounding such matters as confidentiality, public interest, accountability, freedom of speech, employment rights, truth telling, resource allocation, personal responsibility and an employee's right/duty to speak out when a public service fails to provide a minimum level of care and puts service users at risk. Speaking out has been given the inelegant label of 'whistleblowing'[1] and my personal involvement in the 'Stockport Affair' has prompted me to address this subject in these pages. Whistleblowers are those who make revelations meant to call attention to negligence, abuses or dangers that threaten the public interest. They sound an alarm based on their expertise and inside knowledge. Highlighting such situations in the NHS is far from a new phenomenon, as problems in our psychiatric institutions since the late 1960s illustrate. The Ashworth Hospital Inquiry (1992) found inhuman and degrading treatment and punishment carried out by nurses and an unacceptable standard in much of the patient care. Those very few people who tried to expose what was going on were harassed, victimised and felt obliged to resign, until five non-nursing staff stood up and publicly denounced the neglect and abuse.

Most of this book is taken up with the account of my attempt to gain sufficient staff to provide adequate nursing care on the three wards of the unit for care of the elderly in one hospital. It went no further than this. However, to reflect on some of the wider ethical and legal issues, which these efforts exemplified, including what has become the scandal of gross negligence in some hospitals in recent years, a final, up-to-date chapter has been added. Whereas the spotlight usually focuses on the individual who speaks out,

---

1   I believe one of the best definitions is that used by the Australian Senate Committee on Public Interest Whistleblowing: 'The whistleblower is a concerned citizen, totally, or predominantly motivated by notions of public interest, who initiates of his or her own will, an open disclosure about significant wrongdoing directly perceived in a particular occupational role, to a person or agency capable of investigating the complaint and facilitating the correction of wrongdoing.'

there is a need to understand why the majority of the workforce, those who see the misadministration, danger or negligence day in, day out, but choose to remain silent in the face of distortion or suppression of the truth and injustice to a colleague.

The British Medical Association has spoken of 'a conspiracy of silence' in the NHS where it is clearly a very risky business to open one's mouth about any matter that managers believe will dent the shiny corporate image that they are so keen to promote. With this ethos, how can speaking out be justified? Is not public disclosure an act of betrayal of both one's colleagues and the institution? Does it not place vulnerable patients in jeopardy? Confidentiality is sacrosanct. Thus ran the arguments of managers, civil servants and, until recently, the political decision makers. The contracts of employment of all NHS workers formerly imposed on them strict confidentiality, while the nurse's code of conduct insisted that patient safety and care was paramount. But what does one do when the two become incompatible? I refused to remain silent about the disturbing scenes I was witnessing nightly and indeed was obliged to be party to. I maintain now, as I did then, that it was my duty, in fact my obligation, to bring to local people's attention what was occurring at night to their loved ones.

Over the years there have been attempts to enable staff to speak up if they encounter this sort of poor care. But the events at Stafford Hospital where up to 1,200 patients could have died unnecessarily, demonstrate that the system is still not working. Nurses are too afraid to raise the alarm about very serious lapses in patient care unfolding before their very eyes. As Robert Francis QC said:

> It is now clear that some staff did express concern about the standard of care being provided to patients. The tragedy was that they were ignored and worse still others were discouraged from speaking out.

ONE
SOMETHING WILL HAVE TO BE DONE

'Health care is one of the clearest and most visible expressions of a society's attitude to the value of life. It is moreover one of the most important dimensions of the way in which we, as individuals and as members of society, demonstrate the value that we place on one another's lives and display the respect that we believe we owe to each other' — **John Harris, bioethicist**

We were about two thirds of the way through another hectic night on ward A14. Our nursing auxiliary was on her second break, while nurse Wilson and I were holding the fort, a fort under siege by a ward full of desperately ill and dying elderly patients. During the four-and-a-half hours of meal breaks each night (some 40 per cent of the shift), when only two members of staff were on duty, we tried to station ourselves to be able to keep in view as many beds as possible. At this time, I was on side two with 13 patients while my colleague was out of sight 30 yards away on side one.

In the first bed was 90-year-old Mrs Tomlinson[2]. She had heart failure, kidney failure and was close to death. She had continuous oxygen running, was catheterised and semiconscious. She needed, but was not receiving, two-hourly turns, mouth care and catheter care. She was prescribed diamorphine by injection as required for

---

2   All patient names have been changed

relief of pain in terminal care, but the chances tonight were that such need might well go unnoticed.

Next to her was 82-year-old Mr Hunter, who had come in with a history of chest pain and dehydration. He had developed a chest infection and needed regular suction of the mouth and throat (at least quarter-hourly) to prevent him choking on his coughed-up sputum. He was restless and worn out.

Opposite was 79-year-old Mr Kaminski with a suspected pulmonary embolism, chest pain and who was likely to cough up blood. To help prevent serious heart complications (a thrombosis, for example) he was on a continuous intravenous infusion of heparin, an anticoagulant drug, via an electrically-operated pump. This would have run safely but for the fact that he was both distressed and confused. Frequently during the night we had to go to him to restrain and soothe him. His agitation was increasing, such that one person was now needed to stay with him. He had the required cot sides in position (ostensibly for his protection), but in his confusion was attempting to climb over them.

In bed four was Mrs Packham. She had Alzheimer's disease with congestive heart failure and should have been given regular mouth care, catheter care, pressure area care and much skilled nursing attention, affection and love. She slept fitfully and when awake, as she now was, called out repeatedly for 'mummy'. Reasoning was of little use, deafness compounding her senile dementia, though she responded to a held hand or stroked forehead and would settle if one of us had a few minutes to stay and comfort her – so little to expect when her 98 years were almost over.

In the side ward lay 85-year-old Mrs Gilmour, paralysed by a massive stroke, doubly incontinent, unconscious and dependent on us for everything. Staff label such a patient as in for TLC (tender loving care) – an inelegant, clumsy euphemism and so often at night a gross contradiction of the truth. Her son had rushed back from

Spain 48 hours earlier, leaving his family on holiday, and had sat by her side for the whole of the previous day. At about midnight I had persuaded him to leave the hospital for a break. He was exhausted. 'Go home, if only for a few hours and try to get some rest, even if you do not sleep,' I suggested. 'Have the phone by you and the moment your mum's condition deteriorates, I'll ring.' Giving advice in such a situation is always difficult and relatives are never pressed to leave. Mr Gilmour agreed to go home for a while but only on the strictest promise that I would keep a very close watch on his mother and ring the moment she seemed worse. 'She mustn't die alone,' he insisted, and I had witnessed too many patients die unattended over the years to disagree with that.

In bed 13, Mrs Hadfield, at 78 years of age the youngest patient, was receiving a third unit of blood for her leukaemia. Were she being cared for by a newly qualified staff nurse Pink in 1952, her blood pressure, pulse and temperature (among other observations) would have been carefully monitored at least every half hour, and woe betide the nurse who failed to do that. Yet not tonight, not in 1990, not on this geriatric ward.

The other seven patients on side two at 4.40am that Sunday in July were also very ill and in need of my care and attention: two had suffered heart attacks; one had pneumonia; one myxoedema (a diseased thyroid); another bleeding from the rectum and then there was Mr Gibb, with advanced cancer of the stomach – by and large a standard group of patients for ward A14.

So confused and agitated was Mr Kaminski that I could not leave him for more than a moment. He was calling out incoherently and attempting to climb out of bed. Even if rational, he would have rightly wanted to leave the bed, it was soaked in urine. I looked over to the other side but nurse Wilson was not in sight. Single-handed with her 13 patients, she had enough on her plate at that moment. All I could do was try to calm the tortured and pitiable man, and attempt to keep him in bed. If he were to fall (as many patients did at night), not only might he hurt himself but the infusion would be torn from his arm. This might lead to problems with bleeding and I would have to call the doctor, who as usual had been up till the early hours, to re-site the apparatus. Three members of staff might have just coped with those 13 patients on side two that morning. Alone I stood no chance. No chance of comforting the deranged, protecting the confused, treating the very ill, providing decent and dignified care; no chance even of meeting the most basic bodily needs of these helpless and dependent old people.

As I restrained the distraught Mr Kaminski, my feelings were not so much of anger as of sadness and despair. How could this dreadful situation occur in view of the events of the previous 12 months? Had all my efforts been in vain? Did anyone care? If I was going to throw in the towel, then now was the time, as the plaintive but insistent cries of Mr Gibb started again on the other side of the partition. In heaven's name, I thought, what has to happen before someone acts?

◆ ◆ ◆

It was almost a year to the day since I had first written to management to report the situation to those who should have already been fully aware of the deteriorating conditions on the unit. Some months previously, in late December 1988, 17 months after being appointed supervising night charge nurse to the geriatric area of Stepping Hill Hospital, Stockport, I had spoken at length to the night nurse manager, Miss Carew. I told her of my concern at the serious shortage of staff on the three elderly care wards, the resulting lack of proper care and the danger to which the patients were so often exposed. She had held out no promise of improved staffing, but I wanted her to have the opportunity to present the evidence to the senior managers. Throughout the spring of 1989, I reminded her of what was going on. As she visited the wards nightly and often stayed for some time to help, she really did not need me to spell it out for her.

When it became obvious that there was to be no improvement in the staffing, I wrote a letter. This would have come as no surprise to Miss Carew, for I had made my intention known to her if any representations she made proved fruitless. I include that letter here.

Mr F Richards, Chairman,
Stockport Health Authority,
District Offices,
STOCKPORT SK7 5AB

August 24th 1989

Dear Sir,

For the past two years I have been employed as a charge nurse on night duty at Stepping Hill Hospital. With another charge nurse, I have responsibility for the acute geriatric area comprising 72 beds on wards C5 (20 beds), A14 and A15 (each with 26 beds). We work a seven-on/seven-off rota from 8.30pm to 8am. My job is to supervise the unit at night, to ensure high standards of nursing care, advise and assist staff, reassure and comfort relatives, attend to administrative matters such as duty, ensure a safe environment and so on. Paramount among my varied concerns is the safety and care of the patients and it is these matters that cause me to write to you.

Ever since appointment, I have been unhappy at the low staff-to-patient ratio on our wards. We accept only patients of 75 years and over who are acutely ill. Unlike most other areas of the hospital, many of our patients arrive with a multiple pathology – for example a lady might be a diabetic, suffer from arthritis, be hard of hearing, partially sighted and be brought in following a heart attack. Additionally, patients frequently have social and psychological problems and are severely stressed at having to leave home and loved ones (so crucial a factor for elderly people). Thus the degree of dependency and amount of care each patient needs is especially high.

Enclosed you will find a typical night report. It is based on the situation pertaining on one night some little while ago when I was 'warded' – that is asked to take charge of one ward only because of insufficient staff. The few details for each patient can only suggest the demands in time of individual people. You will note such words as 'incontinent, confused, unconscious, aggressive, death, collapse, depressed, moribund, and hypothermia', words used singly and perhaps only rarely in other wards. And how many nurses do you consider are needed to guard, toilet, medicate, actively treat and care for these 26 frail and, in most cases, desperately ill ladies and gentlemen over an 11-hour period? My answer would be three or four (with additional non-nursing assistance). The health authority's answer, your answer, is one. I alone, with two untrained nursing auxiliaries, was left to face the night.

NIGHT REPORT (SIDE ONE)

1. Mrs M Burns (78) Carcinoma of the rectum, breaks to sacrum, incontinent of faeces, anal washouts. confused.
2. Mrs A Howard (82) GI bleed, large bowel obstruction, diarrhoea, pain. IVI running.
3. Miss E Clarke (87) CVA, right hemiplegia, dysphagia, Improving, two nurses to transfer.
4. Mrs J Freeman (97) Dense CVA, unconscious, suction prn, oral hygiene, 2-hly. turns, doubly incontinent, VERY POORLY.

5. Mrs J Lloyd (84) New admission,?CVA, vomiting (bile stained), UTI, chest infection, confused and aggressive. IVI, relatives present.

6. Mrs N Jacobs (77) Chest infection, diabetic, dyspnoea, nebulizers, pyrexia. 4-hly. TPR & BM stix, oxygen, POORLY.

7. Mrs E Bell New admission. Gross CCF, diabetic, high blood sugar, vomiting, BM stix 4-hly. Fell on floor today, POORLY.

8. Mrs V Bartlett (84) Hypertension, nausea, headaches, 4-hly. observations.

9. Mrs K Laskey (83) Social problem, ?CVA, TIA, confused.

10. Mrs J Lauchlan (78) Hypertension. Very anxious. 2-hly. BP.

11. Mrs B Mason (82) Falls, fractured pubic ramus, Paget's disease, haematoma, incontinent of faeces, catheterised, POORLY.

12. Mrs A Kelly (75) Gross CCF, emphysema, oxygen, POORLY.

13. Mrs G Potter (90) Dense CVA, right hemiplegia, 2-hly turns, dysphagia, ?UTI, incontinent, IVI, very obese. Three to lift.

(SIDE TWO)

1. Miss E Coyle (88) CVA, incontinent; IVI.

2. Mrs P Reade (87) Dementia, pressure sores, wound, diarrhoea, confused and very restless. Watch carefully.

3. Mrs A Lawson (86) Dehydrated, diabetic, UTI, frequency. 4-hly. BM stix, IVI, confused, calling out. Restless, observe.

4. Mrs K Dobson (87) New lady, collapse, chest infection, oxygen. ?MI, ALL CARE, POORLY.

5. Mrs B Godfrey (93) anaemia, confused, wanders, incontinent. VERY DEPRESSED.

6. Mrs B Lee (90) Chest infection, UTI, arthritis, poor mobility, doubly incontinent. WANTS TO DIE.

7. Mrs A Morgan (82) Atril fibrillation, arthritis, urgent stress incontinence, immobile.

8. Empty Bed (Mrs Hurst died at 7pm.) Admission expected (80) hypothermia, confusion.
9. Mrs P Hardy (81) Falls, vomiting, mass in pelvis, chest metastases. 2hly. turns. CLOSE TO DEATH. No known relatives.
10. Mrs G Cox (88) CVA, right hemiplegia, incontinent, dysphagia, IVI, confused.
11. Mrs L Williams New admission. Arrived on ward in moribund state, acute LVF, doubly incontinent. BP 4-hly. ALL CARE. Relatives coming in. Priest informed.
12. Mrs C Jackson (84) Peptic ulcer, ?oesophageal tumour. NBM Atkinson tube in situ., blood transfusion – 2 more units. CLOSE OBSERVATION.
13. Mrs I Davies (96) MI, Chest infection, UTI, confusion, general deterioration. PAIN, incontinent, turns, mouth care, POORLY.

And my letter continued...

Such is the state of cover at night that three staff (only one of whom usually is a nurse) is the accepted complement (acceptable, that is, to our nurse administrators) for wards A14 (male) and A15 (female) with two staff (one nurse) for ward C5 (female). The dangers, omissions and distress this lack of staff conduces I wish in some detail to convey.

I DRUG ADMINISTRATION
Almost invariably in recent months when warded, and often when not, I have had to administer the drugs alone. This must increase the possibility of error. The 'Rules For The Administration Of Drugs' published by the authority are of necessity flouted each night. For example, Part II, section 2,

refers to correct identification prior to giving medication and
urges use of the patient's Identiband. But repeatedly patients
are found not to have any reliable identity.

The evening drug round can take up to 80 minutes. Elderly
people do not want to be rushed; they may need coaxing,
want tablets crushed, ask what such a medicine is for (and
have every right to know), may be confused or difficult, want
milk or a hot drink to take medicine etc. It all takes time and
one often has to rush and browbeat in a cavalier manner – as
upsetting to the nurse as it must be for the patient.

II TOILETING

On average the ladies on C5 need to be put on commodes
four times a night – once between 9 and 10pm, once between
5.30 and 7.30am, and twice in between. Very few, if any,
patients, are self-caring. This means 40 toiletings between,
say, 11.30pm and 4.30am – about eight ladies an hour. Where
patients have frequency and/or a urinary infection, are on
an infusion or diuretic drugs, the total number can be nearer
50. The staffing quota for C5 is two with, at times, a third
assistant for the evening and morning rounds. Once or twice
a year a third person is allocated for the whole night. You
will not need me to remind you that back strain/injury is
an ever present hazard for nursing staff and that hazard is
accentuated on all geriatric wards where so many paralysed
patients are to be found. Staff are constantly urged not to take
risks and never to lift alone.

A year ago, a considerable fuss was made when I pulled my
back lifting, with others, an obese patient. The assistant night
nurse manager spent close on half an hour explaining how
very concerned nursing management and the health authority were about back injuries and why no risks should ever be

taken. Yet every night then, as now, staff were left alone on C5 ward to drag patients on and off bedpans and commodes. That the lady knew of and approved such staffing levels made her pretentious claptrap all the more difficult to stomach.

When my colleague or I is not warded we make a point of being on C5 to provide cover at break times. This, however, is becoming increasingly impossible. So desperate is the present situation that, to staff the three wards to what I believe is an unacceptable level, I have been removed from my post, without any consultation, and have spent 11 of the past 13 nights on C5 or A14. When this happens, the cover should be provided by the night sister but this has amounted, on average, to less than eight minutes a night. On Saturday 28th July, for example, sister was with me on C5 for a total of five minutes and for eight-and-a-half hours she came nowhere near the ward, nor even phoned to enquire how things were. During the nursing aux-iliary's dinner break I had to move five ladies, three of whom were stroke patients and two large and overweight to boot, onto and, more riskily, off the commode. The hazard to both patient and me was appalling; yet night after night we are placed in this situation and our nurse managers accept such inexcus-able goings on. The danger and neglect that the patients are at times placed in is not only scandalously unprofessional but, I suggest, borders on the criminal.

III   TERMINAL CARE AND DEATH

Although designated an acute area, we regularly have a per-centage of our patients in for terminal care. Some arrive in extremis; others slowly deteriorate over a period which can be weeks long. The care of the dying (hundreds die on these wards every year) is a very special field in nursing (for which, to the best of my knowledge, no proper training is provided) and calls for exceptional qualities and experience from staff. We must provide care for the patient and at times for five or six relatives. So above all, one needs time. What has particularly grieved me these last two years are those occasions when a patient is close to death and no relatives are present. The comfort of a held hand, a gently-caressed cheek or quiet word is incalculable but, so often, not offered; we do not have the staff. To find that a patient has died in such circumstances, as happened twice last week, causes me profound anguish and I have wept. Which manager, administrator or health authority has the right to so abuse our loyalty, our devotion, our very humanity? Until now, my indignation has been submerged at such times by a sense of remorse and desolation.

IV   CONFUSED PATIENTS

At any one time, numbers of our old people are confused. This can vary from a mild disorientation to outright aggression and violence. On one occasion two members of staff had to attend Casualty so extreme had been a patient's frenzy. Such behaviour has a number of deleterious results. A patient moaning or shouting out can keep awake most of the other patients who, in turn, need extra comfort and attention. More disturbed people (for whom sedation may be inappropriate or have proved ineffectual) become restless and irascible. For their own protection (sometimes for that of the other patients), such a person must be removed from bed, or in the bed, perhaps to a corridor (we have nowhere suitable for these cases) and a member of staff must sit by to attempt restraint. Such care is necessary but time consuming. Recently I sat with a patient in great torment from 11.30pm to close on 7am. The problem occurs regularly and makes our normal heavy workload even less manageable.

V INCONTINENCE

A high proportion of our patients are incontinent of urine or faeces or both. On Monday of last week, 10 out of the 24 patients were incontinent, a not unusual situation. One gentleman in his 100th year was changed nine times and when we left at 8am he was lying in a wet bed once more. Another had a massive bowel movement; then in his derangement proceeded to wipe the faeces over his head, face, body, down his excessively long fingernails (nail care went out years ago I am told), the locker and cot sides. It took two of us 20 minutes to make him warm and comfortable. During this time we were out of sight and earshot of half the ward and we were the only two on duty. Less than an hour later, the patient had a second evacuation with only slightly less upsetting consequences. On Tuesday morning we put out 13 bulging bags of linen for the laundry.

There is so much more that you ought to know of – avoidable injuries to patients (one leading to death); important observations for people on blood transfusions for example not carried out; patients offered a wash once a day (would you, Mr Richards, I wonder, eat your breakfast not having washed your hands for 22 hours?); male patients exposing themselves to ladies in adjoining beds; basic nursing care, such as oral hygiene, eye care, intravenous infusions ignored; patients shaken at 11 or later to be given medication; lights on as early as 5.25am so that the morning round can be started; a very sick lady pushed into the dayroom on admission and left there for an hour because a corpse was in the bed she was to occupy (while I had to lie to the relatives); an unidentified body sent to the mortuary; glaring fire hazards reported months ago ignored; dirty wards and sluices; a malfunctioning central heating system that causes patients to shiver, then comes on full-blast in the middle of June's heatwave, twice reported by me over the last six months...and so on, and so on.

It amounts to a catalogue of shame and neglect which must now be brought into the open, for our whole community to know of if need be. One final personal experience, burnt into my psyche, must be told. While warded on A15, I was working on one side (the ward is not the old 'Nightingale' type) and heard a lady call from the opposite side. Leaving the other two staff for a moment, I went to see what the patient required. She wanted the commode. As she was immobile and weighed some 15 stone, I asked if she could wait until we were free. She said that she needed the commode 'now' (few elderly people can wait). I apologised and explained that we were caring for a very ill patient and would be about ten minutes. She implored me to help her and burst into tears.

— 'I'll have to do it in the bed,' she cried.

— 'Then you'll have to do that,' was all I could reply.

Need I tell you how ashamed and debased an old lady can be to be so treated? I was impelling her to soil the bed and, perhaps more offensive still, driving her back more than 80 years. Need I tell you how abjectly degraded I felt to be party to so revolting an incident? The lady 'did it in the bed' and lay in her own excrement for half an hour. Were you not to have heard of other incidents, surely just this one must offend and outrage you beyond words. This alone must cause you and your committee to act.

In the singularly personal situation I have attempted to describe, statistics are perhaps unapt. But the admission figures for Ward A14 over the last few years are pertinent. Total admissions for the last eight years are as follows:

1981	1982	1983	1984	1985	1986	1987	1988
447	476	686	661	700	860	969	981

In three years (1985-1988) there has been a 40 per cent increase and since 1981 a 120 per cent increase. The higher turnover implies a much heavier workload. The nurse managers have been made fully aware of the evidence and the resultant state of affairs yet, far from the position improving, it has steadily degenerated.

To my knowledge, no senior nurse manager has set foot at night on A14, A15 or C4 in two years. One of our night nursing officers very rarely visits. So perhaps our nurse administrators won't be entirely surprised that their apparent complete lack of interest and concern at our predicament causes them to be viewed by many bedside staff with disparagement neighbouring on contempt. Not only are their efficacy and commitment in question but their very suitability for office.

Yet the United Kingdom Central Council (UKCC) – the nurses' professional body – publication Exercising Accountability states: 'Each registered nurse. . .shall act, at all times, in such a manner as to justify public trust and confidence, to uphold and enhance the good standing and reputation of the profession, to serve the interests of society, *and above all to safeguard the interests of individual patients and clients*' (my emphasis).

Nor can we exonerate the geriatric consultants who, knowing the precarious staff position, continue to admit patients so putting staff under unwarranted strain and patients at unacceptable risk. They have much to answer for.

I am assuming that you and the members of your committee are not aware of the conditions that I have delineated but that you will be persuaded to initiate whatever action is called for to ameliorate the situation both immediately and in the long term. You will, I am sure, be distressed and angered by what you have read (and who would not be?) If the relatives of these elderly people could see how their loved ones are at times treated they would be up in arms. The very members of our community who are most vulnerable, yet deserve the greatest respect, care and love, are being humiliated and ill-used.

My aim here has been to present the facts as objectively and substantively as possible, omitting a number of wretched incidents which I have witnessed especially with patients close to death. But I cannot disguise my deep concern at what is happening, nor my repugnance at being obliged by the health authority to act so in its name. Nightly I am forced to violate proudly-cherished, long-held standards and see loyal and selfless staff manifestly fatigued and stressed.

Let me say that in a working life of 42 years I have never come across such a devoted, sedulous, and tolerant group of people as our night staff. My admiration and esteem for them are boundless. Never once, even under the most demanding and exhausting circumstances, have I heard a patient spoken to sharply. Some of the tasks undertaken night after night would repel and sicken (quite literally) many people. Yet they work with a quiet dignity and sublime skill way beyond the call of duty.

Should you or any of your committee wish to see our work at firsthand please do pay us a visit; you would be most welcome. But please do not arrive for 20 minutes on some pre-arranged, magisterial-type visit, but come unheralded and stay for some hours, all night if possible. See for yourselves our problems, our anguish and our reward. For, despite all I have said, there is a deep-seated fulfilment from nursing such venerable members of our society. I am not alone in believing that I am privileged to be entrusted with the care of these revered patients who have given so much to their families, their community and their nation. It is an inestimable honour to be close to them at their parting this life.

I cannot, however, support any longer what is happening nor does my professional body expect me to remain silent. It is essential, we are admonished: '. . .to achieve high standards rather than to simply accept minimum standards. Practitioners must seek remedies in those situations where factors in the environment obstruct the achievement of high standards: to start from a compromise position and silently to tolerate poor standards is to act in a manner contrary to the interests of patients, and thus renege on professional accountability.'

To achieve these 'high standards', assuming wards continue to be maximally utilized, we shall need five staff (at least two nurses) on A14 and A15 and three staff (two nurses) on C5. This would include the provision of sufficient staff reserves to cover for holidays, maternity leave, and unexpected sickness so that these levels were never allowed to drop for a single night. Such arrangements do not now exist. To achieve 'basic' standards on A14 and A15, four staff (two trained) could cope for much of the time but no reduction on C5 should be considered.

Yours faithfully,
FG Pink

The letter took close on a week to prepare and write. A great deal of care and thought went into it for it had to be accurate, honest and well-argued without exaggeration or distortion. The layman to whom it was addressed may have had no experience of caring for the sick so my aim was not only to present the facts but to give him some idea of the revulsion at the lack of care that I had experienced. If it appeared dramatic and alarming, so indeed were the events described and I wanted the chairman to be as concerned, if not as revolted, as was I.

As my charge nurse colleague was referred to on page one I thought it courteous to show him a draft copy (we had previously discussed the situation) which he read without comment. While most of the staff knew of my intention to raise our concerns officially and had offered to put their signatures to any letter, I took the decision not to involve them. The opinions expressed were forthright and deeply-felt and it seemed appropriate that I alone should accept responsibility for what I appreciated might ruffle a few feathers, though I never imagined that what would be set in train would have such devastating personal consequences. Nevertheless, I was aware of the dictatorial regime of our night nurse manager and thought it better not to ask colleagues, who unlike me needed the work, to leave themselves open in any way to further unpleasantness. I posted the letter on the Thursday before the August bank holiday weekend.

◆   ◆   ◆

The following Tuesday (29th August), I was warded on A14 and it was particularly busy. At about 9.30, a patient collapsed and the doctor was urgently summoned. For the ensuing half hour staff nurse Thomson, the nursing auxiliary, the doctor and I were rushed off our feet attempting to revive the lady and keep an eye on the other 25 patients. As we hurried to and fro, I was aware that a man was standing at the nurses' station – presumably a visitor. I offered him a chair and explained that an emergency prevented us from dealing with him then. In the event the lady in the side ward died, doctor dashed off to another incident and we could draw breath before continuing our usual evening round that was by then well behind schedule (it was long after midnight before we put the lights out). I was able then to speak to the visitor, apologise for keeping him waiting and ask whom he had come to see. 'You, Mr Pink,' was his unexpected reply.

He was Mr Milnes, the health authority's district general manager and chief executive. In the absence of the chairman, he explained, he had opened my letter that morning and was disturbed at what he had read. We walked round the ward but he could see that there was no time to spare and in any case, I had said all there was to say. He promised to look into the situation and as we moved through the ward his obvious concern and disquiet at what he was seeing no doubt for the first time were apparent. 'Something will have to be done,' he said. Then of necessity I had to make my excuses and return to the bedside (a second patient died soon after). As Mr Milnes was leaving the ward, Mrs Thomson, one of our most senior and experienced staff nurses, asked to whom I had been speaking. 'I must have a word with him,' she said and hurried to catch him in the corridor. She realised why he had come and wanted to reinforce our need for more nurses. Within a few minutes she returned to the ward. 'Isn't he a nice man?' she said. 'I don't think he'd any idea what was going on here. He's quite upset and told me that something would have to be done.' Certainly we were both impressed by this quietly spoken, thoughtful gentleman who had reacted immediately to my letter and who appeared moved by what he had learnt.

The work kept us constantly on the go but at least now there seemed the prospect of some immediate relief following Mr Milnes' visit. Perhaps my forebodings were unnecessary if his response was to be typical. Driving home next morning, my usual exhaustion was relieved by the thought that the worst was over and the 30-odd hours which it had taken to write the letter had been time well spent. My sleep that day was deep and long and particularly tranquil.

TWO
THE FIRST CASUALTY

In a contemplative fashion,
And a tranquil frame of mind,
Free from every kind of passion,
Some solution let us find.
Let us grasp the situation,
Solve the complicated plot
Quiet calm deliberation
Disentangles every knot — **WS Gilbert**

My seven nights off duty followed that Tuesday in August. On my return, there appeared to be no sign of any change in the usual minimal staffing. The only outcome was that Miss Carew told me in no uncertain terms that I had no right to approach the health authority chairman and that my action was completely out of order. I reminded her of our conversation the previous December and subsequent discussions. 'You are fully aware of the situation. There seemed no point in telling you what you already knew.' I told her that some weeks previously I had discussed the staffing with the senior sister (days) on ward A14, Mrs Field, who told me of her own difficulties with increasing workload and too few staff. So concerned had she become that she had written to the hospital's assistant manager, a Mr Geraghty, the most senior nurse (equivalent to the 'matron' of former days), alerting him to the serious problems she was experiencing and her worries that basic care was having to be neglected. When I told Mrs Field that I was considering a similar move, she said, 'Well, don't send it to Mr Geraghty; that'll be a waste of time. It took him three weeks to acknowledge my letter and three weeks after that nothing has been done.' Not wanting to have the matter pigeon-holed or ignored, I decided to take Mrs Field's advice. Hence my decision to write to Mr Richards, the chairman. No slight or discourtesy towards Miss Carew was intended but some, I fear, was taken.

The reaction of senior colleagues to my efforts to obtain more nurses has always been a mystery to me. I thought that they would have applauded a reasoned, well-evidenced case for more staff. They could not deny the need or the benefits that even a slight improvement would bring. Though they themselves appeared not to be under undue stress (they were not working at the bedside), they were, or should have been, aware just how harassed ward staff were. If our lay managers were unaware of the serious problems on many wards, and not just those in the geriatric area, as they appeared to be, then my efforts to enlighten them should surely have been welcomed. But no. The prevailing, if unvoiced, attitude of nurse managers and night sisters in charge of other units was one of resentment and/or hostility. This truly baffled me and still does. What strange logic were these people applying? My regard for the work of my ward-based colleagues was boundless. They were a superb group of people, alongside whom it was a real pleasure to work. Whichever two or three of us found ourselves together we invariably worked as a team with great respect for the patients and for each other. No matter how wretched, repetitive or wearying a task might be, it was carried out in a positive, friendly way with no hint to the patient of how distressed or tired we might feel. Despite what I have written, the atmosphere was often cheery and bright with the odd bit of banter with any patient well enough to appreciate a joke or leg pull. I cannot find the words to say how highly I regarded these colleagues. Be assured, they wanted to provide a skilled and dedicated standard of care that was second-to-none.

It has been suggested that the senior nurses were less than happy at my action because they interpreted it as a threat. This seems to make little sense. Perhaps they were upset because I had spoken up to highlight unacceptable standards that they had witnessed and come to terms with over the years. If they thought my views and action suggested arrogance, I can understand that. It could be argued that I was assuming responsibilities well beyond my station and if that is a fault, I hold up my hands and plead guilty. In one sense, I was out of order in bypassing the normal line-management. Any representations I thought it proper to make, should have been handed to my immediate superior for her to do with as she saw fit. However, I believed the situation was so serious and urgent that my direct approach to the most senior person I knew of was justified. I must leave others to judge the wisdom of that assessment.

On 7th September, the chairman Mr Richards replied briefly to my letter to say that Mr Milnes, following his earlier visit, was 'initiating some action', though what that was I never discovered. The chairman offered to visit the wards himself and this was arranged for the 16th, his earliest availability. I was not on duty but went in to show him round the unit. In every respect, however, the visit was less than satisfactory. He arrived at 9 o'clock, always a busy time when staff have little chance to stop and talk to anyone. The chairman's manner, unlike that of Mr Milnes, was distant and guarded. We spoke briefly on the corridor before entering the patient area of ward A14. I decided that he should not have me at his side as he moved about. I kept at a distance and out of hearing so that staff would feel free to speak to him without being overheard. The regular auxiliary on duty was busy with nurse Williams, so Mr Richards spent some time speaking to the other assistant who, as it happened, we had never had on a geriatric ward before. This was unfortunate since she had no experience with our patients and as a new member of staff would not feel easy speaking to this authoritative figure. During this encounter the nurse manager arrived. My 'Good evening, Miss Carew' was met with a glare as she swept past me to seek out the chairman.

Mr Richards continued round the ward with Miss Carew at his elbow as I waited at the nurses' station. They stopped to have a word with nurse Williams, but later she told me that there was a great deal she would have liked to say to the chairman (and she was not the sort to be reticent when something needed to be said) but felt unable to speak honestly and openly with Miss Carew 'glowering at me over his shoulder'. As the pair made to leave the ward I joined them, but Mr Richards' curt and dismissive thanks and 'Goodbye' (more significant than I then appreciated) made it clear that my further presence was no longer required, despite having come in specially to be on hand to answer his questions or suggest possible ways that our crisis might be alleviated. I had been in his presence perhaps three minutes, he on the ward perhaps ten. My words in the letter: 'but please do not arrive for 20 minutes on some prearranged, magisterial-type visit. . .' had obviously been missed. No meaningful discussion took place. I did no more than restate our position; he did not question any of the evidence nor challenge my assessment. He appeared to want to accept nothing and admit nothing. His brusqueness dispelled the optimism that my colleague Mrs Thomson and I felt after meeting the chief executive.

The chairman's visit then continued, I assume, to wards A15 and C5, but what Mr Richards could genuinely learn from so controlled and contrived a circuit must have been limited and distorted. Rather than question my evidence and opinions, if not challenge them directly, his presence seemed almost preordained to confirm disbelief and unconcern. *He that nothing questions nothing learns.* Mr Richards later wrote to Mr Nicholas Winterton MP, Chairman of the House of Commons Select Committee on Health, that he 'spoke to every member of staff on duty on the three wards'. All I can say is, I beg to differ.

♦ ♦ ♦

I returned to work on Thursday 21ˢᵗ September with no sign of change. The following Monday I arrived at about 8pm as usual. This routine enabled me to walk round the three wards before handover, say hello to those patients I knew and assess the general situation. Clearly A14 was particularly busy with new admissions, relatives on the ward, much active treatment and several confused/disruptive patients. When I reported to the night office, Miss Carew announced that, once again, I was to be confined to A14 for the night (the system known as 'warding'). When I was first appointed I had been told that my job was to supervise the three wards and divide my time between them as needed. This meant that on average each ward was provided with an additional three-and-a-half hours of registered nurse cover each night and I tried to ensure that no ward was left in charge of an auxiliary if at all possible. Sadly this was often not possible and by the summer of 1989 warding was becoming the norm rather than an exception, but only for the geriatric area. It was almost unheard of for the sisters covering other areas to be confined to one ward.

On that Monday night, instead of our two regular and experienced auxiliaries, I found two unknown ladies waiting to join me for the night's work. One was new to the hospital; neither had been on the ward before, nor had cared for elderly people in hospital. Neither had been given any training, knew any of the patients nor wanted, it seemed, to be where they had been placed. There was, again, going to be no way of providing proper care, attending to anxious relatives or ensuring a reposeful environment for those few patients well enough to sleep. The prospect was disturbing and this just a few weeks after raising these very problems at the highest level. Miss Carew may have done her best but as far as I, and more to the point the helpless patients, were concerned the 'best' was unacceptable.

I picked up the phone, dialled the switchboard and asked to be put through to Mr Geraghty at home. He was the Stepping Hill assistant general manager and the most highly placed nurse in the hospital hierarchy. On reflection, I see that this, while carefully considered, could be seen as provocative. Yet my only concern was then, as it has always been, the safety and welfare of the patients and for that I was prepared to break any conventions. I knew nothing of Mr Geraghty and we had never met. In the subsequent BBC 40 Minutes programme, *Dear Mr Pink,* he stated that it was 'not uncommon for me to be in the hospital one night a week – one night a fortnight' and this may well have been the case. I can only say that in the 18 days and 272 nights that I had worked at the hospital, our paths had never crossed. Nor, as far as I was aware, had he ever been sighted at night on any of the geriatric wards. Yet when asked to comment on the reports in my first letter to management he replied, 'I found this quite difficult to accept and no evidence of this had been brought to my attention by anybody. I was happy and confident that I knew what was going on in the hospital at night time as well as during the day time.'

These words struck me as disquieting and a little smug. If Mr Geraghty did not already know what was going on in the wards for the elderly, he should have done. If he did know, one must assume that he was fully satisfied that all was well. If he was not satisfied, we can ask what steps he had taken to stop the neglect. It seems more likely and more charitable to believe that he was completely unaware of the night-by-night dilemmas which we were experiencing. It is unthinkable that he would turn a blind eye to such goings on.

But as I waited at the end of the phone that September evening, more immediate problems occupied my thoughts. A young man answered and I asked if Mr Geraghty was available. 'This is charge nurse Pink at Stepping Hill Hospital,' I added. A moment's pause and then the assistant general manager was on the line. Quickly and politely I explained the situation we faced. 'The needs of many patients will have to be ignored tonight,' I told him. 'There is no way we can properly care for so many severely ill and dying people.' I suggested that if no other nurses were available then 'you'd better get in here yourself and give us a hand. The situation is desperate,' and apologising for having no time to hang on, I put down the receiver.

Sometime later, as we were attempting to carry out the essential work, a stony-faced Miss Carew arrived with a gentleman who introduced himself as Mr Geraghty. If I'd have had my wits about me, I should have directed him to the lady who had been calling for the commode for more than ten minutes or asked him to start the medicine round, then an hour behind schedule. If he had come genuinely to help out, he would not have needed any invitation from me. As it was, I told him to see for himself and left them to parade unhelpfully round the ward. Then they were gone. Miss Carew returned later to help and severely reprimand me for having the audacity to phone a manager at home and without her permission, but no extra staff were forthcoming. The chief nurse said he would call a meeting, a move which I suggested would not solve our problems nor put more staff at the bedside.

A week later on 3rd October I wrote to Mr Geraghty thanking him for coming in that Monday evening and sending him a detailed report on the patients and their conditions for that night. My letter continued:

> As for nursing staff to minister to their needs and to protect these helpless people, I alone with two helpers was expected

to cope for 11 hours. Surely this state of affairs cannot be legal? But even if legal, can it be morally right for any nurse manager, consultant or administrator to place me, or a fellow nurse, in such an alarming and intimidating predicament? I regard it as a scandalous outrage which cries out for amelioration or exposure. The neglect and suffering nightly caused to our patients leaves me angry and anguished. And has anyone considered the effects on the staff?

Monday night was not an unusual or even heavy night by our standards. We had but one intravenous infusion, no admissions, no grief-stricken relatives to cope with, no deaths, no one on a monitor, no unduly frenzied or violent patients, no arrest or medical emergency, no gross faecal incontinence, no accidents...Our nursing officer, Miss Carew, dispensed the late drugs and spent close on an hour helping us on the morning round, lights on at 0525 hours. What a tower of strength and support she is; always ready to work at the bedside despite her responsibility for the whole hospital. And how sad that her colleague, the assistant nursing officer, never lifts a finger personally to help, even in our most dire moments. So you can imagine the pressure and stress on our devoted staff during a busy night. Not infrequently, especially in recent weeks, I have gone to bed at 9am and found it impossible to sleep. The utter fatigue, both physical and mental, can leave one's mind in turmoil.

Two weeks ago, one of our staff nurses (an ex-full-time sister, a most diligent and skilled nurse) had a quite harrowing and arduous night during which three patients died in as many hours. Such was the pressure on the staff that we could not prevent one group of relatives, whose mother was still breathing, from having to move aside while the mortuary trolley was brought past. Another gentleman, distraught at his mother's death, could not be consoled nor would he leave the body. It took staff nurse all her considerable tact and resourcefulness to gently ease him out. Her bearing and shining fortitude that night were magnificent, but by 5am she was close to breaking point, barely able to stem her tears. People like you, Mr Geraghty, who force these insufferably oppressive conditions on us and are prepared to condone them, must accept our condemnation. Your tacit approval of these totally unreasonable staffing levels (and I choose my words with nicety) denigrates the patients and abuses the staff.

During August I was warded for 11 nights; more nights in a two-week period than most sisters are warded in a year. The reason, according to Miss Carew, was the poor timekeeping of the geriatric night staff. Has anyone, I wonder, enquired more deeply here? Could an above-average absenteeism be significant? Is the constantly excessive work and grinding stress perhaps taking its toll? Certainly our area is very wearing and can be most depressing. Yet no relief is ever considered, as far as I am aware. Why isn't some form of staff rotation offered, three months on a surgical ward every two years, for example? One of our nurses, after eight years' toil in geriatrics with no respite, longs for a change. Original and imaginative thinking would appear to be at a premium.

As I briefly said to you on Monday, there are two approaches to the equation. Either more nurses are provided or fewer patients catered for (or some combination of both). If we are to continue with current patient numbers, and to provide the basic nursing care, we must have at least TWO NURSES on each ward every night without exception, with two auxiliaries on each of A14 and A15 and one on C5. This requires another 16 nurses (two nights per week) allowing us to cut back on our present heavy reliance on bank staff.

With our present cover, most patients are out of sight and earshot for much of the night. You know of the tragic accident last year which led to a lady's death a few days later and which could clearly have ended in litigation. It is sheer good luck that we have not had a similar situation this last six months. It seems inconceivable that a court of law would consider our present cover anywhere near adequate and this consideration alone must give the health authority pause for serious thought.

Both Mr Richards and you have implied/stated that there is no money available to employ more nurses. As we must not be made to endure the conditions I have described any longer, only one alternative appears possible. At present we have 12 nurses employed on the area. Given, say, another six (part-time) nurses we could staff two wards, and two wards only. This would seem more sensible than the alternative of reducing intake on each ward by half, to 14 (A14), 14 (A15) and 10 (C5).

Clearly there is a very serious situation – no doubt about that which, I suggest, will not yield to tinkering. Rather is needed a bold, radical decision to produce relief within days. It is now five weeks since my letter of August 24th to the health authority yet no improvement is in sight.

POSTSCRIPT
I am doubtful that any purpose would be served by our meeting; what else can I say? But should you so wish it, I hold myself available. . .

On the same day I also wrote to Mr Richards to say that his visit and that of Mr Milnes were 'much appreciated'. Then I wrote to the three consultant geriatricians, Miss Carew and Mrs A. Matthews (the day nurse manager in overall charge of the care of the elderly wards) enclosing copies of the letters to Mr Richards and Mr Geraghty. The three doctors appeared to show no interest whatsoever in my letter and none of them spoke to me at any time about the standard of care. Considering that the night shift constitutes all but half the total time a patient spends in hospital, this silence speaks volumes. One can only assume that what they read they either disbelieved or found acceptable.

Mid-October arrived with no response from the authority and no additional staff. On the 17th I wrote a short letter to the top man. Mr Duncan Nichol, chief executive of the NHS, enclosing copies of my letters to the hospital chairman Mr Richards and the chief nurse Mr Geraghty. It read, in part:

> Could you please clarify the legal position regarding the number of nurses (registered or enrolled) required to the number of patients. Our chief nurse, Mr J Geraghty, does not know the answer. While very much appreciating the health authority's difficulties over financial restraints, our present situation must surely be unacceptable.

A week later I wrote to the two local MPs, Mr Tony Favell and Mr Tom Arnold, asking for their advice and possible intervention. At Mr Geraghty's request, I attended a 45-minute meeting on 23rd October with him and Mrs Matthews, the clinical nurse specialist for the elderly. He agreed that nursing levels were 'not ideal' but 'compared favourably' with levels throughout the rest of the hospital and throughout the other districts in the region. He produced no data to support this statement but I accepted it. I pointed out that our needs were real and substantive. I was making no comparisons with other wards or hospitals. To my mind such information was unhelpful and irrelevant. As far as staff and patients were concerned, comparisons were inappropriate and invidious. I emphasised the acute danger to staff as well as patients which existed. He knew, and if he did not I told him, that every night on C5 one member of staff (repeatedly an untrained helper) was left alone during the three hours of meal breaks (unless I was able to make myself available) to care for the whole ward of ladies and that for 90 minutes that person was an untrained, unqualified helper, sometimes without experience of acutely ill, elderly patients. 'You know that, Mr Geraghty,' I said, 'and so does the health authority, but you appear not to share my profound disquiet at the situation.' I explained that ladies had to be man-handled onto and off commodes by ONE person. 'Do you approve of this practice?' I asked. No answer.

It had been reported in the nursing press a few weeks earlier that a record settlement of £157,000 had been awarded to a nurse by the Northumberland Health Authority following a lifting injury. 'Will Stockport similarly compensate one of our night staff who seriously injures themself?' I asked. The question was ignored. Mr Geraghty's principal concern, and no doubt the reason for calling the meeting, was to ensure that I would not go public by contacting the press as this would, he told me, 'undermine the public's confidence in the hospital and cause unnecessary worry to patients and relatives.'

It did not appear to cross his mind that perhaps the public should not have confidence in the hospital (or at least one area of it at night), and that patients' and relatives' worries would be fully justified if the truth was known. His thinking, as with that of everyone I was up against, made no sense to me. I do not wish to be unkind, but his worry, and the authority's worry, did not seem to involve patients. My response was to state that I had no wish to speak to the press. That course of action would be fraught with problems and had never crossed my mind. Still, he put the idea there. As the meeting ended, he and Mrs Matthews (who had played little part in our discussion) were left in no doubt that my resolve to improve the care of the patients and banish forever so many quite dreadful incidents was unshakeable. This declaration was not one that I had prepared, and I was rather taken aback when I heard myself saying it. The seeming lack of concern for patients, the prevarication, procrastination and inability to address the real issues, must have roused me (normally a placid, accepting individual) to speak as I did. This may have been influenced by yet one more disturbing experience a few nights earlier.

It was during the first break and I was covering for staff nurse on C5. My bleep sounded to summon me to an emergency a quarter-of-a-mile away on A14, which had no nurse on duty. All was quiet on C5, but even if that was not the case my responsibility was to attend such a call immediately. A short while later as we were coping with the collapsed patient on A14 (doctor had arrived) I was urgently summoned to the phone. It was the auxiliary on C5. 'Mr Pink,' she said, 'Can you come back up straight away. Mr Peters in the corner bed; he's moaning and looks awful. What shall I do? I think he's dying!' 'Stay with him,' I said, 'and someone will come.' Who would come was unclear, for the only doctor on duty was still working on the collapsed patient and I could not leave A14. I bleeped Miss Carew and waited for her to respond. It seemed like an age, as 20 seconds can do at such a time. She rang. 'Why aren't you on C5 yourself?' was her rather fractious comment. I explained. 'I'll see if I can find someone,' she responded. And she did, one of the sisters. But all this took some five or six minutes. Sister arrived but to no avail. Mr Peters died just before she walked onto the ward. In a letter to Mr Geraghty a day or two later, I wrote: 'I find such an episode quite dreadful and unacceptable. It is anathema to all I know to be right and proper both as a nurse and as a human being.'

I now awaited a detailed and substantive reply to my first letter, perhaps with news of the promised 'action'. Despite the negative meeting with the assistant manager, my faith in Mr Milnes remained. The chief executive seemed a man of decency and integrity, a man not to go back on his words – 'Something will have to be done.' But it was not until early November, after a two-month wait, that a response came from the chairman, Mr Richards; a brusque few lines. It read:

> Dear Mr Pink,
>
> I am in receipt of copies of the correspondence you have addressed to officers of the Authority about the staffing situation on the wards for which you have responsibility, and I also note from the correspondence you addressed to Mr Favell, Member of Parliament for Stockport, that you complain you received no written response from the Authority to your letter.
>
> May I remind you I spent some time with you during the late evening of 16th September, to discuss the subject with you and to see for myself the position on the wards. I would have thought this was adequate acknowledgement of your complaint and I made plain to you that I would speak to Mr Milnes, the District General Manager, in order to have the matter fully investigated.

There had been no discussion with me when the chairman visited and this second letter was his last communication. We never met or spoke again. Both MPs appeared concerned and quickly replied. On 6th November, Mr Favell MP wrote to say that he had been told by Mr Richards 'that this matter is being thoroughly investigated by the health authority'. What those words mean I do not know. Whatever investigation was carried out did not involve any member of the ward staff. Its methods of enquiry and results were never made known to us. Meanwhile, the neglect of patients continued. If management remained unconvinced of this, another occurrence on

C5 in early November affirmed, better than any words of mine, the case for more staff.

It was 11.45pm and I was alone on the ward, alone that is apart from 20 stricken ladies, most someone's dear mother, grandmother or great-grandmother. Two ladies were on commodes and a third had called me. As I jerked and heaved Mrs Gowan, an overweight stroke patient, towards the bedside commode, I heard footsteps shuffling unsteadily along. Drawing back the curtains a little I saw that one of the demented ladies was about to leave the ward. Immediately outside the door is a flight of stairs by the lift. We were on the second floor. What on earth was I to do? Mrs Gowan, half-in and half-out of bed, should not be left to perhaps fall on the floor. Yet in her confusion, Mrs Neal was in considerable danger. 'Can you just keep still for a moment, Mrs Gowan?' I asked. 'I won't be a moment; Mrs Neal is wandering.'

If Mrs Gowan falls, I decided, she may damage herself, break an arm or her pelvis perhaps, but she should not be fatally hurt, whereas tragedy was in the offing on the corridor. I dashed out and took hold of Mrs Neal who by now was close to the stairs. This frightened the bewildered lady, for she took me to be a burglar in her own home. Thus her confusion was compounded by fear, and try as I may she would not move. Recourse to dialogue and reason was pointless. Meanwhile, the ward door had closed leaving the patients abandoned. I needed to get back into the ward and was reduced to manhandling the lady in a most unseemly and almost violent way.

The whole episode was utterly sickening for me. One can only guess what Mrs Neal thought was happening. Even now, years later, revulsion and despair flood into my mind. No doubt Mrs Neal is now at rest but that scene, despicable and degrading as it was, will haunt me for the rest of my days. In a letter to Mr Geraghty on 13th November I detailed the events adding:

How I forcibly impelled this dear old lady back into the ward would be as distasteful to recount as it was loathsome to execute; and I say again that those in authority who accept our inadequate staffing cover and drive me to such maltreatment of a patient, not only insult and affront patients and staff but shame themselves. Yet you, Mr Geraghty, believe that our staffing levels do not put patients in danger. Can we be using the same language I wonder?

The following day Mr Geraghty wrote to me.

I would confirm my statement to you, that it is not possible to increase the staffing levels in the geriatric area at night, without depleting levels of staff in other areas.

He made it clear that from management's point of view, there was nothing more to be said. 'I should like to take this opportunity of thanking you for bringing this matter to my attention.' A very strange sentence indeed. If the quality of care was to management's complete satisfaction, why thank me? Would not a reprimand be in order? If, as it seemed, my account of events were discounted and discredited, my action seen as frivolous and vexatious, a more critical letter with the suggestion of possible future disciplinary action, if only for wasting managers' valuable time, would surely have been more appropriate. I have little experience of management, but have gaped in disbelief at the ham-fisted, irrational and tactless way they blundered along. The greater the evidence that something was wrong, the more unresponsive and less open to reason they became.

Had someone spoken candidly and said: 'Look, we accept what you're saying; no one is questioning your descriptions; we know how things are and have done all that's possible but just do not have the money to provide more nurses,' that at least would have been open and honest. It would have avoided so much unnecessary unpleasantness and waste of many people's time and effort that could have been better used. Had management or the health authority so spoken, then my efforts, however limited, could have been joined with theirs in an attempt to: (a) improve the deployment of existing staff; and (b) try to obtain extra funding. Instead of ignoring the evidence, why could it not have been used to persuade the regional health authority or central government to provide the staff needed? As in war it seemed, truth (at least for management) was one of the first casualties.

Late in November, following a wait of six weeks, some civil servant replied to my letter to Mr Nichol. Another brush-off:

> Once again, I do not think it is appropriate for us to attempt to establish nursing arrangements in a particular hospital within the NHS precisely because the Management Executive and the Government are convinced that responsibility for decision making should be placed at the most appropriate level.

Would the writer, I wondered, like to come and tell Mrs Neal, Mrs Gowan or Mr Peter's widow about 'responsibility for decision making'?

THREE
AN UNEXCEPTIONAL, AVERAGE NIGHT

Democracy substitutes election by the incompetent many
for appointment by the corrupt few
— **George Bernard Shaw**

It was now early December 1989, close on a year since I had raised the question of staff shortage with my nurse manager and over three months since writing to Mr Richards. And what had been achieved? Nothing. This was quite incredible and difficult to understand. I was sure that the first letter would be the last; that the managers would be so concerned by what they read that within days the staffing would be improved at least to the minimum suggested. Of course, they would want to check that my descriptions were true. Quite right. It never crossed my mind, though, that they could in all conscience just ignore them. Rather than critically consider the evidence, and perhaps discredit it, managers seemed to have been suddenly struck blind and deaf. No one asked me to defend my assessment; none of the other staff was asked to comment; no manager spent time on the ward to observe how so few people coped for over 11 hours under the described conditions; none of us was invited to put forward suggestions. Scepticism, even extreme scepticism, would have been understandable; but to me this appeared to be little short of nihilism. It was a strange and completely unexpected response and to this day makes no sense to me. Had I been a senior nurse or administrator who received that letter of 24th August, I'm sure I would have disbelieved what I was reading and would have wanted at once to either disprove or at least check the accounts. This would have been done carefully and thoroughly but in double-quick time. I would have wanted to speak, not just to the writer of the letter, who might have ulterior motives or just be some sort of crank, but to meet as many bedside staff as were prepared to discuss the situation with me; perhaps call a staff meeting to confirm or confound what I had read. Until this was done, I doubt if I could sleep easy in my bed for fear that what was written, or even the half of it, was correct.

During my years as a teacher, I worked in a number of schools in three countries. A common feature was that regular staff meetings were held. Staff took it for granted that every month they gathered to discuss the many topics affecting their work, especially how to enhance the quality of school life, improve pupils' behaviour, attendance, examination results etc. In the more enlightened schools, the pupils were represented by one or two senior students, a most sensible idea I always thought. Although these meetings often ran on beyond 6pm, the time spent was never begrudged if the outcome was to benefit the most important people concerned, the pupils. Each member of staff was entitled/encouraged to contribute and even if our proposals were not accepted, at least we felt better for speaking up and having our opinions listened to. Staff wanted to be involved and committed to the organisation. A wise and experienced head teacher realised that staff responded better by being consulted rather than directed and was keen to hear of colleagues' problems, suggestions etc. Many of the best ideas came from classroom teachers. No such forum existed in the hospital for the night staff (nor day staff, to the best of my knowledge) and consultation, so I am told, is the rare exception rather than the rule in most hospitals. Democracy is an unknown concept in our NHS, and patients' views are generally of no interest to anyone. I remember asking a colleague who had worked in the hospital for more than ten years, when staff meetings were held. She looked at me quizzically and said: 'What's a staff meeting?'

I subsequently wrote to Mr Geraghty:

> Among our 26 night staff, a group of devoted and perspicacious individuals, there resides, by my reckoning, well over 250 years of nursing experience; experience gained in diverse areas and more significantly perhaps, in many different hospitals. This huge reservoir of expertise and wisdom lies virtually untapped. The staff is not aware of anyone in management caring to know its opinions on anything. When, some weeks ago my colleague and I tried to arrange a unit meeting, an idea supported by staff, every obstacle was put in our path. I was told 1) it was not necessary, 2) an agenda must be submitted and approved, 3) half-an-hour would be quite long enough, 4) the nurse manager would need to be invited – all caveats designed to kill off our suggestion stone dead. What we saw as a worthwhile and well-intentioned gathering, designed to improve our care of the patients, was construed, I suspect, as subversive if not seditious. How sad; how desperately sad.

The nurse manager was obviously alarmed at my suggestion of a staff meeting and implied that I was meddling in matters that were none of my concern. 'There is no need for one,' was her response. My questioning of her pronouncement seemed to irritate her no end, as if anyone who challenged her ordinance must be unhinged and/or a dangerous revolutionary. Such words as 'discussion, consultation, co-operation and agreement' were unknown to our managers. Rather than talk things over and seek mutually acceptable solutions to problems, diktat ruled. It was a style of management more in keeping with 1930 than 1990. So if nothing had been achieved, was it time to withdraw, retire, or see a psychiatrist? Had I got it all wrong? Was I perhaps imagining these incidents? Surely the chief nurse, two members of parliament, three consultant geriatricians, two nurse managers and the chief executive of the NHS could not all be wrong, could they?

On 11th December I wrote to the government's secretary of state for health, the Rt Hon Kenneth Clarke, enclosing copies of all the correspondence with the words: 'I appeal now for your help.'

On 3rd January 1990, Mr Tom Arnold MP sent me a letter which he had received from Mr Geraghty dated 28th December, Mr Geraghty wrote: 'With the assistance of bank nurses, the minimum cover provided on each ward is three staff and where possible we endeavour to have four staff available per ward.'

This was not my experience. C5 ward had never had four staff on at night and three perhaps once in a blue moon. A14 and A15 once or twice a year had four staff and the minimum cover should read 'two staff for 40 per cent of the night'. This was but a foretaste of the tenor of management statements to come. To Mr Arnold MP I wrote:

> The enclosed copy of our duty sheet for the week of 15th January starkly reveals our desperate plight. We are not even able to staff the wards to the standard which managers regard as appropriate. As you can see, on five nights no trained staff are available on one of the wards. No doubt bank staff will be found and auxiliary ladies moved from other areas. You can appreciate, I am sure, the weight of work for a full ward of acutely ill, very elderly patients, many in a parlous state, some close to death. It is an awesome and at times unbearable charge.

Hospital patients prefer to have regular staff that they can get to know and trust. This applies particularly with the elderly who like to see a familiar, friendly face. While this may have been the position for our patients during the day, it was not so at night. Because most of the night staff were part-time, they worked only two nights a week, making it difficult for patients to build up any sort of relationship with them. Presumably there were advantages (of a financial nature, I shouldn't wonder) to the hospital in employing part-time and bank staff, but from the patients' viewpoint, so often the last to be considered, it was far from ideal.

If sufficient part-time staff had been available, these difficulties could have been minimised. But rather than see a familiar face, the geriatric patients at night might have an unknown nurse, unfamiliar with both ward and patient routines. Often when I did my early walk round, patients would make some kind remark about seeing someone they knew. If repeated changes of staff were necessary (which I doubt) why not see to it that they affected the wards with younger, more adaptable patients? Just one more example, I fear, of hospitals being run more for the convenience of management than patients.

♦ ♦ ♦

On 11th January 1990, I wrote to Mr Geraghty. Not wanting to raise contention and discord I made no mention of his letter to Mr Arnold but put a suggestion to him which I hoped would present a more constructive approach. Part of the letter ran:

> Our best guide to future outcomes is past experience. Using this criterion, let me detail two recent ward-based nights.
>
> **THURSDAY 14th DECEMBER 1989   WARD A15**
> Twenty six patients, staff nurse, nursing auxiliary and me. The attached handover report shows three or four patients

with incontinence; three senile ladies; five confused; one violent; eight critically ill and four dying, an unexceptional, average night. But the report can barely hint at the distress and disturbance with which we three had to contend. For example, Mr Knowles died at 10.27 and within six minutes we were informed that another patient for that bed was on her way in. The speed and manner in which Mr Knowles' body was disposed of by the nurse manager sickened both staff nurse and me. I hope never again to see anything so improper and discreditable. Mrs Flatley had to be left – 'Special Care' out of the question, and I was compelled on my own to heave and drag her off the floor back into bed on a number of occasions. Other and worse things happened that night which were a disgrace to our noble and proud profession and which I would feel shamed to describe.

WARD A15   HANDOVER REPORT (SIDE I)   14.12.89

1. Mrs B Mott (94) Senile dementia, pressure sores, incontinent of urine. Calls out for long spells. All care, POORLY.
2. Mrs D Grout (89) Heamolytic anaemia, chest infection, congestive cardiac failure, social problems. Restless. NB husband died 5 days ago, VERY POORLY INDEED.
3. Mrs S Brett (78) Anaemia, chest infection. NB she is blind, deaf and dumb. IVI running. Oxygen.
4. Mrs A Urwin (76) Senile dementia, blackouts, confusion, NEEDS WATCHING CLOSELY; disorientated and wanders out of ward.
5. Mrs J Gooch (88) MI, septicaemia, renal failure, diabetes (BM stix 4-hly.), sliding scale insulin, BP 4-hly. Drowsy, tremor, pressure areas, turns, POORLY. OBSERVE.
6. Mrs E Sheldon (89) General deterioration. UTI, chest infection, doubly incontinent. Very Ill. All care needed.

7. Mrs G Cavanagh (79) CCF Parkinsonism, 16 stone plus, hugely oedematous legs. Incontinent, very concerned about her daughter, a patient in our psychiatric dept. Can be very demanding.
8. Mrs M Wheeler (83) CCF, MI, renal failure, anaemia, obese lady. Incontinent. TIA this am ?CVA, POORLY. All care.
9. Miss P Chorlton (89) Senile dementia. Comfortable.
10. Mrs K Lang (86) Dementia, weight loss, confusion, chest infection, social problems, vomiting. Fairly settled.
11. Mrs E Harris (70) MI, cough. Comfortable.
12. Mrs N Smith (74) Diabetic neuropathy, wasting of lower limbs. Incontinent. Poor nights.
13. Mrs T Rigby (82) Anaemia, collapse, confusion, TIA's, alcohol abuse. Restless.

SIDE II

1. Mrs H Bradley (76) Angina, ?M.I. Diabetic. VERY ILL. Deteriorating. Poor output. BP 4-hly. Now on diamorphine, oxygen continuously, POORLY.
2. Mr E Glasgow (75) COAD, chest infection, coughing up thick, green sputum, dyspnoea. Very distressed. Oxygen continuously, POORLY.
3. Mr W Knowles (86) M.I. Very ill indeed. Another MI this afternoon. Relatives present. Diamorphine at 1600 hrs.
4. Mr R Nolan (77) M.I. chest infection. Making good progress but very upset at impending death of Mr Knowles
5. Mrs B Povah (78) MI, bronchitis, pneumonia, chest pain. Epileptic (controlled). Congenital deformity right hand and arm. O_2 running. Fairly comfortable.
6. Mrs O Flatley (82) Overdose (amitriptyline, paracetamol and whiskey). Suicide note. Very confused and grossly agitated talking/shouting without pause to imagined person;

hallucinating. Seen by doctor from psychiatry. Won't stay in bed. NEEDS SPECIALING.

7. Mrs L Myers (81) CCF, hypertensive, hyperthyroid. Temporary pacing wire in situ. FAIR.

8. Mrs M Greaves (76) UTI., chest infection, general deterioration. IVI running, VERY POORLY.

9. Mrs W Cobb (89) CVA, general deterioration, drowsy, POORLY. All care needed.

10. Miss K Lyons (76) Leukaemia, general deterioration, diarrhoea, nausea. IVI. Poorly and sinking. For TLC.

11. Mrs T Karbowski (90) CVA, UTI, chest pain. Polish lady who speaks no English. Distressed and upset.

12. Mrs B Taylor (88) Senile dementia, acute confusion. Watch carefully. Wanders.

13. Mrs V Grey (89) Hypothermia, vomiting, arthritis, falls, POORLY. All care needed.

SATURDAY 6th JANUARY   WARD A14
Twenty five patients – two nursing auxiliaries and me.

I'll spare you the details. Suffice to say that it was a heavy and difficult night. The drug round (carried out alone with the concomitant dangers that ensures) took till 2240 hours; the general round was complete at a quarter to midnight when the last lights were put off. Thence we were on the go till about 0300 hours when a lull gave us a little respite. At 0425, a lady with a heart condition developed distressing chest pain and from that moment on we were flat out again. Miss Carew arrived to give us, as ever, monumental support for over two hours. Her staunch backing and untiring slog never cease to amaze me and to earn our huge appreciation. The one lady who had just suffered another infarction (heart attack) seemed to monopolise much of my time, though drugs were dispensed, nebulizers given and patients' immediate care attended to. But much had been neglected, no clinical observations taken and recorded, even for the very ill patients, no detailed enquiries made of our admission (at about 0600 in the midst of all else, a new patient arrived) and no written reports made on 22 patients, a glaringly unsatisfactory situation.

When I left for home at 0840 hours, I had been on duty without leaving the ward for a break for well over 12 hours. During that period I alone carried responsibility for the ward with its frail and endangered inmates. I had been on my feet for some 12 hours. During a long working life, I have always taken a quiet pride in a job well done. Now, for the first time, that record is tarnished. I returned to the hospital on Sunday evening after a sleepless day in bed.

Since last August, as you know, I have done all I can to highlight the gross understaffing at night on the geriatric area. On our one occasion of meeting (October 23rd) I did voice my appreciation of your own problems of monetary constraints and limited resources. With these in mind, may I make a suggestion, something small but positive perhaps in what may seem an otherwise negative position?

As from February 1st, I am prepared to be employed without salary for an indefinite period. The money (top of scale F) could then be utilized to employ staff nurses (say low position on scale D) for I estimate up to six nights every week. If the health authority can match, or slightly improve on, my offer we could raise enough money to employ two nurses (one for A14, one for A15) for the whole week, every week. Please ask the health authority to give the suggestion its most urgent and serious consideration. I remain optimistic that we can together resolve what seems an insuperable predicament.

That night of 6th/7th January 1990 was such a good example of every-thing I had been reporting to managers. From 4.25am the place was hectic beyond words and I doubt if a single patient could have slept through it. Even with the addition of Miss Carew and the doctor we just could not attend to more than basic needs. I managed to sit down to write reports (a 90-minute task) at 7.40am. The four critically important ones were written by 8am when, 15 minutes late, I handed over to the day staff. Then I returned to work at the bedside for another 20 minutes before taking myself home, thoroughly exhausted and upset that so much obvious neglect had once again occurred.

Following that trying night's toil I was stunned by a letter I received from Miss Carew on 9th January listing the nursing duties that I had failed to carry out on that shift. This included two inaccuracies. In her position I would have thanked the staff and congratulated them on the superb way they had managed. But instead she wrote:

> I must advise you that if, for any reason whatsoever in the future you are unable to carry out essential tasks, it will be necessary for you to advise me at the time. I am extremely concerned that these matters were not brought to my attention so that I could examine the possibility of re-deployment of staff in order to assist you.

Rather than visit the ward and discuss her concerns in a friendly manner, she wrote this unhelpful letter. I do not doubt for one moment that the massive responsibility which she bore caused her concern from time to time, but there are ways of encouraging staff, gaining their co-operation and admonishing if necessary, especially when the people concerned are so pleasant and amenable. Four weeks after writing to the secretary of state, Mr

Clarke, I wrote again to ask if my first letter, sent by recorded delivery, had been received. In late January, the chairman of the north western regional health authority, Mr R B Martin QC wrote to me as follows:

> I have read the related correspondence and noted your concerns. I am heartened to read of your commitment to your profession and of the care and devotion that you manifest towards the elderly patients that you nurse.
>
> I feel, however, that I must point out that it would be wholly inappropriate for the Region to interfere in the local management of the District's affairs.
>
> One of the roles of the region is to allocate funds to its Districts. It is then up to each district to manage its resources in order to provide the best possible health care for its population. Local managers are in the optimum position to plan for the health needs of their District and to ensure the best delivery of the service within the resources available to them. However, within a service with finite resources, there are many competing areas and managers have difficult decisions to make, particularly prior to the end of the financial year.

Mr Geraghty replied to my letter on 25th January 1990:

> I have discussed your offer of being employed without salary, with effect from 1st February, with Mr Caldwell the Unit General Manager. We considered this to be an extremely generous offer. However I must inform you that regretfully we are unable to accept. Difficulties regarding conditions of employment, contractual arrangements and insurance make it impossible.

It was now five months since my first letter, and in view of impending changes in staffing, the very antithesis of what was needed. On 1ˢᵗ February I wrote my first letter to Mr Milnes, the man I presumed made the ultimate decisions for the authority. I reminded him of his visit in August and commented on his 'professional and dignified approach', which nurse Thomson and I had found so reassuring. The letter continued:

> Far from our position improving, it is about to deteriorate and I would like you, as district general manager, to be in no doubt as to the present situation. When I took up my post at the hospital in August 1987 we had 15 nurses working 31 nights a week. We now have nine nurses on duty working 19 nights a week, a drop of 40 per cent! Since the enclosed duty sheet was prepared the situation has worsened with two trained staff on long-term sickness, one on maternity leave and one on medium-term sickness, a 30 per cent loss of trained staff. I employ no exaggeration when I state that our nurse cover is in crisis. And at such a time my charge nurse colleague and I are to be permanently warded. My appointment was as supervising charge nurse to provide block cover for three acute wards. Apart from covering for sickness, no mention was made of working nightly on one ward.
>
> At no time since have I been consulted about this change in my job description. Doing the job for which I was appointed, I make myself available to all three wards, providing on average some three-and-a-half hours help each night. When warded as sole nurse that extra assistance is lost, a 25 per cent reduction. The lost cover is not replaced by a night sister. For example, when warded on Saturday 13th January, the sister made one visit to the ward at 6.25am and stayed for 45 seconds. When I asked our manager why no cover is provided

when I am warded, she replied: 'There is no cover because you are a charge nurse'; a response as enigmatic as it is meaningless. Does management think that a charge nurse has two pairs of hands, that patients' needs are reduced when I am on the ward? The illogicality of such a statement seems to escape our managers.

Thus, five months after you promised that 'something would have to be done', it has – nurse cover is to be reduced. Reduced overall since August 1987 by 40 per cent and additionally, from today, by 25 per cent when I am warded as the one qualified person in charge. That my exposition of our desperate situation and this paradoxical and incomprehensible reduction in nurse hours appear to be correlated, is of less import than the menacing consequences which must ensue. An idea of the danger and neglect our patients are likely to be more frequently exposed to and the stress and exhaustion imposed on staff can be appreciated from my experience on December 14th and January 6th.

Our nurse managers appear to be so insensitive and so out of touch with the actual weight of work involved. Take, for example, the writing of reports. Before writing in the nursing Kardex one needs to take a close look at the patient, consult the recorded observations of such measures as temperature, pulse, blood pressure, intravenous infusion, fluid balance, BM stix reading (where appropriate), drug regime etc. One needs to discuss with other staff such matters as incontinence or level of confusion, to speak to the patient if possible and enquire regarding pain, sleep, bowel function and so on; to read, perhaps for the first time, the previous day's report or look through the medical notes; all this before one puts pen to paper. It takes, I find, on average three to four minutes to write one report with the thoroughness necessary for such acutely ill patients. So, when the only nurse on the ward, one has to find some 90 minutes for reports. To write a report any earlier than say 4am would be irresponsible and inaccurate. At between 3.30am and 3.45am our second break commences leaving two people on A14 and A15 and one on C5. The demands can then be such as to make report writing difficult if not impossible, and by the end of second break we are about to start the morning round. If an emergency develops, as happened on January 7th, something may have to be neglected. The nurse alone in such a situation may decide that patient care, safety and treatment must take precedence, a professional judgement available only to the nurse on the ward at the time.

Such was the situation on A14 on the morning mentioned. All important patient needs were met, all necessary care and treatment given. Do the nurse managers thank us for coping in such very trying circumstances? (I remained on duty for 12 hours without a break). Are we three perhaps commended for undertaking the work of four or five people? I returned home that morning utterly jaded in mind and body, so over fatigued that I was unable to sleep, the turmoil of the night gyrating through my head. And the night manager's response to all this? An officious and pretentious letter offering provocation and offence rather than credit and respect; implying censure rather than understanding.

It is disturbing that such tactics are resorted to by a nurse manager but at least the damage is contained within the hospital. More unsavoury, surely, is it to send out spurious and incorrect information, especially when the recipient is a member of Parliament. In all my contacts with others these last five months, I have taken great care to present evidence and facts with no disguise, no pretence.

Can you be surprised, Mr Milnes, that having so little in common with our nurse managers, I would prefer to deal with you. When presented with a problem our nurse managers seem to have a number of strategies:

1. Deny any problem exists.
2. Ignore it and hope it will go away; failing that
3. Procrastinate.
4. Deny responsibility; blame someone else/anyone else.
   If all else fails:
5. Attempt to discredit the problem-raiser.

To date I have experienced all five stratagems. My offer of January 11th stands. It is a genuine attempt to help implement a promise which I cannot get out of my head:

'Something will have to be done'.

Yours faithfully,
FG Pink

In retrospect, I can see that if managers had been concerned at what was going on they would have so indicated in response to this letter. My regard for Mr Milnes, as the letter shows, remained intact, and even after what had transpired, there still seemed hope that he could retrieve the situation if only by being truthful and admitting, if such was the case, that there was nothing the authority could do. That I would have accepted. Sadly, this opportunity was not taken. Mr Milnes wrote to me on 26th January to say:

I have seen the correspondence sent to you by Mr Geraghty and I know that the issues you have raised have been considered very carefully in the Unit. Before responding to you further on this point Mr Caldwell has asked Mrs Frederiks, the chief nursing officer, to assess the situation and to advise him, taking into account the workload and staffing levels on the wards. I will write to you again when this assessment has been carried out.

That was, as it turned out, an empty promise for, when he did write again, after a wait of three months, his eight lines failed to address the issues, rebut the evidence, offer any countervailing evidence or make any positive proposals. When asked by Peter Dale, the producer of the *40 Minutes* programme, what action he had initiated following his visit to the ward in August 1989, Mr Milnes replied: 'Erm...I made sure...I asked for the unit general manager to satisfy himself about staffing levels and the standards at night in the care of the elderly wards.'

Not, you will note, 'I asked for a report, an appraisal, a denial of the claims made'; none of these. And why wait six months to assess the situation? A question, like all the rest, never answered.

As Mr Milnes had referred to a Mrs Frederiks – of whom I knew nothing nor had ever heard spoken of – it seemed appropriate and courteous to write to her with copies of all the relevant correspondence. This I did on 1st March 1990. A letter enclosed said, in part:

> As you can see, over six months after raising our serious staff shortage with the health authority, far from the position improving, it has seriously degenerated, as bizarre and absurd a piece of maladministration as one is ever likely to experience. And when you consider that this has occurred in the full knowledge of our desperate predicament, it must cast a sobering shadow over the reasoning, competence and capacity of our nurse managers. Certainly, were I chief nursing officer I would be acutely dismayed by such behaviour.

At my meeting with the chief nurse on October 23rd, and in subsequent correspondence, he stated that our nurse cover at night was on a par with other wards in Stepping Hill and with other hospitals within and beyond Stockport. This is not in question. Our argument makes no comparisons nor is based on some notional, relative norm. The need is substantive and independent, a concept which managers appear unable or unwilling to grasp. When a nursing auxiliary, alone with 20 acutely ill patients, is obliged to stand and helplessly watch a patient die before her eyes, she draws no comfort to know how 'properly staffed' nurse management believes us to be. When I on my own have to drag a deranged and demented lady off the ward floor for the umpteenth time, and almost throw her onto her bed, it brings no solace to me (nor relief to Mrs Flatley) to be told that we 'have as many staff as . . .' Such information is irrelevant and meaningless.

Administrators, managers, consultants, NHS executives listen but do not hear. They do not want to know, do not I suspect, care. Are you not enraged to know what is going on? Were you reduced to the state that we are when you were a bedside nurse? Were your patients so abused and staff so disregarded? When in God's name will someone hear and act?

By mid-March I had received no reply, let alone acknowledgement, from the secretary of state for health, despite two further letters asking if he had received the first one. So on 15th March, after waiting 13 weeks, I wrote to the House of Commons speaker Mr Weatherill to request his intervention. A few days later, an assistant secretary replied to say: 'The speaker has asked me to explain that he cannot be responsible for the way in which ministers or members of Parliament deal with correspondence.' Mr Kenneth Clarke never responded to any of my letters.

As a last-ditch hope of arousing some interest in the patients' predicament, I had written to No 10 Downing Street on 4th February. I say 'Downing Street' because I was under no illusion that my letter would get anywhere near the lady to whom it was addressed. Presumably sack loads of mail arrive daily and have to be shunted off elsewhere. My letter read:

Dear Prime Minister,
May I request your intervention and help over a very distressing situation? The enclosed copies of correspondence dating back to last August outline my profound concern for the elderly and infirm in our area who are admitted to our wards. As you will see, the area health authority, the regional health authority and the Department of Health all appear unable to act. I do so hope, as busy and overloaded as you must be, that you are able PERSONALLY to read the letters and know of our plight. You are our last hope.

Yours faithfully,
FG Pink

A reply, dated 2nd April 1990 reads:

The Prime Minister has asked me to thank you for your letter. Mrs Thatcher receives so many letters from members of the public that she must in the normal course of business, delegate to her staff and Government Departments the responsibility of dealing with many of them. Your letter was forwarded to the Department of Health from which you will be receiving a reply in due course.

L Gonan

On 5th April I received a few lines from the health department. It read:

> Thank you for your recent letter [sic] to the Prime Minister and Kenneth Clarke. Once again, I must stress that I do not think it appropriate for us to attempt to establish nursing arrangements in a particular hospital. Responsibility for such decisions lie [sic] with the District Health Authority. I understand that Mr Milnes, wrote to you on 26th February advising you that he has asked Mrs Frederiks, to carry out a thorough assessment of the situation.

FOUR
TIME TO CARE

One must wait until the evening to see how splendid the day has been — **Sophocles**

One night in March 1990 a disturbing and significant experience had a lasting impression on me. There were three of us on duty, but as the only nurse I was dashing round, leaving this, only half-doing that, and trying to attend to essentials. I had started the medicine round but this was repeatedly interrupted. A number of infusions, including blood, had to be watched, while keeping an eye on oxygen therapy running on two ladies, a heart monitor kept in sight when possible, two very confused patients attended to every few minutes, a lady to commode, doctor to assist in examining a newly-admitted gentleman, and constant phone calls to answer. Such important responsibilities as clinical observations, injections, seeing that patients were given drinks, restarting a blocked infusion, providing assistance to a vomiting lady or making someone comfortable would all have to wait or even be ignored. As for the luxury of talking to patients in any meaningful or supportive way, that was out of the question. It is too easy for nurses, doctors and all of us who work in hospitals to forget that the place seems strange and intimidating, especially to the old. As Dr Wendy Savage observed in her book *A Savage Enquiry* (1986) we feel perfectly 'at home in hospitals, the surroundings are familiar, we know all the people, we have the pleasure and satisfaction of having accomplished worthwhile work in the building, and it is hard for us to see the place as an outsider does, frighteningly impersonal, overlarge, filled with remote people in a rush, and often associated with unhappy memories of illness or death.'

If younger people feel as Dr Savage describes, how much more upsetting must it be for an 80 year old. Remember that some of our patients had not been in hospital since childhood; for others the only recent contact was the illness and death of their spouse, perhaps in the very same ward. And now, when in need of peaceful surroundings and someone to listen and give comfort, they find themselves surrounded by mayhem.

The one thing (perhaps the only really important thing) that a very ill, conscious patient may want to do, is talk to someone. The physical aspects of care – bathing, pressure area relief, mouth and eye care, toileting, suppression of nausea and pain control, help with breathing, drugs and nourishment are all necessary, and we did our best to attend to these bodily matters, albeit often poorly. But a sick, elderly patient needs so much more than this. They need: companionship, respect and unstinting affection. The lack of opportunity to sit quietly and converse with a patient was particularly disconcerting. Approaching death can be an anxious and lonely time, and for many, very frightening. The mad-rush environment of a busy hospital ward at night is far from conducive to the serene, reflective atmosphere that the terminally ill need as the end approaches. Once all the lights were out, usually around 11.30pm, it would have been good to have enough staff to allow us to sit with worried, unsettled patients who might want to talk to a caring listener. As it happened, that night there was one such gentleman on A14, Mr Haviland. He had been informed by doctor the previous day that he had cancer and I ought to have had time that night to sit with him but there was just too much to do.

At about 9.30pm, with little progress made on the drug round, the phone rang again. It was Mrs Haviland. She phoned each night at about the same time. She was in some considerable distress having received from the doctor earlier in the day confirmation of what she had been dreading, that she was soon to become a widow. She was alone at home and needed someone to talk to. The drug round and the other work could wait. Even the doctor, who was impatiently requesting my assistance, got a rare, curt answer to her 'Are you going to be much longer?' Indeed I was. We spoke for close on ten minutes. Their only child had died the previous year, following a lifetime of handicap, and now Mrs Haviland had no other relative but her husband. She seemed to take comfort from our chat, she talking and I mainly listening. I think I said all the right things and she took heart from my assurance that Mr Haviland was settled and pain free and would be carefully and constantly watched through the night, a justifiable untruth, I thought, in the circumstances.

As I put the phone down, an unknown staff nurse came onto the ward. She had been sent to help out from the intensive care unit which was quiet. I was able to get on with the drugs while she saw to the observations, testing, charting, treatment and other nursing care. By 10.40pm the lights were out, an unheard of achievement, and nurse had been able to sit with one gentleman who was in pain until he calmed. I was free to speak quietly to some relatives who were with their dying father. In other words, by having the level of cover I was requesting, the patients were properly cared for and the staff unstressed. A more convincing example of the truth of my case would be difficult to cite.

In conversation later with staff nurse, I learned that four nurses were allocated to her unit each night, and I could not help wondering about the equity and morality of a system which provided *four* nurses for four patients in one department – high-tech, expensive, glamorous intensive care, and *one* nurse for 26 patients in another – ours! Does this say anything of management's attitude to elderly sick people? Do not these patients deserve better than this? They have devoted a lifetime to their families; they have served their communities and their country through a world war, some on the battlefield. We owe them a debt of honour and respect that can never be repaid, yet assign them, so often, to a degrading ordeal in their last hours on earth. But nurse managers are not alone in needing to hang their heads in shame. The whole community must accept responsibility for what is happening,

Once all was settled on that March night, I took the opportunity provided by our proper staffing to go to Mr Haviland, sit by his bed, and tell him of his wife's call. I knew that, despite sedation, he was awake and restless. He welcomed someone to talk to and spoke of many things, especially his fears and concerns, not for himself but for his beloved wife. He thought that she was unaware of his condition and wanted to protect her from unnecessary suffering. 'We've had 52 years of love and happiness,' he said, 'and now it's time to part.' He went on to recall so many cherished memories of what must have been a wonderful life together. He did most of the talking. I doubt that I have ever spent, or ever will spend as long as I live, a more intensely poignant yet worthwhile 30 minutes and was thankful that the ward lights were out. As we clasped hands, the morphine took effect and he drifted into sleep.

The demands and pressures of a nurse's work can be very difficult and at times oppressive, but the rewards are sublime. What an inestimable privilege it was to be so close to Mr Haviland at such a time. If I achieve nothing else in my lifetime, that one experience will suffice. In the early hours, I phoned Mrs Haviland to say that her husband was peaceful. She sounded relieved and promised to lie down till morning.

In a letter to Mr Milnes some days later, I wrote:

> Had I been in any doubt these recent months of the justice or morality of my stand for more nurses, that one night dispelled

it. I am now convinced, beyond peradventure, how compellingly valid is the claim. Would that I could persuade others.

Our night passed pleasantly and the morning round was carefully and thoroughly carried out without rush or frayed nerves. We went home tired but in the knowledge that the patients had been properly cared for. I felt a sense of contentment, the depth of which defies description. How honoured and blessed I felt to be in such a glorious occupation as nursing.

Mr Haviland did not regain consciousness and died the following night, his sweetheart of over half a century at his side. So my conversation with this brave, selfless and gentle man was his last in this world.

♦ ♦ ♦

As the March daffodils bloomed, any hope that our difficulties might soon be at an end faded. In fact, perversely, the nursing cover was reduced by the warding of myself and my charge nurse colleague. This ill-considered and dangerous move was foisted on us without any consultation or agreement. I found it inconceivable that important changes directly affecting those of us who worked on the wards and who were directly concerned with the patients could be taken in such a high-handed and arbitrary manner. It was a style of management which I thought had gone out of fashion decades ago. But nursing, in this respect at least, hasn't heard that the Crimean War is over. 'It is still a rigidly hierarchical profession. Nurses are not trained to question those in authority. They are trained to get on with the job, more in the manner of the military than anything else' (Jay Rayner, *Guardian*, 15.1.93). What a way to run a so-called caring profession. Certainly at Stockport at night, the military comparison was most apt. Few staff were prepared to step out of line or question management's command. I did, and paid the price.

Miss Carew told me that the warding of the two unit charge nurses was an 'experiment' but was not prepared to discuss the matter or consider reasons why a ward for the elderly might not be the best place to carry out an experiment. None of the other night supervisory nurses, all sisters, were warded, though one might suggest that the medical or surgical areas with younger, fitter patients would be more suitable for trying out something new. It was difficult not to wonder at least if my loud and long protestations were the real cause of our warding. For management, it did have the advantage that I then could see only the one ward and be denied nightly access to two thirds of the staff.

Time to take stock. Was there anyone else who might be approached for advice or help? Having written in excess of 17,000 words in 49 letters to everyone I thought might be concerned, and having had negative responses or no response from them all, it seemed that there was little else to be done. Even the nurses' regulatory body, the United Kingdom Central Council for Nursing, Midwifery and Health Visiting (now the Nursing and Midwifery Council) had chosen to ignore me. And, I suppose, to some extent it was this complete rejection by everyone that strengthened my resolve to fight against what to me, and only to me it seemed, was a glaring wrong.

It was during March that someone suggested contacting the local authority and enquiries led me to meet Mrs Anne Coffey, leader of the labour group on Stockport Council. She advised me to see Mr Andrew Bennett MP who represented the Denton and Reddish constituency. This was arranged for a Saturday morning. He had had an opportunity to read the correspondence and was most complimentary about my efforts. We talked at some length but he was not hopeful that his intervention would add anything or provoke the health authority to provide more staff. The massive Conservative majority in the House of Commons was cited as reason for his pessimistic/realistic outlook. He hinted at publicity. However I was strongly opposed to that as my opinion then of the press and other media was such that I wanted to avoid going public at all costs. I did not want the story sensationalised, trivialised or personalised. The situation was too serious and too wretched for that. 'But you've done everything possible,' he said, 'and far more than any other one individual I've ever come across. There's little else left, and I know someone who'll treat the case seriously and sensitively.' We parted on the understanding that I would give the idea some thought, but it was not what I wanted. He promised to raise the matter in the House of Commons as soon as he could.

I pondered long and hard on the difficulties of publicity. Apart from anything else, the idea of possibly becoming public property was unsettling. I had managed to live for 60 years unknown but to a small circle of family and friends and that suited me well. On the other hand, where else was there to go if the events I was nightly witnessing were to be stopped? Was there the danger that the story could be distorted in such a way that relatives and future patients would be unduly worried about admission to Stepping Hill, which might, for all I knew, have a high standing in the eyes of the local community? My bedside colleagues, not seeing what I had written about them, might infer that I was criticising them, when in truth the opposite was the case. But the overriding fact was that no one I had approached seemed in the least concerned. And it was the case that the potential harm of 'adverse' publicity was just that – potential, whereas what I had described was actual. But would the readers of some small article be any more likely to believe me, and if they did, what could they do faced with the wall of silence and indifference that I was up against? After much heart-searching, I agreed to let Mr Bennett MP show the letters to someone in the press, subject to a later veto on publication. There was, of course, no certainty that a paper would consider the affair of sufficient interest to warrant writing about, so the possibility passed from my mind as the work continued.

One night in early April, the assistant night nurse manager, Miss O'Donnell, made one of her rare visits to the ward. She told me that the chief nursing officer required an account of one night's activity. No reason for this request was proffered. We agreed that I should record the next night's work. Other nurses had been so instructed. It seemed to me most unsatisfactory to expect us to add to our usual routine the task of writing down everything we did but I duly carried out my instructions. Rather than hand in some scrappy piece of paper, I carefully wrote up my notes two days later during my off-duty period and sent them as a letter on 9th April.

Dear Mrs Frederiks,
The nursing officer has requested me to prepare for you an account of one night's activity on Ward A14 and this I shall attempt to do. I have, though, a number of reservations as to the objectivity, comprehensivity, and reliability of such a narrative.

To jot down contemporaneously is a skill at which nurses are untaught and inexpert. With practice, and acting as an observer, the technique can be mastered. But to attempt such a task unprepared, with no guidance, and acting as a participant, observing and reporting on oneself, must be particularly difficult, if even possible. Add to this the time and pressure factors of night duty, where very often it is a struggle to keep one's head above water, and the value of such notes must be highly suspect. For example, one set of such observations, which I believe you already have, was started at 2am, five-and-a-half hours after commencement of duty.

Nurse tells me that as the only trained member of staff on duty she was run off her feet that night and wrote something of what had happened up till then. She said that it was quite impossible to relate more than a very general impression; she was unclear as to what was wanted; had to keep leaving the account to attend to patients' needs and had no idea why she had been given such a task, digressive and time-consuming as it seemed. The adequacy and usefulness of such accounts must be very much open to question.

May I suggest two alternatives, the findings of which would perhaps carry some validity and credibility.

A. An objective enquiry carried out by trained and experienced observers throughout a good number of complete nights, unannounced and randomly chosen.

B. A series of interviews with staff, willing to participate, to gain views on staffing, workload, patient care and safety, stress, solutions to problems, etc (*vide* my letter of January 11th to Mr Geraghty). Such interviews should, I suggest, ideally be private, conducted outside working hours, and fairly informal. Observers and interviewers need not be nurse trained but should be independent of the hospital and health authority.

A combination of A and B would provide evidential and authoritative witness to substantiate or refute the detailed observations and submissions that I have made.

On the night in question, I did attempt to keep running notes of my work and these I propose now to use to delineate the sequence. Additionally, whereas others requested have, I imagine, written immediately and consequently with circumscription, I am writing a day or two later with time to elaborate and comment. The night was not typical, for there is no such thing. The notes are recorded chronologically and relate mainly to myself.

WARD A14   WEDNESDAY APRIL 4th 1990.
Number of patients; 26 (8 ladies & 18 gentlemen). Number of staff: 3.
20.30 – Day report taken during which a new patient arrives.
20.55 – Report finished. Colleagues start the bed round whilst I inform doctor by phone of Mrs Bryce's arrival, then attend to the lady. Basic details (age, next-of-kin, religion etc.) taken, a number of essential forms/charts made out, Identiband placed on patient's wrist, details entered into admission book etc. and patient made comfortable. Have a quick word with relatives. Called to help lift Mr Moon (80, CCF, confusion, gross obesity, weighs 25 stone). Phone – doctor wanted.
21.15 – Start drug round. Doctor arrives, leave drugs, doctor needs assistance taking blood. Phone, Admissions' Office with enquiry regarding Mrs Bryce. Relatives arrive to visit Mrs Sykes (75, weight loss, confusion, general deterioration, UTI, falls, VERY POORLY); briefly speak to relatives, return to drugs. No Ventolin on trolley, go to cupboard, stopped on way by Mrs Bryce's relatives who need advice and reassurance. Say a few words but explain that I am too busy to stay with them.
21.25 – Try to calm down Mr Murphy (92, general deterioration, neglect, arthritis, pressure sores, very agitated) who is shouting and trying to climb out of bed. Patient requests me to pour a drink. Back to drugs, set up nebulizer. Coughing lady asks for tissues; go and search for some, phone, another ward requests a drug, look in two locked cupboards, we do not have. Speak to doctor re. IV infusion; phone, laboratory, blood

results on Mrs Bryce, take down, read back to technician, enter into 'Results Book'. Try to return to drugs, phone, patient enquiry.

21.35 – Relatives in side ward most concerned about their mother (Mrs Sykes); they are clearly very distressed and I know want to talk. I apologise but say I have no time to spare, feel wretched about this. Patient asks me for another pillow, go to look for one in linen room, none. For months I have been requesting more pillows, a stock of 20 or so is needed. Night after night I request. Result? never any pillows; go over to ward A15 to look for one, they have none either. Return and apologise to patient who cannot understand the shortage; nor can I.

21.40 – Try to continue drugs; now on fifth patient. Lady calls me to help her put on cardigan; patient asks what his drugs are for so I explain, having to look one up in book. Find we have no verapamil on trolley, look in cupboard, none, go to A15, none there. Phone, doctor wanted by another ward, look for her, she's not on ward.

21.50 – Porter arrives to take Mrs Bryce to X-ray. Discontinue drugs and a nebulizer. Lock trolley, six patients have been given medication in 40 minutes, find blanket for patient in wheelchair. Hand over keys. Leave for X-ray. By now other two staff are on side two. I have left for X-ray, so half the ward is completely unattended with the staff well out of earshot, let alone sight.

21.55 – Arrive X-ray.

22.27 – Return to ward. Mrs Bryce, who has not had a drink for five hours or more, asks for some hot milk and this I prepare. Return to drugs, have to shake awake patients for them to be given their tablets. Mr Fitton says he needs loraza-pam, has been on them for ten years at home and won't settle without; says he so told day staff on admission earlier today but they appear to have overlooked this. Look for doctor to write prescription, not on ward; no erythromycin on trolley, none in cupboard, phone, enquiry about patient we do not have. Go to A15 for erythromycin.

22.43 – Doctor arrives and writes up lorazapam but on looking, we have none. Go to A15. Mr Murphy continues to shout and disrupt his side of ward. Dr prescribes sedative and I draw up, have checked and administer. Dr wants IV frusemide, I prepare.

22.58 – Lights out. Assist Dr prepare IV erythromycin, eye drops for Mrs Bryce prescribed and I administer. Phone, enquiry by relative about Mr Robertson (80, CVA, right. hemi. chest infection, incontinent x 2, very agitated and restless, unable to swallow).

22.58 – Sister visits for first time; does not do a round, look at Kardex or show the slightest interest in the patients; is on ward for 1 min. 45 secs.

23.30 – Take my break, first chance of a drink since leaving home four hrs ago.

Thus passed the first part of the night. It had not been unusual or out of the ordinary in any way as far as the work was concerned. Yet there was something different, the unique aspect mentioned above, in that we had three trained staff on duty. Our normal complement is two auxiliaries and one nurse. Had such been the situation on April 4th, then much would have had to be neglected and patients put at risk. It is unlikely that any clinical observations could have been recorded, and infusions (eight of them) would not have been kept running on time. There is no way that one nurse can cope properly even on a quietish night like this. You must now know this to be true as do nurse managers and everyone else. There can be no one in the authority, and way beyond, who is unaware that neglect of patients and abuse of staff nightly occur at Stepping Hill and, were I in your position, I would feel a sense of deep shame and disgrace.

It should not have been necessary to tell Mrs Frederiks, a nurse, how unreliable her method of collecting data on a night shift was. In her position, I would have put myself onto the ward for a few whole nights and seen what was happening at first hand. To run the nursing services of a large general hospital by sitting in some remote office issuing this sort of edict is surely not the way to do things. My colleagues who were told to record their activities at night, found it meaningless and just one extra chore and did it, they told me, with reluctance. As conscientious as I was trying to be that night, it was impossible to keep stopping to scribble down exactly what I had just been doing the previous few minutes. That would have added at least one minute to every ten throughout the night. Thus, as detailed as this account may appear, much of the night's activity went unrecorded. This is no way to carry out a serious investigation into staffing levels and one must wonder if it was laid on intentionally to produce a false and distorted picture. And how reliable can information gathered on so unusual a night be? It was utterly unheard of for three nurses to be on duty all night on any geriatric ward but on 4th April, the night the nurse manager knew I was to record our activity, this was the staffing position. Amazing! Subtlety was never a hallmark of our senior nurses.

My letter to Mrs Frederiks continued:

00.10–01.10 – Charting, checking IVIs, trying, without much success, to calm Mr Murphy and Mr Robertson; change bed for patient who split urinal, provide a drink for patient, put lady on commode, read some Kardexes.

01.10–01.50 – Incontinence/turns round. (Note, from 11.30 to 01.45 hrs two staff only on duty.)

01.50 – on – Quiet period. Complete paper work for admission of new patient; walk round ward every ten minutes or so to check on each patient individually, empty and renew urinals, change two wet beds, try again to calm confused patients, answer a number of phone calls, put two ladies on commodes, prepare morning medications, keep an eye on the infusions and change as necessary, talk briefly to sleepless patient, make him a cup of tea, go in search of pillows from other wards, take gentleman to toilet, lift another up the bed, check and suction Mrs Brown's mouth (83, CVA, right hemi., cerebral signs, blind, nauseous, taking nil orally, chest infection, turns) which is constantly filling with large amounts of phlegm, provide pain tablets for Mr Moon, two-hourly turns, provide blanket for a patient who is cold and linctus for another with a cough, set up trolley for morning round.

At 03.30 – Second break started.

I trust that this outline, fragmentary as it is, conveys at least a feel for what's involved. Keep in mind that every patient is frail and acutely ill, many incontinent, confused, demented, immobile, paralysed, blind or deaf and distressed. On average, seven patients at any one time will be dying. In 1988, for example, of 981 people admitted to A14, 261 died on the ward, that is 26.6 per cent. To say that many of these deaths go unnoticed is alarmingly true. Some time ago, after a frantic night on C5 ward, the nurse, as ever the only nurse for 20 people, found when the lights were switched on at 5.20am, three patients DEAD IN BED. Do you, Mrs Frederiks, find that situation acceptable or reasonable? I do not, nor does our night staff, though your nurse managers and everyone else appear to.

There remains the morning round to be described, but permit me to highlight one problem here. On average two staff need five minutes to devote to each patient each morning. I say 'on average' for, on the morning of April 5th, it took all three of us 12 minutes to attend to Mr Moon. Four porters had to be employed to move him into bed the previous evening. It took over ten minutes to wash, change and settle Mr Robertson. So five minutes for each is not excessive. Two pairs could thus complete the ward round in 65 minutes. But one pair (we never have two) needs two hours and 10 minutes. So we are compelled to start at 5.30am, sometimes earlier, and to rush in an unceremonious, offhand manner. Remember that it might have been close on midnight before the lights went out. What an unseemly and unwarrantable performance. It does not appear to bother the nurse managers unduly but it sickens me.

While staff nurse and I undertook the round, an exhausting and punishing two hours any morning but particularly back-breaking that morning, our companion took the observations, collected the required specimens, answered the phone, gave out the medication, kept an eye on the infusions, helped with Mr Moon and Mr Robertson, made and gave out the tea, fed the helpless, charted the drinks, bundled up the linen (nine bags), put some ladies on the commode, sucked out Mrs Brown, gave oxygen, brought out extra linen to the trolley as required, collected the pots, washed and dried them, rinsed patients' teeth prior to replacement, took Mr Jackson to the toilet etc.

The night sister collected the report and stayed for all of 30 seconds. Her total time on A14 that night, 2 minutes 15 seconds. Her contribution to the patients' comfort and safety, ZERO. Yet one more shameful aspect of this whole disreputable saga.

Yours faithfully

FG Pink

Not only is nursing management often Byzantine, but ward-level practice in so many respects is premised, not on what is best for the patient, but on what suits the staff. With so few nurses in relation to the demands this is understandable, at times unavoidable. When I was a nursing student it would not have been thought decent to wake patients for the morning wash before 6am. But 40-odd years later, here we were routinely putting on the lights between 5.15am and 5.30am because there was so much work to be done and, believe it or not, providing a bowl of water for those patients who wanted one was not included. Most of a patient's timetable in hospital is, as it always has been, organised to fit in with the doctors', nurses' and others' schedules and to some extent this is acceptable. But do we have to be waking up elderly patients at such an unearthly hour because the day staff, so the night nurses are convinced, expect everyone to be ready for breakfast at 7.40am when the food trolley arrives? Must those patients well enough to sit out be put in a chair at crack of dawn (or earlier) to spend so many long, wearying hours in the one position just for us to say that everyone has 'been seen to'? Shouldn't the day, to some extent, be arranged to suit patients? Surely 6.30am or 7am is early enough to start the morning round, especially after a disturbed night. Routine has its place but in hospitals it is too often seen as sacrosanct; we do it this way because we've always done it this way. The fact that the patient's stay, and care, is continuous, not compartmentalised, is overlooked and the old, well-worn pattern slavishly followed. Change and questioning existing practice are too often somehow seen as suspect. Many nurses are suspicious of new ideas and innovation but, I am told, this attitude is changing. Great. But how long will it take?

The task of writing at length to as many people as I did was certainly time-consuming. I would gather all the required details, reports, figures etc. and put them in some sort of reasoned order, write a first draft, edit it then write a second, sometimes a third draft

all in longhand. One letter could take several days. It was essential
to give a great deal of thought and care to everything I wrote. Once
satisfied with the script, I took it for typing to the agency four miles
away. A day or so later I returned to collect the work, read through
and post it off. This needed to be fitted into my normal life and I
was aware from the beginning that the whole thing could dominate
much of my time. This I was determined to avoid. I suppose in
reality there was less time for other things but I managed somehow
to fit the letters in to an otherwise busy existence.

Getting out into the country, for example, perhaps became a
more necessary and more enjoyable relaxation. I could walk for
miles either to reflect on what was going on or, more likely, to forget
all about it. I recall one glorious day in April 1990. I was up early
and by 8.30am out in the Derbyshire Dales beyond Buxton. The
refreshing air, the bird song, nature exploding on all sides, the
silence of a bright spring morning overwhelmed me with joy. Then
to cap it all came a magical encounter. Coming along the valley
towards me I saw a large dog. I waited for the owner to come into
view but no owner appeared. I stood stock still as the animal steadily padded towards me. It was a fox in immaculate condition. Either
it was unaware of my presence or saw me as no threat. I froze as
it imperiously trotted past some 15 feet below where I stood. For
a 'townie' like me this was an awesome sight. What a magnificent
animal it was, lord of all it surveyed and no doubt off to find some
juicy, newborn lamb for breakfast; a simple but wonderfully happy
memory to cherish for years to come.

FIVE
DEAR MR PINK

*Give me the liberty to know, to utter, and to argue
freely according to conscience, above all liberties*
— **John Milton, *Areopagitica (1644)***

As promised, Mr Andrew Bennett MP forwarded my correspondence to a journalist he knew. It was David Brindle, social services correspondent at the *Guardian*, and on Wednesday 11th April 1990 the newspaper devoted a whole page to extracts from the correspondence below a photograph of me sitting with a patient. It must have been quite a problem for Mr Brindle, to edit so many words to something less than 4,000, but at least I was relieved to see that the story was presented in the words of the participants themselves, leaving the readers to draw their own conclusions. In a brief introduction Mr Brindle wrote:

> Only in his dedication could Graham Pink be described as a typical nurse. At the age of 60, when other men would be winding down or already retired, he is not only working 12-hour night shifts, but is taking an MA with the Open University. Some would see his approach as over-emotional; his style as precious. Others, reading his words, would say it must be hard to remain detached in such stressful circumstances.

Management was aware that the extracts were to be published and had made a short response. 'We are taking the matter very seriously,' commented Mr Milnes. 'The matter is still under review.' What this

means is anyone's guess, but how could it be still under review?
A week or two, a month at most, would have been more than long
enough to establish or discredit my reports; but well over seven
months? Either the accounts were true or they were not. It would
have been straightforward enough to check the facts if management
wanted to know the truth. Quite patently, it didn't. If that had been
done then my conclusions as to the need for extra staff could have
been challenged and discussed. But managers would not talk about,
let alone admit, my descriptions, and this perhaps was a shrewd
tactic. If you ignore an unpalatable fact, you can pretend that it
doesn't exist. It's an approach that I do not understand; never have;
never will.

I was soon to learn, though, that the matter was not to be
discussed either with me or among the staff. The coded message was
flashed along the bush telegraph: 'Do not talk to charge nurse Pink
about the staffing or the *Guardian* extracts,' and by and large few
did. The million-plus *Guardian* readers and thousands of nurses all
over Britain could and did discuss the affair, but for those directly
involved it was a taboo subject. If you think that strange, as did I,
remember that there is no medicine for fear.

On Good Friday the paper published two letters. Alastair Heron,
professor emeritus, wrote from Sheffield:

> The situation described so graphically could certainly be
> replicated in many health districts nationwide. Once one had
> begun to take in the human implications of the conditions for
> the very elderly and multiply-ill patients, for their relatives,
> for Charge Nurse Pink and for his all too few colleagues,
> there could be no question of anyone being too 'emotional'.
> For his single-minded dedication, and for his determination
> to leave no stone unturned to get matters improved, there can
> be nothing but grateful praise.

After months of frustration it was uplifting to read that someone apart from Andrew Bennett MP thought that my efforts were worthwhile.

For me the effect of Dr Heron's words were a mixture of relief at a burden shared, sadness that I had been reduced to publicising the case, plus great humility. And I found Dr Heron's belief that all the officers to whom I had appealed would find unacceptable the described conditions 'for their mother, father, wife or husband' compelling. If, as he believed, they would reject outright such treatment for their own loved ones, how could they possibly condone (or ignore) it for others?

Some nights after the *Guardian* piece appeared, one staff nurse, who hadn't perhaps heard of the manager's 'advice', or more likely dismissed the possible consequences, spoke to me about the report.

'You know, when my husband read your account in the *Guardian*, he said he didn't believe it and asked me to confirm that you were making it up or at least exaggerating. I had to admit that everything you'd written was completely true. 'But you've been working on those wards for years and you've never described anything like this to me,' was his response. This made me think and brought home the fact that we are just so used to what goes on here, that we take it for granted.

'It was not until I read your words in cold print that I appreciated how the system dulls our senses and leads us to abandon our standards. But here we all are, long-serving nurses, knowing that so much of what happens is unacceptable and at times dreadful, yet we do not complain and it takes you, a newcomer, and a man, to do what we ought to have done years ago.'

She thought that the fact I had been out of nursing for many years was significant; I had returned with a less-jaded perspective and hope of improvement had not yet been driven out by 'reality' as it had for her and her colleagues.

This was the time of the Strangeways Prison riots in Manchester when nightly on our television screens we saw inmates rampaging on the prison roof, and it made one wonder how much all this destruction would cost (in excess of £80 million in the end) and how many nurses we could employ for a fraction of this. Roger Brockbaub from London SW11 had the same thought in his letter to the *Guardian*, published on 16th April.

> Thank you for the article on one member of the NHS and his struggle with his daily work, as well as his tireless devotion in advocating humane care for the lost souls of his ward, and on the soul-less people who manage such institutions. Peter Milnes, the general manager of Stockport Health Authority, should hang his head in shame. I worked as a student nurse and staff nurse for five years at Manor and Springfield Hospitals – mental handicap and psychiatric institutions in Epsom, Surrey and Tooting, London, respectively. It was the norm for student nurses to be in charge of geriatric wards at night alone, with up to 40 geriatric patients in their care.
>
> Institutions do not like 'whistleblowers'. My complaints to my nursing hierarchy about conditions, nursing levels, ill-treatment, etc, frequently resulted in nurses' notes I had written on incidents disappearing from patients' case notes, and to disciplining from superiors with reminders to 'keep my nose clean' (otherwise I would fail my training) and veiled threats from colleagues. Mr Pink is a brave man fighting a form of care that we all share some blame in. Unfortunately, apart from Mr Pink, there is little likelihood of Mrs B Mott (94), Mrs D Gout (89) or Mrs S Brett (78) getting our attention, even if they climbed onto the roof of ward A15 and threw tiles!

Ann Davies, a registered nurse from Bradford, wrote:

> How many more times do we have to hear of the plight of the NHS before any changes are made? Mr Pink's experiences are not unusual but typical of those faced by thousands of nurses. Few nurses can say that they have never been in a similar situation. I was frequently left in charge of a ward at night from the beginning of my second year of training at a London teaching hospital. Assisted only by a first-year student, I had no qualified help actually on the ward. This practice was the norm then and I suspect still is. Many occasions spring to mind when patients' lives were in danger as a result of the low standard of care provided. Only when realistic levels of staff are provided, will the dangerous and abusive treatment of both nurses and patients stop. Until then the possibility, indeed likelihood, of a patient or nurse in any of our hospitals experiencing conditions similar to those described by Mr Pink is almost certain.

The response to the paper's coverage was overwhelming. I started to receive letters via the paper or the health authority and letters flowed in to the editor. Speaking some time later in one of the television documentaries about my case, David Brindle said:

> Initially, a substantial file of Mr Pink's early correspondence arrived on my desk from Andrew Bennett MP with a simple covering note saying, 'I think you may find this of interest'. It was not unlike other files I receive from people who've got axes to grind and frankly the thickness of it was rather intimidating and I didn't look at it for several days. But when I did, I found a very special combination of factors which made me realize straight away that here was something which would make a very good package for us.

The response was enormous. We had countless phone calls;
scores of letters from people identifying with what Mr Pink
was saying, and people trying to get in touch with him to congratulate him and really it was the most enormous response
I've ever experienced in journalism.

One of those letters came from Stepping Hill on 21ˢᵗ April.

In your in-depth account of one man's opinion of staffing levels
within the geriatric department at Stepping Hill Hospital,
Graham Pink expresses his concern about the quality of service
we can offer. Indeed, over the past 12 months we have enhanced
the establishment of staff through an investment of £28,000, to
provide night bank nurses. If problems do arise, the night nurse
manager can be contacted to request assistance. The instances
Mr Pink mentions which are not unique to geriatrics, are certainly not every-day occurrences. I do not dispute that the ideal
situation would increase these levels to four members of staff.
Unfortunately, resources do not permit this.

We believe the quality of care we offer meets the physical
needs of all our patients, and their emotional and social needs.
The staff working in geriatrics have chosen this area as their
speciality, and each possesses the special qualities which this
demanding work requires. An additional ward is to be opened
later in the year, and an extra £250,000 is being provided
for this development. After reading your article and the
subsequent replies, I fear families throughout the country will
be subjected to undue concern over standards which, though
not ideal, are not as black as has been painted.

D Caldwell, (General Manager),
Stepping Hill Hospital, Stockport, Cheshire

The letter accepts for the first time that limited resources are a problem. But where Mr Caldwell speaks of four staff as the 'ideal' situation, my evidence shows that four would provide only basic to reasonable care. And much of what he writes is either irrelevant or misleading. The suggestion that a bank nurse can be provided at a moment's notice is spurious (it never once happened) and an extra ward does not address the highlighted difficulties; in fact it might exacerbate them. To say that staff choose to work with the elderly may have once been true, but not today. Many nurses are in geriatric care because that is where the jobs are. For example, one young man who had just qualified as a registered nurse was offered a placement on ward A14 as a staff nurse (days). It was not his first choice, he told me, but no other posts were available. (Many newly qualified nurses leaving training are going straight into unemployment or casual non-nursing employment.) This young man had recently set up home and become a father. He lived locally and was not in a position to seek a post miles away. Work on our area of the hospital for him was Hobson's choice; not the best reason for nursing the elderly. What the general manager fails to grasp or admit is that local families (and perhaps families throughout the country) have every right and reason to be concerned over standards of care for their ageing relatives. His failure to deny or discredit (publicly, or privately to the staff) any of the described incidents or to produce any counter evidence speaks volumes for management's case.

The first communication to me from management following the publicity was sent by Mr Geraghty nine days later, requesting a meeting with Mr Caldwell and him 'as soon as possible'. In response to an earlier invitation to a meeting, I had written to Mr Geraghty on 16th March offering seven different dates and times in April when I would be readily available but not one of these was convenient. Now, following the publicity, they were most anxious to meet. A date was set: 17th May 1990.

Meanwhile, on 23rd April, Mr Andrew Bennett MP asked questions in the House of Commons and received the following answers:

W408 Mr Andrew F Bennett MP (Lab Denton and Reddish): To ask the secretary of state for health what assessment he has made of the staffing levels on the geriatric wards at Stepping Hill, Stockport and whether he has discussed the matter with either the Regional or District Health Authorities.

MR ROGER FREEMAN

We have been assured by the Chairman of the Stockport District Health Authority that local managers, with the agreement of senior nursing and medical colleagues, have assessed and will continue to keep under review the nurse staffing levels on the geriatric wards at Stepping Hill Hospital. We do not intend to erode local responsibility for managing the hospital services by intervening in this matter.

W409 Mr Andrew F Bennett MP (Lab Denton and Reddish): To ask the secretary of state for health, if he will review staffing levels in geriatric wards in the light of correspondence from Mr Pink, a charge nurse at Stepping Hill Hospital, Stockport.

MR ROGER FREEMAN

The Department of Health does not and could not prescribe the staffing requirements on geriatric wards across the country because, for example, nursing requirements depend on the number and individual needs of patients, the design of wards, and the skills and experience of nurses. That is why general managers working with medical and nursing colleagues decide such matters at the local level.

These answers manage to be both misleading and astute. Perhaps senior nurses had assessed the situation, though how and when I do not know, but never had senior doctors done so. Had they visited the wards at night, they might have been moved (or shamed) to act. Once the consultant geriatricians each received my detailed account of the nightly neglect I fully expected all three to arrive hotfoot if only to discredit me and disprove what I had reported. As it was, never once in three years of full-time duty did I, or anyone else, see a consultant come onto a ward at night, nor was one known ever to speak to any night bedside staff about the situation. Without visiting and talking to the staff how could they possibly obtain any assessment? I am prepared to accept that prior to 3rd October 1989, when I wrote to each individually, they might have been unaware of what was going on, but after that date they could have been in no doubt and it is to their everlasting shame that not one of them took the opportunity to spend time on the wards at night, to take steps to improve the situation or to show the slightest interest in how 'their' patients were cared for while we were on duty.

The astute aspect of the replies is that no mention is made of the quality of care, only that the nurse staffing levels have been 'assessed'. This is saying nothing at all. That the levels might have been assessed as inadequate, poor or downright dangerous is ignored.

Four weeks after writing to Mrs Frederiks, the chief nursing officer, I sent my third letter to her. Part of it read:

My letter to you of April 9th was, I trust, received.

Some ten weeks ago Mr Milnes wrote to me to say that you were to assess the situation on our wards and I am concerned that, despite so long a time, you appear not to have completed the task. You will have seen the latest issue of the Authority's bulletin – NEWS, in which, under the heading, "AIMING FOR EXCELLENCE", Mr Milnes writes: "The authority is keen to ensure the highest possible standards of care for its patients at all times and in striving to achieve this, recognises the need to involve staff at all levels."

Such an unequivocal statement from the district general manager is most propitious and supportive to bedside staff and encourages me to believe that, when pressing for improved care for patients and reduced stress for staff, I am pushing an open door. Both nurse Thomson and I were particularly impressed by Mr Milnes' discerning and accurate observation of our plight and his determination, despite what must be the enormous constraints and difficulties he faces, to ameliorate the most unsatisfactory situation which he experienced at first-hand on August 29th. I agree wholeheartedly that staff at all levels need to be involved, a sentiment that you, as CNO, must espouse.

Over the years I have always aimed to be positive and to see the other's point of view. To date my attempts to raise standards at Stepping Hill had perhaps lacked a more constructive side and this I regretted. So much of what I had written must have sounded negative, but if only someone in management had invited my advice I'd have done my best to assist, and this section of my note to Mrs Frederiks clearly restates my faith in Mr Milnes and my willingness to contribute to any strategy for improvement. Here was an opportunity for Mr Milnes to 'involve staff at all levels' but the involvement of bedside night staff was nil. In the light of his behaviour throughout the case, these words come across as cynically guileful. My letter went on:

Thus you can appreciate my unease at the slow progress of your assessment. You will naturally want to know the views and opinions of our 12 nursing auxiliaries and the ten nurses now working permanently on our three wards, yet neither my charge nurse colleague nor I is aware of any such discussion having taken place over recent weeks, or ever. Such enquiry would, as I have previously advised, need to involve independent questioners. The necessity for this was brought home to me a few days ago in discussion with one of our long-serving members of staff. When I mentioned your impending enquiry, adding that I hoped she would speak out as support-ively and openly if asked, she responded: "No chance. I do not want to lose my job," a harsh but perhaps understandable comment...

...A year or two ago, I spent 12 months as a nurse tutor and was greatly impressed by the students' idealism and eager devotion to their calling; they were a tonic and inspira-tion to everyone, patients, relatives and fellow nurses. All too often, though, the reality of the conditions and experienced colleagues, knock such "nonsense" out of them. Forgive me if I appear a touch cynical, the last eight months have not been easy.

Among the evidence you will wish to consider in your assessment will be our "patient dependency" statistics. No doubt you have these on your desk now. I refer to the yearly summary (1989) for ward A14. On average more than 18 patients (70.38per cent) each day fall into dependency groups III, HIGHLY DEPENDENT and IV, TOTALLY DEPENDENT (with 42 per cent falling into category IV). As you can see, bed occupancy could hardly be higher, with three or four (the record I am told is five) patients using one bed in one night.

What more can I say? Perhaps this, for any person not yet satisfied that our situation demands action. Prisons have been much in the news of late, especially the insani-tary and degenerate conditions in our Victorian jails. Having been in Strangeways myself, I know the problem. Even in Strangeways, though, as sordid as it was, no inmate was forced to empty his bowels in the bed and then left to wallow in his own excrement.

Yours faithfully,
FG Pink

The letter was acknowledged but there was no response.

Patient dependency figures were gathered each day on a special form which detailed five areas of concern: personal care, feeding, mobility, nursing attention and other intervention. While the form might be suitable for the average medical or surgical ward (although even this is doubtful), it was quite inadequate for a geriatric ward, concerning itself with physical wellbeing only (and not all aspects; toileting, for example, was not included) and making no allowance for patients' confusion, depression etc.

While it seriously underestimated the actual dependency of our patients, it did give some idea of their handicapped state. And even with these unreliable data, the yearly average in 1989 shows over two fifths of patients as totally dependent on others' intervention for their physical needs. Such patients would usually be comatose or unconscious, able to do nothing but breathe for themselves, in need of constant monitoring and hourly or half-hourly attention. Forty two per cent of 26 is more than ten so, on average, on any one night we would have ten patients who needed, but so often failed to receive, total care.

The bed-occupancy figures I found initially puzzling because at times the percentage was over 100 and this seemed to make no sense. But it was explained that the multiple use of a bed within a 24-hour period accounted for this. Even within our spell of night duty this could happen. For example, a patient would die at, say,

10pm; another would be admitted to that bed at 11.30pm and die within three or four hours allowing a third person to occupy the bed at 5 or 6am. For the year as a whole the figure for A14 ward was 97.7 per cent.

In my efforts to explore every avenue, I decided to write individually to each of the health authority members. I had been informed by one sympathetic member that my letters to date had not been seen by them, and guessed that this was a deliberate decision by Mr Milnes. So I set about preparing 16 sets of 48 pages of correspondence, a time-consuming and expensive business, running to more than £110. These were posted on 8th May. Two of the recipients discussed the case with me and were very concerned. The other 14 did not bother even to acknowledge receipt.

As with so much else, this amazed me. How could members of the health authority, appointed I assumed to represent the public, no doubt prominent and supposedly public-spirited members of the local community, take so little interest in what they read. It is beyond me why such people accept these positions if they do not want to be involved, or cannot be bothered to take an active and direct interest in the running of the hospital. What possible use are they to patients? Weren't they concerned, if not disturbed, at what they read?

By early May I must have received some 50 letters from members of the general public which was quite unexpected but so encouraging. In fact I was knocked sideways both by the number of letters and by the appreciative things people were writing; here are some extracts:

Dear Mr Pink,
To tell you that I was moved by your series of letters in today's *Guardian* would be the understatement of a lifetime. I have just read your correspondence with the powers that be. We

live in a materialistic and Godless world and as far as they are concerned these old, senile patients are just flotsam, people who have outlived their usefulness and their manner of dying is of no relevance.

I have just returned home from a meeting with my senior nurse. Sitting down with a coffee to read my paper your letters brought tears to my eyes. I am not altruistic, 15 years in the health service has seen to that. I need the job security for selfish reasons, a high mortgage and two children!

What saddens me beyond all expectation of disillusionment is that as a student nurse the greatest shock to me was that some people didn't *really* care two hoots about the care being provided.

I want to express my gratitude to you for your long-running battle to improve the appalling staffing levels at Stepping Hill Hospital. . .

. . .The plight of the people for whom you care is enough in itself to move any human being with an ounce of compassion. What makes it particularly poignant for me is that, although I am only 26 years old, my parents are both well into their seventies.

I am a final-year medical student at the Middlesex Hospital in London and while I am mostly occupied with preparation for my exams in June, I must say that I and many of my colleagues are deeply concerned about the deteriorating conditions throughout the NHS. I would like to thank you for your bravery and commitment in speaking out.

I sympathise with your plight and hope that you and more like you find the courage to speak out against what is at the least a loss of basic human rights. Those of us who are frustrated and angry at the sharp end of the NHS owe you a debt. I wish you every success.

These comments are typical of the generous remarks many people were making. It seemed strange that my letters should so disturb and move newspaper readers when the officials to whom they were written were untouched and indifferent. I responded to each of the letters as best I could but I'm sure inadequately. What can one say in response to letters like the following:

> After reading about your campaign to improve the quality of care for old, sick people, I felt compelled to write. Your dedication and commitment to the patients in your care is utterly admirable. It has been said that 'for evil to triumph it is only necessary that the good do nothing'. Thank you for raising these issues which must affect most of us at some time in our lives. You are an inspiration and an example.

SIX
I WANT TO SHAKE YOUR HAND

Comment is free but facts are sacred — **C.P. Scott**

When these events were unfolding, nursing was regulated by the United Kingdom Central Council for Nursing, Midwifery and Health Visiting (the UKCC) forerunner to the Nursing and Midwifery Council. The council was established by Act of Parliament in 1979, taking over from the General Nursing Council. Its duties related largely to standards of nurse education and training, maintenance of the register of qualified nurses and the disciplining of nurses and midwives reported to it for misconduct. In its own words, the "Council's functions are concerned with serving the public interest and protecting the vulnerable public – not that of serving the interests of the professions it regulates." Like today's NMC, the council had a code of professional conduct and early in 1990 I gave it some attention. My action has always been based on simple decency and justice; I did not need a handbook to tell me what is acceptable or how I should behave. It occurred to me, however, that this body might be in a position to assist by supporting my attempts to improve care. The code at that time was unequivocal and started:

> 'Each registered nurse, midwife and health visitor shall act, at all times, in such a manner as to uphold and enhance the good standing and reputation of the profession, to serve the interests of society, and above all to safeguard the interests

of individual patients. Each registered nurse, midwife and health visitor is accountable for his or her practice, and, in the exercise of professional accountability shall...'

There then followed 14 clauses setting out the behaviour expected of a nurse or midwife. This introduction seemed to suggest that my every action to date was in keeping with the requirements of the code. With this in mind, I wrote to the Registrar, Mr Colin Ralph, on 4th January 1990. In part the letter read:

> To cover our three wards properly we need six nurses every night, two on each ward, with five nursing auxiliaries in support. To provide this 42 nurse nights per week, my estimate suggests a complement of at least 26 nurses (each working a two-night week). The enclosed copy of our duty sheet for the week of January 15th starkly reveals our plight. We are not even able to staff the wards to the standard that nurse managers regard as appropriate.
>
> From a reading of the enclosed letters you cannot fail to experience my despair and anguish at what is happening. Our professional code (sections 1, 2, 10 and 11) exhorts me to speak out and 'make known to appropriate persons or authorities any circumstances which could place patients in jeopardy...or constitute abuse of the individual practitioner and/or jeopardise safe standards of practice'. This have I done as precisely and honestly as I am capable. And to what end? A blank wall. Your advisory document, *Exercising Accountability*, very aptly states the position:
> 'The primacy of the interest of the public and patient provide the first theme of the code and establish the point that, in determining his or her approach to professional practice, the individual nurse should recognise that the

interest of the public and patient must predominate over those of practitioner and profession.'

Not only have my arguments and protestations failed to achieve any improvement but, so I have just been informed, the situation is to be worsened by warding my colleague and me. Rather than relieving the staffing crisis, my efforts perversely seem to have hastened, perhaps caused, retrogression. No consultation has taken place; our views or opinions have not been sought. More crucially, I am now to be placed in a cruel dilemma. Having made such trenchant representations against what I regard as an intolerable situation, my warding cannot but exacerbate matters. While aware of, and not unsympathetic to, the financial constraints of management (a point I have always made) my primary and overreaching responsibility is to the patients, their loved ones, to my fellow nursing staff and to my own integrity. The last thing I wish to do is further endanger patients or overburden colleagues.

While uncertain of my legal standing were I to refuse to co-operate with being warded (and I fear legal costs would be beyond me), I believe morally that I have right on my side and think that I may have to make a stand. My reading of the UKCC's code seems to support such a stance. Thus I now write to you, the chief executive, for your advice and support. If I refuse to be warded in three weeks' time the management would, I presume, be in a position to suspend me and in time dismiss me. About this I have no illusion. Such action, 'pour encourager les autres', would surely follow. Yet so deeply and ineffably am I concerned that I am prepared to accept such a consequence.

May I specifically ask: 1. Has management the right to change my job description and work pattern without a) consultation and b) my agreement (nothing has been put in writing) and 2. if suspended or dismissed do I have rights? Would my ethical reservations stand up in an Industrial Tribunal or Court of Law?

Yours faithfully,
FG Pink

What Mr Ralph's observations on the letter were or what his advice would have been, I do not know for he never replied. Nor did he have the courtesy to acknowledge, let alone reply to, any of the six letters that I wrote to him over the ensuing two-and-a-half years. It took the UKCC six weeks to acknowledge this letter and 16 weeks to respond. When an assistant registrar for standards and ethics, a Mr R Pyne eventually wrote, I found his reply evasive and non-committal.

> The contents of the documents you have sent to the council certainly reveal that you have done as the council expects in making known that, as you perceive it, there are circumstances which place both the patients and standards of care in jeopardy. I must add, however, that it would have been the council's expectation that those of your professional colleagues who experience the same problems in their practice settings would, like you, have expressed their concerns in writing to their managers and reported their inability to provide adequate care if they believed that to be the case.
>
> You refer in your letter to a change in your work placement and your job description. Those are matters in respect of which you should involve whatever professional organisation or trades union of which you may be a member. Careful consideration of the exact wording of your contract would be necessary before any attempt could be made (even by

experts in the labour relations field) to advise you. That does
not mean, however, that you should not make representations
about those matters which obstruct the delivery of safe care
and the achievement of satisfactory standards of care. The
council would expect you to do so if you believe that to be the
case and would assert your right and responsibility so to do.
Further to that, it would expect the same of your fellow registered practitioners if they believe such a situation to exist.

Although I do not feel able to respond to the specific questions with which your letter concludes I hope that I may have
been of some assistance. I would simply add that there may well
be merit in drawing to the attention of your registered nurse
managers (including any now employed in general management posts) the wording of clause 2 of the Code of Professional
Conduct and the introductory stem out of which it grows.
The words 'omission' and 'sphere of influence' were carefully
and deliberately chosen to try to ensure the registered nurses
employed in management positions recognise that they are
joined in accountability for standards of care.

In my response, I expressed concern that it had taken the UKCC
all but four months to reply to my January letter and said that the
explanation for this delay was unsatisfactory. There must, I said,
be something seriously amiss with an organisation that treats cor-
respondents in such an apparently inconsiderate manner. Many
nurses have contacted me since with stories of long delays, ignored
and 'lost' letters, what appears to be an uninterested and inefficient
reply to nurses' correspondence and a generally thoughtless and
arrogant approach by the people who run the council.

My suspicion was that the mass of detailed information that
I had sent to the registrar had not been seen by Mr Pyne. It was
just too vague and general to provide the advice or support I was

hoping for. His reply seems to imply that my evidence is less reliable, perhaps less valid, because other nurses ('professional colleagues') working on the wards ('practice settings') failed to write to managers as did I. The logic of this somewhat disapproving comment is not easy to fathom and displays an unfortunate remoteness from hospital reality. Any nurse working directly with the public and subject to nurse managers knows what the problem is. The whole indoctrination into the job, certainly in my day, lead to, and is traditionally designed to lead to, a compliant, uncomplaining, and uncritical person whose job is to manage no matter what the circumstances and never to complain. Good nurses do not complain, moan, remonstrate, demonstrate or appear unhappy. Nurses like to be liked and some need to be liked.

I am well aware that nurses have to think twice, and twice again, before stepping out of line. But are there no limits to compliance? This account of my experience is not the place to try to understand this apparent widespread subservience to authority found among nurses. Suffice to say that it goes back to Scutari, is well-entrenched, and was certainly the accepted norm at Stepping Hill where the authoritarian and exploitative regime had passed unchallenged for years as far as I could see. This was not difficult to maintain with an almost entirely part-time workforce. Most staff worked two nights a week 'at the requirement of the service' which means as and when told. This condition is quite properly made clear at engagement. Naturally the staff had preferences, on a permanent or varying basis. Some were single parents; others had husbands with shift difficulties; some would request to work extra nights; care of the children had to be organised and so on. Few were able to wait and accept the duty as allocated. So each month requests were received and generally approved (or swaps sanctioned). Holiday requests were usually accommodated – the sort of civilised arrangement you would find in most work places, no doubt. As most colleagues saw it, though, this did place them under a tacit obligation to their manager and in a constrained position when it came to 'causing a fuss' or speaking out of turn. Mr Pyne's implied assumption that if matters were as serious as I stated, then others would have "written to their managers and reported their inability to provide adequate care" suggests that he may have been out-of-touch with bedside nurses. As I said to him in my reply:

> Is it any wonder that so few are prepared to speak out, let alone put pen to paper? Fear can be a very compelling inhibitor. I am in a most fortunate position. I have nothing to lose for I do not work out of necessity; a privilege not available to my colleagues. Do not assume that silence means acceptance of and approbation for our present staffing levels. Such a conclusion would be incogitant and naïve. My experience and that of others would suggest that nurses, for a variety of reasons, do not speak out nor should we expect them to.
>
> It could very reasonably be argued that I, a charge nurse, am transcending my responsibility by speaking as plainly as I have done in what could be construed as a presumptuous manner, and I would have considerable sympathy with that belief. But if nurse managers accept the conditions for patients and staff that I have adduced, and which have been disavowed by no one, what am I to do? Your advice is to draw to the attention of nurse managers clause 2 of the code. Can you be serious in advising me to quote the code to the managers; to the chief nursing officer herself? Surely that is the job of the UKCC.
>
> In raising the situation in the first place I may have already appropriated management's responsibility. Am I now to do your job also? The advice seems improper, and ill-considered. The managers may well know the code by heart, but what

use is that if they choose to discount it? I have acted as urged, that is: "Have regard to the workload of and pressures on professional colleagues and subordinates and take appropriate action if these are seen to be such as to constitute abuse of the individual practitioner and/or to jeopardise safe standards of practice" (clause 11). This is precisely what I have done and now I await your unequivocal support and clear advice. Your letter gives me neither.

If the code is to be respected, the council must be prepared to intervene decisively where the code's circumvention or abrogation is established. Otherwise the code, and the Council itself, are brought into disrepute. As you are well aware, when the UKCC was established by the Nurses', Midwives' and Health Visitors' Act, 1979, it was charged 'to provide advice for nurses, midwives and health visitors on standards of professional conduct'. This I now call on the council to do.

In his reply, the assistant registrar pointed out that the council has no powers to investigate complaints of poor standards of care unless a nurse is reported for misconduct when the situation can "then become the subject of public comment," whatever that means. He stated that problems "often come to light" during misconduct hearings but implied that even then there was nothing the council could do to rectify unacceptable care, insufficient staff or manifest danger to patients. In other words, the UKCC is impotent in these areas. It claims that unsafe and improper individual practice will lead to a nurse or midwife being disciplined, but is indifferent when it comes to institutional mismanagement and poor quality care. Even the assertion of its concern for nurses' behaviour (and thus patients' wellbeing) was to be shown bogus when faced with the power of Stockport's managers. There was some mild support in the letter. No doubt it was well intentioned but management ignored or dismissed it. Mr Pyne wrote:

> I have found the correspondence very informative, disturbing and (in places) deeply moving. I have noted in particular the suggestions contained in your letter (9 April 1990) to Mrs Frederiks for two alternative methods of assessing the workload and the adequacy of resources when compared with need. Those two approaches, either separately or in combination, would appear to provide an objective means of testing the assertions you have consistently made about the inadequacy of nursing resources. I would agree with you that no nurse, while delivering nursing care in a busy and demanding ward to highly dependent and vulnerable patients, can possibly prepare a contemporaneous, comprehensive and objective report on his or her activities.

What Mr Pyne's letter displays, as so clearly does this whole case, is at local and national level, it seems, no one is prepared to accept responsibility; to say 'the buck stops here'. As a body, nurses are two thirds of a million strong but our mouse-like demeanour ensures that we are too often treated as an easily-pushed-around bunch of willing handmaidens, the tame 'gofers' of the health service.

On 17th May I met Mr Caldwell the general manager and Mr Geraghty, the assistant general manager. Mr Caldwell did all the talking from their side. His principal concern was with the publicity. The essence of the situation which had brought about the publicity appeared not to be on the agenda. This I found unacceptable, and I insisted on raising the substantive issue of patient care. While he seemed concerned about appearances and public perception, I wanted to talk about what was going on at the bedside night after night, but it was like speaking to the deaf.

He announced that: (a) the health authority was satisfied with the present staffing of the geriatric wards at night which was 'adequate to produce the level of care that we feel is necessary'; and that (b) as manager he, not I, took responsibility 'for the staffing levels and the standard of care that those levels produce'.

This was the first intimation that members of the health authority had taken an interest though, as I was to learn later from a member who was present at the authority meeting, it was the publicity rather than the quality of care that exercised members' minds. Mr Caldwell expressed the belief that harm was being done to the hospital by the publicity. He produced no evidence. I accepted that this might be so, whereas he was not prepared to discuss the care of the patients as Mrs Fredericks, the CNO, had assured him (and he later wrote) that 'patient's [sic] lives were not being put at risk'. In short, I should get on with my job and stop interfering with matters that were no concern of mine and which management had no intention of discussing with an employee in my position – a one-sided and particularly fruitless half hour.

The prospect of management taking any notice of what we the bedside staff thought was now all but nil, but that seemed no reason to give up trying. From the meeting I had learnt that the chief nursing officer had carried out some form of review and declared that lives were not at risk. This terse statement it seemed needed some clarification, so on 25th I sent Mrs Frederiks a letter, part of which read:

> Is it in order for the nursing staff to ask how your review was conducted? As stated in my May 7th letter, we are unaware of any enquiry. To us it is inconceivable that you could have reached any significant or valid conclusion without seeking our experiences and opinions. Mine you know; but there are 20-odd others who might like to be asked and whose

views, not all by any means of a like mind, would enhance a properly-conducted review adding veracity and validity to its findings. Our hard-pressed but uncomplaining workforce must not be taken for granted, ignored or browbeaten any longer. Each member has a right to be heard without fear of disfavour or recrimination. Not to provide this opportunity is as ill-considered and tactless as it is insulting and presumptuous...

...Exceeding my position I may be, but I must challenge you to justify your method of review. If you have in fact already done so to the health authority, for surely its members must have needed some assurance as to your procedures, numbers and status of people involved, statistics consulted, wards visited at night, dependency figures used, etc, then perhaps that justification can be given to our staff. If protocol precludes you from responding, though such convention might appear as an anachronistic pretence where patient safety and recovery are at stake, then some more senior person or body, the UKCC for example, might be called on to authenticate your methods and results. If future staffing levels are to be predicated largely on your review, then its scope, thoroughness and comprehensiveness must be irreproachable and seen to be so. As Mr Caldwell said at a night sisters'/charge nurses' meeting on March 12th this year: "Everything we do should be in the public arena." Over the last nine months I have produced a considerable body of evidence to substantiate our need for improved staffing. I have:

1. Detailed the manifold pathology of our ageing patients, most of whom are in a veritably helpless and prostrated condition.

2. Produced copies of reports to illustrate the degree of immobility, infection, dementia, neglect on admission,

disorientation, collapse, anxiety, incontinence, confusion, fear, unconsciousness, paralysis, rapid deterioration, worry, aggression, exhaustion, insomnia, violence and despair from which senescent people suffer.

3. Provided statistics on admissions (120 per cent increase in seven years), bed occupancy, dependency (42 per cent totally dependent), terminal care, deaths (520 in 12 months), nursing and non-nursing cover.

4. Described, in considerable detail, routines, ward rounds and duty rotas.

5. Recorded the lack of basic nursing care, the neglected procedures, dangerous drug administration (flouting the health authority's own rules and the UKCC guidelines), the unacceptable distress caused to patients, a ward full of patients with but one person, often unqualified, to minister to their multifarious needs.

6. Indicated the misuse of patients where toileting is concerned; the distress and danger occasioned to very frail people; the inseparable likelihood of staff injuring themselves when struggling alone.

7. Cited the loss of full-time charge nurse cover and the subsequent paucity or complete absence of sister support.

8. Exemplified the near-total lack of consultation with nurse managers and the disdain and discourtesy accorded to many staff.

9. Attested to the often unsparing and overbearing strain and fatigue which staff have been, and continue to be, placed in.

10. Made some positive, objective and I trust reasonable suggestions to help resolve the situation.

To support these data I have quoted certain bedside experiences which have clearly indicated the problems we face. Not one iota of this prima facie evidence has been questioned; no single detail challenged. Your response to this enumeration contained in 59 pages of text I have sent you? *Seven words.* No explanation, no evidence, no rebuttal, no vindication, no disproof, no denials; no attempt to demonstrate or verify your statement, a statement which appears to conspicuously disregard the critical issues. You, Mrs Frederiks, may find this situation satisfactory. I do not; most of the geriatric carers do not, nor, I suggest, would our present and future patients, their loved ones, the nursing profession, the UKCC, the people of Stockport and the wider public.

At our meeting on May 17th, Mr Caldwell voiced his concern at the possible loss of confidence and unnecessary worry caused to patients and their relatives by extant and perhaps future publicity. To which my reply is to question his use of the word 'unnecessary' and to say that actual events happening nightly and directly influencing patient wellbeing must take precedence over assumed, possible future concerns...

...To underline the point let me quote from a most interesting study very recently carried out by nurse Vernon of Ward A14's night staff. She looked at accidents in hospital with special reference to Stepping Hill. Using accident reports for the whole of 1989, figures you will have seen, she examined the 782 reported accidents. Of this total, 317 occurred on the geriatric wards. When you consider that 20 medical and surgical wards, the children's and maternity departments and other areas such as X-ray, outpatients and physiotherapy were surveyed, and that there are but three geriatric wards, comprising at a rough estimate less than 10 per cent of the surveyed population, a figure of 317 is revealing as it accounts for 40.5 per cent of all accidents.

The study made a careful assessment of when accidents happened and shows graphically that they are most likely to occur when inadequate staffing pertains; for example between 11.30pm and 1am 'when staff are further reduced due to meal breaks, and depending on the type of ward some are left with only one member of staff' making 'supervision of all patients impossible'. Nurse Vernon adds, pertinently: 'This is highlighted even further when according to the survey only 21 per cent of all accidents had any witness', a sobering and disconcerting statistic.

Mrs Vernon discusses the interplay of advancing years, loss of self-esteem, drug therapy associated with multiple diseases, most of our patients are on a variety of medications, and declining sensory and motor capabilities in the aetiology of falls. We do our best at night to prevent accidents, but far too many occur and relatives must often be dismayed to think that, in hospital of all places, their loved ones are at extra risk. In our area less than 7 per cent of all accidents are witnessed, 22 out of 317. Does not this figure alone ram home the justification of our need for more staff, 93 per cent of accidents on our three wards last year happened out of sight of staff – 93 per cent.

How much more evidence do you need to be convinced that night in, night out, these helpless people are put in mortal danger and for you to say otherwise implies a startling abrogation of your responsibility? As nurses we all have a massive obligation to our patients. 'It is clearly wrong for any practitioner', states the UKCC, 'to pretend to be coping with the workload, to delude herself into the conviction that things are better than they really are, to aid and abet the abuse and breakdown of a colleague, or to tolerate in silence any matters in her work setting that place patients at risk, jeopardise standards of practice, or deny patients privacy and dignity.'

I must now tell you that Mr Pyne of the UKCC has advised me to draw to the attention of my nurse managers the wording of clause 2 of the code of conduct and the introductory stem out of which it grows. As the most senior nurse in Stockport we look to you for leadership, backing and encouragement in pursuing the highest ideals and standards in our nursing code. Unlike the non-professional general managers, we have our Code which commits each one of us morally to our patients. Thus, it disturbs and saddens me that nurse management in general and our chief nursing officer in particular appear so remote, even out of touch, with both staff and patients and so impotent and cowed when it comes to speaking out for proper nursing care. As Gayle and Robert Quick put it (the *Guardian*, 18.4.90): 'Professionals must not make excuses for health authorities and general managers who force such circumstances on the patient and the nurse. The UKCC's code makes it very clear: it is the duty of the ward nurse to report her superiors for professional misconduct if such circumstances arise.' And, if all else fails, such a course of action would need to be seriously considered.

I do appreciate that mine appears to be a lone voice, but 'appears' is the significant word here. A considerable number of staff have quietly expressed support for my endeavours but for a variety of reasons, fear being not the least, do not wish their views to be known openly. Only a few nights ago, a member of staff who has occasionally worked in our area, stopped me and said: 'Mr Pink, I want to shake your hand,' and she did so most warmly. 'You are a very brave man to have said openly what we all know to be true. You have my greatest respect and admiration.' This from someone who has cared for patients in Stepping Hill for more than 20 years. Note the use of the word 'brave'. There must be something seriously wrong in an organisation where colleagues are so reluctant to speak openly and where bravery is equated with speaking no more than the truth.

Following coverage in the *Guardian*, the *Nursing Times* commissioned an expert analysis of the Stepping Hill situation by Jean Ball, lecturer in quality assurance at Leeds University. 'Based on a staffing formula from the manpower planning system Criteria for Care, Ms Ball maintains that for the 26-bed ward the minimum staff required to cover an 11-hour night duty was six each – preferably four trained nurses and two unqualified staff. For the 20-bed ward, she concluded 4.5 staff were needed with a staff mix of 65 per cent trained and 35 per cent untrained. Ms Ball also pointed out that the concentration of all over-75s in one area creates a *"highly intensive care ward"* [my emphasis], and that it was unlikely that the needs of these patients were much reduced at night.'

♦ ♦ ♦

Within a few weeks of the case becoming public, three quarters of the night staff had been to see me to offer support, but invariably each spoke when no one else was within hearing. They expressed admiration for my stand, said how brave I was to speak out and agreed that we needed more staff. Additionally, quite a number came from other wards, sometimes on the pretence of wanting to borrow linen, and if the coast was clear, quietly expressed their respect and approval.

One nursing auxiliary who occasionally helped out in our area told me, as had others, that the staffing situation was no better on other wards. She recalled one night on an acute surgical ward when the nurse was on her break and she was left alone and in charge. There had been many operations that day and she was doing her best to manage but was not trained to note important signs should a patient's condition change. One young post-operative patient collapsed and in the struggle to cope on her own she did not immediately appreciate this. By the time she did, vital time had been lost. The night sister and doctor were called, but the young man died. Even though some time had elapsed since the incident, no more staff had been provided for this very busy ward and the auxiliary was clearly haunted by guilt and distress.

I was both embarrassed and encouraged by the generous and kind remarks that these staff were making. I did not ask for their support, though it was interesting to hear most of them add that they felt unable to go beyond speaking privately to me. This I accepted, making it clear that our conversation would go no further. Their attitude brought home to me how strong was the general sense of apprehension.

Since starting work at Stepping Hill, I had been aware of Miss Carew's iron grip on the night staff. No one, I was told, was prepared to cross her and for those who stayed in line there was, I'm sure, no sense of undue discipline. She was prepared to help staff with suitable off duty and additional nights. It must be said, too, that she was a Trojan when it came to helping out at the bedside, and whenever her responsibilities allowed she came down, rolled up her sleeves and got stuck into direct patient care which I think she quite enjoyed. Her assistance was always appreciated.

Against this, however, Miss Carew did have considerable problems in getting along with others, especially those below her in rank. She seemed able to cope only by adopting a domineering and blustering attitude (not untypical, I'm told, of many nurse managers).

At the end of May 1990, I wrote briefly to the UKCC's Mr Pyne to keep him up to date with the situation and explain why other staff were unable to openly support me.

You have clearly outlined the council's position. What it amounts to is that I am on my own. This is not unexpected but does not lessen my resolve to provide better care for our patients. My suspicion is that disciplinary action is just around the corner and I presume if that happens you can in no way assist me.

My brother was involved 50 years ago in a certain operation on the French coast. Perhaps he passed on to me some of the spirit associated with that episode, defined, I see, as:

"Refusal to surrender or despair in time of crisis."

SEVEN
THE GREATEST OF FAULTS

The greatest of faults, I should say, is to be conscious of none — **Thomas Carlyle**

Sometime in early May 1990, staff nurse Peel decided to start a petition to back up my efforts. I was not involved and did not see what she wrote but it was, I am told, quite short and stated that what I had reported was correct and those signing agreed that more nurses were urgently needed. Over two nights Mrs Peel openly and readily obtained signatures from 80 per cent of staff on duty. She then left the single sheet of paper in an envelope on the night duty notice-board for others to read during her nights off.

A day or two later she began to receive phone calls at home from colleagues who had signed to say that on reflection they thought it had been a mistake to give support and asking that their names be deleted. It transpired that Miss Carew had taken down the petition, strongly disapproved of it, told staff that Mrs Peel was a 'trouble-maker', made it clear that others were not to have anything to do with it and that those who had signed 'knew what had to be done'. Under the circumstances, Mrs Peel felt unable to continue (the petition disappeared), for she did not want to put her colleagues in an impossible situation. To the best of my knowledge, no inquiry into Miss Carew's action was undertaken; no fellow senior nurse or manager suggested that she had acted improperly and when the matter was reported to the UKCC that body showed no disapproval or even interest. To her credit, Mrs Peel was not prepared to quietly accept such disgraceful behaviour and wrote on 25th May to the chief nursing officer.

> I am a staff nurse at Stepping Hill Hospital, working two nights per week on Ward A14. I have been following Mr Pink's efforts to improve patient care through increased staffing levels with great interest and concern. I believe an investigation has been carried out into the subject and the conclusion reached that staffing levels are adequate. How this conclusion has been reached is beyond me. Neither I, nor any of my colleagues, to my knowledge, have been consulted about this problem. Surely staff at ward level are better qualified than anyone else to give an opinion on this matter. I understand that because Mr Pink has not received any visible support from his fellow staff his claims are being dismissed.
>
> I personally have tried to start a petition in support of Mr Pink's request for higher staffing levels thus improving patient care. I know most of my colleagues agree with him on this, but unfortunately many were reluctant to sign fearing recriminations. It has come to my knowledge that I have already been branded a "TROUBLEMAKER" for my efforts. I was not aware that nurses at ward level were not entitled to express an opinion. It is precisely this sort of reaction that caused some of my colleagues to withhold their signatures. Those signatures I already have I now feel reluctant to pass on to you for fear of further recriminations against them.
>
> I have worked on the geriatric unit for nearly six years. I work amongst extremely dedicated, caring and hardworking staff, both trained and untrained. I am not the most experienced nurse on the unit as many of my colleagues have worked in other fields of nursing; many have been sisters running

wards. There is clearly a wealth of expertise and experience amongst them. I feel therefore that it is a great shame, if not an insult, that their opinions were not sought before you arrived at your decision. Our patients are old, many with total dependency, and poor quality of life. Many patients are terminally ill and will not go home again. These patients are entitled to EVERY possible care and attention, and TIME spent on the individual, to make their last days as comfortable as possible. We do not need thousands of pounds for new technology but simply ask for a few more pairs of hands. There have been many occasions when I have started my night knowing full well that the workload would be too great for the staff provided. This has often meant my being the only trained member of staff on duty to cope with many medical and ward administrative problems.

Frequently I have come off duty totally exhausted and utterly depressed because, despite the outstanding efforts of the staff we cannot always give the complete care, just the basics, due to the heavy workload and inadequate staffing levels. It is certainly NOT ideal that patients have to be woken at 5.30am to prepare the ward for hand over to the day staff (whose workload is just as heavy). A lot of patients sleep very little during the night, as it is. I would like to say that I support Mr Pink wholeheartedly, and that we most definitely need more staff. I appreciate that Miss Carew does her best to send us help when she can, but this is not good enough. I am NOT a "Troublemaker" but merely a concerned nurse.

Yours faithfully,
JL Peel, SRN (Mrs)

It must have taken a great deal of thought and heart searching for Jo Peel to write this letter, for she was aware of the danger it placed her in. If only one or two others could have summoned up the strength of character to do likewise, how different might have been the outcome. But, of course, it is easy for me to say this; I had little to lose. At my interview for the post in July 1987, I made it clear that I did not need to work and would not wish to accept the post if it meant denying it to a younger person who needed it. My colleagues, on the other hand, worked out of necessity, their first responsibilities were to their families. They did not have the luxury of being able to make the sort of stand I did.

It became clear as May progressed that not only were many people throughout the land writing to me but to the health authority as well. A Miss Pardoe in Bath sent me a copy of the reply she had received from Mr Milnes. He wrote:

> When I read Mr Pink's first letter I was as concerned as you appear to be at what he said. Having had the opportunity of reviewing the position and having taken professional advice from senior nurses, my view has changed. I hope you will appreciate that I have to base my judgements on hard evidence. The facts of the matter are different from those described in The *Guardian*'s edited account of Mr Pink's very eloquent but highly emotive correspondence.
>
> Having said that, I am in no doubt about the toughness of the job of nursing very old and sick people. I admire the stand Mr Pink has taken and I am sure he is absolutely sincere in his view. However, it is not shared by other nurses in Stockport.

In view of the fact that throughout the whole of my dealings with management and the health authority next to nothing was committed to paper to me by the various people I was up against, it may be worth taking a closer look at these words of Mr Milnes. I must assume that it was a group management decision not to put any responses in writing to the mass of evidence I submitted over a period of two years. Had I been a manager, my reaction would have been to respond either in writing or face-to-face to the observations being made, addressing the writer's claimed incidents and opinions. The one thing I could not have done was to ignore the reported situation. Nor, I hope, would I have wanted to personalise the matter. It seems odd to me that in this letter Mr Milnes does not say 'I was concerned at the described events' or 'the account of how patients were being cared for disturbed me' or something similar. No. He immediately directs attention onto the writer with the words 'at what he said', with the implication that the focus of concern is the person making the statement rather than the substance of the evidence.

As it was to turn out, this was management's approach throughout: don't seriously consider or discuss the writer's accounts and possible truth of what he claims; don't become involved in countering his arguments; on no account engage in a serious discussion as to how the situation might be ameliorated and above all don't drag patients into it. A close rereading of managers'/officers' 32 letters to me (average length nine lines) prior to suspension is revealing. No mention is to be found anywhere of the reported incidents and no serious attempt is made to address the central issues. Whereas my letters refer directly and repeatedly to patients, the replies studiously avoid the subject. In fact the word 'patient(s)' is used only five times.

Mr Milnes speaks of 'hard evidence' but produces none. He was later challenged to say what this evidence consisted of but never did. The only conclusion is that he had none. If he had properly surveyed the 24 staff concerned and collected the evidence he speaks of, why keep it to himself? He goes on to say that my view is not shared 'by other nurses in Stockport'. What does this mean? How could other nurses in the authority know what was happening on one small area at night? After nearly three years' full-time duty at the hospital, I had no idea, for example, how many staff worked on or what the standard of care was on the ophthalmic ward, or how long patients waited for treatment in casualty, or what patients or nurses thought of care in the psychiatric department. When Mr Milnes writes of 'other nurses', how many of the 2,000 or so nursing staff comprises 'other' and how were their opinions ascertained?

♦ ♦ ♦

We had an unexpected visitor on ward A14 for the night of 31st May/1st June. Mr Caldwell, general manager, spent most of the night sitting at the nurses' station. He thought it would be improper as a layman to follow us around and closely witness our work and this we quite accepted. Unfortunately, from where he sat no patient was visible and only for a short while in the early morning (he left at about 6am to get some sleep before turning in to his office) did he speak to one or two patients. Thus he was not in a position to witness directly what our work involved. Nevertheless, he deserves great credit for spending so long on the ward. No other manager showed the same concern, though it should have been one of the senior nurses, Mr Geraghty or Mrs Frederiks, who visited us. Following my spell of duty, when life consisted of work, travel, sleep, travel, work etc, for six or seven nights and little time for anything else, I wrote on 9th June to thank Mr Caldwell for his interest.

> Your visit to the ward was much appreciated. I believe that nothing but good can come from such an experience. You were able to see staff nurse, the nursing auxiliary and me, three experienced and permanent members of our geriatric night team, at work and coping well; coping not so much because of our skill, acuity, insight or toil, qualities all our

staff possess, but due to the minimal workload on that particular evening.

As you saw, we had no admissions, deaths, arrests, collapses or medical emergencies; no doctors (after 11pm), relatives, monitors, accidents, outbursts from deranged patients or violence; no obese or grossly incontinent people; no one on blood, for close observation, dying, vomiting or in pain; no dementia, shouting out (apart from the lady in the side ward for an hour or two), injuries (to staff or patients), insomnia; no aggressive or wandering patients. We had but one intravenous infusion, one gastric feed, one incontinent gentleman, one unconscious patient and one with mild confusion; three ladies to commode, two turns, two BM stix, one heparin pump, two early morning specimens to collect and one medication. There were no injections to give, no drugs to be borrowed (amazingly), no suction, no one on continuous oxygen, no suicidal or bereft patients, no plague of ants to cope with or items to be borrowed (see later); no one was blind, deaf or non-English speaking. To cap it all, night sister did, uniquely, three rounds. On a continuum from zero (peaceful night with 100 per cent care) to, say, five (manifest neglect of patients and excessive stress to staff) the night would rate no higher than 0.5. A number of our alert patients said how well they had slept and from the patients' viewpoint (the one that matters most), it was an almost ideal night.

May I amplify two concerns mentioned above: 1. Borrowing. In recent weeks we have wasted so much time borrowing, among other things: linen, aprons, charts and other forms, pillows, plastic bags, countless drugs, equipment such as sage pumps, bed pans, urinals, gloves, IV infusion sets, suction and Foley catheters, BM stix, sputum pots, linen bags, lancets, CVP line apparatus, denture holders, blood culture bottles,

THE GREATEST OF FAULTS

bandages, incontinence pads, and (of all things) shrouds. 2. Is the ant invasion over? Patients find it distressing to have these insects swarming everywhere. One very ill lady, within days of death, was acutely upset and dismayed to have ants on her locker, all over the table (she would not eat her food), on the chair and in the bed. She was dreadfully ill and this extra burden seemed so undeserved and extreme.

♦ ♦ ♦

The events that were to lead to my downfall began around the night of 7th June. It was 8.45pm and the day staff were leaving, for once on time. With the usually long and detailed reports it was seldom that we were able to start work at a quarter to nine. When this happened, the day staff would generally remain on duty until we were ready. I say 'generally' because it was becoming more common for staff to tell the nurse in charge at 8.45pm that they were going off duty. To me this seemed quite incredible. As a young nurse, it would not have entered my head to leave the ward until the report was finished no matter how long it took. One evening on C5 the two members of the day staff came into sister's office when we were no more than half way through the report, not to ask if they might be allowed to go off duty but to announce that they were leaving. The fact that no one would be available to attend to the patients, all of whom would be out of sight of a member of staff, was of no particular concern to them. When I later questioned the sister about this she said that staff were paid only until 8.45pm and she had no way of insisting that they stay. Certainly, the times they are a-changing. Nurses of my generation never thought we would see the day when staff walked out on patients because they 'weren't being paid'.

On 7th June, however, the day staff were ready to leave on time except that one staff nurse was in X-ray with a patient and needed to be relieved and allowed to go off duty. Before our being warded, this was the sort of duty my colleague or I accepted. I would go immediately to X-ray and take over. If that was not needed, the first task was to go to ward C5 and administer the drugs. This allowed the evening drugs on two wards to be undertaken by one person, easing the burden on the ward nurses. It meant that some drugs were given an hour or more too soon but no doctor or nurse manager questioned this practice. What both my colleague and I had observed was that as we were setting off to start work on C5 at about 8.20pm, the three or four sisters and the nurse manager were settling down in the office to a good chin wag and a nice cup of tea. The first task after the office night report was completed was to get the kettle on and the cups out, a sacred ritual that was clearly of some importance to the ladies concerned. My heavy commitment precluded me from joining the ceremony even had I wished to do so.

Thus it was, I assumed, that the sister nominally down to cover for ward A14 for the night, would go to X-ray and relieve staff nurse. This was particularly necessary that night for we were extremely pushed and a bank nurse had arrived who was new to the ward. I duly rang the night office and asked if the covering sister would go to X-ray. 'Send the bank nurse' was the senior sister's curt response. 'That will leave only me and the auxiliary to cover a very hectic ward at one of our busiest times,' I said. 'I am quite aware of that,' she snapped in return and put the phone down on me, no doubt to get on with her natter and cuppa that I had thoughtlessly interrupted. If sister had explained that an emergency was in progress or that all the sisters were out on the wards I would have understood. She said neither. In reporting this incident to Mr Caldwell I said:

> Such a situation places me in an impossible dilemma. Either
> I heed my superior's instruction, ill-considered and mala-
> droit though it may be, and further endanger patients' safety,

or I so respond to protect patients, as the code of conduct enjoins, and leave myself open quite properly to a charge of indiscipline. Your comment at our May 7th meeting that the unit general manager is responsible for staffing levels and the consequent level of care, thus absolving me from account-ability for any possible neglect of or danger to patients as a result of such levels, I find unacceptable.

From a legal standpoint you may well be correct but I have a higher, more solemn, and to me more profound obligation to the patients which your assurance in no way diminishes or supersedes...

...It is your 'adequate staffing', Mr Caldwell, that places me and my colleagues in an untenably iniquitous predica-ment and before I or the patients are again similarly put at risk it would seem sensible to initiate protective measures, distasteful though such action might be. Nothing would give me more satisfaction than to avoid such a move, but your belief that management has done everything possible to assess the situation, (a belief I am sure you sincerely, if misguidedly, hold) and consider no improvement in staffing necessary, inevitably leaves me after ten months of represen-tation with few acceptable options.

The 'protective measures' were to report to the UKCC for unpro-fessional behaviour Mrs Frederiks, Mr Geraghty and Miss Carew. At the time this seemed a drastic measure that I felt was forced on me by circumstances. I assumed that once reported, the UKCC, so concerned 'with serving the public interest and protecting the vulnerable public' etc, would step in smartish and stop what was going on, discipline the culprits if necessary – another pipedream soon to be shattered. I was to learn that the council turned a blind eye to much reported wrongdoing.

Whether I ought to have been aware by early July that my days as a nurse were numbered is not for me to say. The management ploy was to ignore all my reports and observations while planning my removal, but even had I been aware of this, I fail to see what further action I could have taken to protect myself. Though to be honest, my own fate seemed insignificant compared with that of the patients. I had passed the point of no return. Come what may, I would continue to press for more staff.

In nursing, it seems, there is a tradition that managers manage and nurses get on with what they are paid to do and no more. Thus it is no part of bedside nursing for staff to be interfering with how the establishment is run. I have a vague feeling that our class system is somewhere at the back of this. The workers (lower and middle-class) are not expected to question the bosses (the ruling class). We must show deference to our masters who know what is good for us to know. As workers move upwards in the hierarchy, they take on the mantle of upper-class managers, assuming the attitudes and practices which perhaps they once condemned. Once nurses gain management positions, they so often appear to do a volte-face and divorce themselves from both patients and junior staff. Suffice to say that both my nurse managers (each of whom once worked full-time at the bedside, though not, I suspect, for long with the elderly) and lay managers appeared remote, insensitive and lacking any concern for patients or staff. That such people can in any way be connected with a hospital (let alone be nurses) I find most disturbing.

A second incident that was to precipitate matters took place one Tuesday night early in July. A phone message from Miss O'Donnell, the assistant night nurse manager, at 10.15pm told me that the assistant general manager (Mr Geraghty) wished to speak to me in the office to clarify some points in my letter to the hospital general manager. I replied that I would gladly meet the assistant manager as he requested. On my arrival at the office there appeared to be a meeting in progress (Mr Geraghty, Miss O'Donnell and Miss Carew, who was not on duty that night). I knocked and waited outside. A voice called me in. I remained outside.

Miss O'Donnell emerged to invite me in. The ruse obviously was to get me to the office on the pretence of a one-to-one meeting with Mr Geraghty when there were actually three of them. So suspicious was I by now of these people that I made it clear to Miss O'Donnell that I was due to meet Mr Geraghty and was ready to do so when the 'present' meeting was concluded. The gentleman himself now appeared and asked me to enter. 'As soon as you are available we can start,' I replied. 'As there are others in there, is there another room where we can meet?' Seeing through the ambush, I remained quiet and positive, making it clear that I was very happy to attend the meeting to which I had been invited.

Eventually Mr Geraghty admitted that the meeting was intended for four people, not two. 'In that case,' I said, 'I'll need to be represented.' 'There's no need for that,' he replied. I stood my ground as Mr Geraghty became increasingly agitated. He refused me representation and ordered me into the room.

In contrast to his mounting loss of control, I remained calm. This seemed only to further annoy him. I suspect no other junior nurse had ever had the audacity to stand up to him. As he raised his voice I decided the time had come to return to the ward. I quietly told him that this was my intention and turned away as he loudly ordered me to return, his voice echoing behind me as I walked back along the corridor. The whole performance was most distasteful. Thus did managers manage, at least at Stepping Hill. Once my spell of duty was over, I set down the events of that evening in some detail in a letter to Mr Caldwell, part of which read:

> I shall not be surprised, Mr Caldwell, if you find this episode difficult to comprehend and accept. I did, and it left me

disconcerted and shaken. Such an unseemly outburst from any professional person would be unexpected; from the assistant general manager it is just unacceptable. But, regrettably, Mr Geraghty's attitude and approach is so typical of the authoritarian, heavy-handed and clumsy manner we are accustomed to at night, where management appears more concerned with tittle-tattle and misinformation than open discussion and co-operation...

...Meanwhile the work continues and the problems duplicate. The unreliability of statistics in reflecting the scale of our task was very clearly illustrated the other night. We had a full ward of 26 ladies and gentlemen (average age 84 years) but much of the night was dominated by one lady, Mrs Kent, who had been admitted in collapse with aortic stenosis, severe confusion and dementia. Despite having had oral sedation at 8pm she was still in a highly disturbed, incoherent and hallucinatory state at 9pm, requiring very close observation and restraint. She moved about erratically, oblivious of her and other patients' safety and shouted wildly if touched. As best we could we tried to get on with the normal care of our patients. The dependency figures that night were: Level I (some help needed): none; Level II (moderate dependency): 2; Level III (very dependent with movement and toileting for example): 8; Level IV (totally dependent); 16. That is 61.5 per cent of our patients could do nothing for themselves and another 31 per cent could do very little.

When doctor visited the ward and saw Mrs Kent, he prescribed additional sedation by injection. This involved all three of us plus doctor in a most unpleasant, forced procedure, unpleasant for the patient who in her deranged and frenzied condition lashed and kicked out, screaming deafeningly the while; for the other patients who suddenly heard terrified yelling, and not least for us who had to inflict such oppressive action on an 82-year-old great-grandmother. I found it most distasteful. For the ensuing two hours, two of us could not leave Mrs Kent for a moment despite the fact that so much needed to be done. The irony is that the lady had been listed as at dependency level II.

Considering the frequency with which such incidents occur with similarly disturbed patients, one must wonder why no specialist training for all our staff has ever been provided. Why is it that such training, so much needed not only on confusion and psychotic states, but on care of the dying, pain control, care of the unconscious patient, bereavement counselling, diabetes control, incontinence, drug use and misuse, the suicidal patient etc. is so noticeably denied to our staff? Does this say anything perhaps of management's attitude to elderly people in general and geriatric patients in particular? When considered alongside our staffing levels, the only possible answer is a resounding "Yes".

The staffing position steadily deteriorates. For example, of our nine staff nurses: one I understand has left; two I believe are on long-term sickness and one is reported to be on maternity leave, four out of nine not available for work, a 44 per cent loss. I say "believe, understand, is reported" because, although appointed block charge nurse, the position I still hold, the nurse manager has not had the courtesy to discuss staff changes, availability, staff development, sickness and so on with me for the last nine or ten months.

This past week has been a relatively quiet spell on A14 and I have managed to catch up on my reading. One health authority paper is entitled "ACUTE UNIT QUALITY ASSURANCE CHARTER" (8.3.90). On page 3 appear the words: "Caring passionately about services we provide...

participative decision making...Sound communication systems which are based on trust, openness and feed-back at all levels of the organisation..." and I could not help wondering if it is nurses whom you employ to dream up such fine-sounding rhetoric. Maybe 17 years' bedside nursing makes one sceptical of page after page of such magniloquent and repetitious ("quality" used 21 times) verbiage – a sort of Newspeak which to us, as we violently force Mrs Kent on to her bed, thrashing about, screaming and crying, sounds like a lot of platitudinous jargon.

Assuming that your "quality assurance" nurses still have their bedside nursing skills, perhaps they could be more usefully employed caring for Mrs Kent or ensuring that night after night an untrained carer is not left ALONE on C5 ward with the lives of 20 desperately ill and dying ladies, the mothers, grandmothers and great-grandmothers of hundreds of people who presumably have no idea what goes on at night in Stepping Hill Hospital.

Yours faithfully,
FG Pink

None of the points raised was ever responded to.

EIGHT
THE LAST STRAW

*. . .and when he saw him, he passed by
on the other side* — **Luke 10:31**

Within a few days of writing to Mr Caldwell, he wrote to me:

> You are required to attend a disciplinary interview on Tuesday,
> 17 July, 1990 at 3pm in my office, 2nd Floor, Oak House,
> Stepping Hill Hospital. The purpose of the interview is to
> investigate the allegation that at approximately 10.30pm on
> Tuesday, 3 July, 1990, you were required to attend a meeting
> with Mr J Geraghty, assistant general manager (surgery and
> paramedical services) and the two night nurse managers, but
> you refused to attend. I enclose a copy of a statement regard-
> ing this incident prepared by Mr Geraghty.
>
> As the interview may result in disciplinary action being
> taken against you, you are advised to be accompanied by
> your trade union representative or a workplace colleague of
> your choice.

Mr Geraghty's statement, addressed to Mr Caldwell and dated 4th
July, read:

> Following our meeting on Monday 2nd July, at which we
> discussed the contents of Mr Pink's correspondence dated
> June 9th to yourself, I attended Stepping Hill Hospital at
> 10.30pm on Tuesday night the 3rd July. Mr Pink was requested

by Miss O'Donnell to come to the night nursing office, as I wished to meet with him and the two night nurse managers, in order to discuss with him the points raised in the above correspondence.

Shortly afterwards, Mr Pink arrived at the office but refused to come in. Miss O'Donnell went out on to the corridor to ascertain what the problem was. Mr Pink stated that he wished to meet with me alone. I went out on to the corridor to ask Mr Pink why he was refusing to meet with me and the nurse managers. I informed Mr Pink that it was your wish that I meet with him and the managers, so that the management's position would be crystal clear to him, in the event of his refusing to carry out a legitimate order. Despite this, Mr Pink refused to enter the office, stating that he was awaiting a response from you to his letter dated 9th June.

I again requested Mr Pink to attend the meeting. He refused to do so. I advised him of the position that he was placing himself in, by refusing to carry out my instructions. Mr Pink stated that he was quite clear what position he was placing himself in, however, he did not wish to attend the meeting and was refusing to do so. At this point, Mr Pink stated that he was returning to his patients and he walked off down the corridor in the direction of Ward A14.

Apart from the last sentence, the rest of the statement is but a pale reflection of what actually happened on the corridor that night. Because I was unavailable on the proposed date, the meeting was rearranged to take place on Thursday 9th August at 8.30pm. On 12th July I wrote to Mr William Reid, the health service commissioner (ombudsman). 'You have, I believe, a wide remit to act on patients' behalf, so, as no other person seems able to act, can you be of any assistance?' His reply reads:

The commissioner's jurisdiction and powers are determined by the National Health Service Act 1977. His function is to investigate specific complaints made by, or on behalf of, people (or organisations) that they have sustained injustice or hardship resulting from a failure in a service or maladministration by a health authority of the National Health Service. It is necessary for such a complaint to be supported by some evidence both of the failure in service or maladministration complained of and that injustice or hardship has been caused.

Your papers reveal two main categories of potential complaint. First, there are those matters where you and some of your colleagues might claim to be aggrieved by the staffing levels and other working conditions which you describe. The Commissioner could not investigate complaints of that sort for the reason explained in section 4(e) of the enclosed leaflet. Subject to the advice of your professional and/or trade union organisations, I can suggest only that you pursue these grievances through your employer's grievance procedure.

Secondly, there are those matters where it appears that certain patients in the geriatric unit of Stepping Hill Hospital are aggrieved in the sense that it is they who might claim to have suffered injustice or hardship. Apart from the exceptional situation mentioned below, the procedure for making a complaint to the commissioner is outlined in section 7 of the leaflet from which you will see that the health authority concerned must first be given a reasonable opportunity to reply to the specific grievance(s).

You will see from section 6 that as a general rule a complaint to the commissioner should be made by the person directly concerned (that is, the person who has suffered the injustice or hardship). Someone else (or a suitable organisation) can make a complaint on behalf of the person directly concerned when he or she is unable to do so. If the person directly concerned is dead, a complaint to the commissioner can be made by a member of the family, preferably the next of kin, or some other suitable person or organisation. A member of the staff of the health authority can make a complaint to the commissioner for the person directly concerned but the commissioner would have to be satisfied that there is not someone more suitable to make the complaint. Depending on the circumstances the commissioner might, exceptionally, accept a complaint sent to him in this way even if it has not first been made to the health authority.

Using quotations from the ombudsman's leaflet, I responded on 1st August:

My initial impression is that most of my submission to you on behalf of the patients in our care is covered by the commissioner's jurisdiction. The Office of Health Service Commissioner was established: 1) "...to investigate complaints about actions of Health Authorities..." (section 1) where 2) there is "a failure to provide a service which it is a function of the authority to provide" (section 3b) and 3) that evidence must be provided in support of a complaint (section 3). In each above particular, my submission appears to comply.

Regarding my complaint that patients are degraded, neglected, denied essential care and protection and have their well being and lives put at risk (claims which I and so many others believe I have established beyond denial) the health authority has been "given reasonable opportunity to investigate" (section 7), an 11-month opportunity.

A rereading of your letter would suggest that the commissioner is unable to offer any help because the complaint is not "made by the person directly concerned". Yet section 6 states that someone else may make a complaint "when he or she is unable to do so" which I submit, is precisely our case. Most, if not all the situations I have described have occurred out of sight of relatives and because so many patients are unconscious, disturbed, confused, aphonic and acutely ill or close to death, next of kin and/or friends are not made aware of these incidents.

When relatives are aware of neglect, they may be persuaded not to put in an official complaint. My code of conduct requires me to "act, at all times, in such a manner as to justify public trust and confidence, to uphold and enhance the good standing and reputation of the profession, to serve the interests of society, and above all to safeguard the interests of individual patients". By asking for the commissioner to initiate an enquiry I am doing no more than this. As a citizen, let alone a nurse and a magistrate, my duty is to report such happenings. Many of our patients, especially single ladies and gentlemen, have absolutely no one. *Who speaks for them?*

Do please reconsider my submission. Your leaflet provides no reason why my complaint is invalid. Someone, somewhere, some day, must be prepared to stand up and say that there is a case to answer. Why can it not be you?

As with everyone else, the ombudsman was not prepared to intervene and his reply of two months later (government departments seldom seem able to answer in a reasonable time) made that clear. Responsibility never rested with any of the people whom I asked for help or intervention. 'No buck is going to stop with us' seemed to be the clarion call from far and wide. So why was I bothering?

Interestingly, in all the subsequent radio, press and television coverage, no journalist thought to ask this question. I would have had some difficulty answering if one had. The best I can do is refer to George Leigh Mallory's 'because it's there' answer in 1923 to the question: 'Why do you want to climb Mount Everest?' I would like to think that the question did not arise because the answer was too obvious. For me, what I was nightly witnessing was just unacceptable by any standards of human decency and dignity. Perhaps had I kept my mouth closed a little longer, I might have come to accept it as normal and unavoidable. Perhaps. I must assume that that is how my colleagues coped. If you live with anything for long enough, you can cease to question it. The reality is that on a busy, geriatric ward one is immersed in the suffering of patients and relatives. Some mirth and joy there is no doubt, but by and large there is little letup in the daily round of distress and death, and as thoughtful and involved as staff might aim to be, the danger is that they can become inured to the pain and affliction on all sides. This is something that nursing and medical personnel are aware of and on most wards the recovering younger patients with a ready quip prevent even the busiest staff from becoming too disheartened by the minority who are very ill.

The situation on wards for the elderly, though, is quite different. There are no youngsters around (with their whole lives ahead of them) to brighten up the place; the ward wag is not to be found; the usual banter and badinage between patient and nursing staff is generally absent; there is an environment of sorrow and finality. Lighter moments there are, but rarely outright laughter. Bright young nursing students bring in a breath of vitality but those who have spent year in, year out with the elderly, can too easily become remote and blasé. What is one more death among so many? Of course, carers have to some extent to remain detached but I see nothing wrong with staff being upset. When time has allowed, I have sat with relatives who've just lost a loved one in an attempt to show compassion and to share in some small way their grief. The skill is to be able to return quickly to the living without allowing the upset to mar your capacity to care. My impression is that most nurses see the show of emotion as a sign of weakness which might render them less able to cope with the more demanding and distressing aspects of the job. I disagree. To allow one's own upset to show is a sign of deep compassion and inner strength and can, I know, bring to others, especially grieving relatives, some comfort. It is, of course, un-British to let one's emotion show, and nurses tend to put on a mask of sangfroid and detachment that to others may suggest, sadly may in fact be, indifference and insensibility.

Among the continuous stream of letters that were arriving was one from a Mr W Baxter in Kent who enclosed a letter he had received from the Department of Health. It was from Baroness Hooper, the Parliamentary under secretary of state for health (Lords). It was clearly duplicated with gaps left for the insertion of names of respondents. In part it read:

> Very great efforts have been made to discuss the problems that Mr Pink has raised, to ensure that nursing levels at night especially were safe, and to look into what aspects of nursing might reasonably be improved through better organisation.
>
> Had the *Guardian* article given this information Mr — would know that the district general manager visited the wards at night to discuss with nurses on duty the staff levels in the geriatric wards. The district chairman also visited the hospital on 16 October and interviewed Mr Pink. A senior manager at the hospital has written to Mr Pink on seven occasions from 3 October 1989 to 14 March 1990 answering issues raised by Mr Pink. So there has been no lack of response on the part of the local managers.

Let me assure Mr — that there has been no significant change of nurse staffing levels on the elderly medical wards referred to by Mr Pink for a considerable time. It follows that there has been no attempt to reduce nurse staffing levels. Secondly, there is absolutely no evidence that the number of very elderly, unwell and chronically fragile patients who have died has any connection with ward nursing levels. Thirdly, there is 24-hour cover at senior nurse manager level with authority to engage agency nurses to maintain safe nursing levels in the case of unexpected staff absences. Fourthly, let me emphasise that there should never be need for the 26-bed elderly medical wards to be single-manned for any substantial time because there is a minimum of three nurses available to each ward at night.

Let me say frankly that no one supposes that the nursing levels at night on geriatric wards cannot be seriously stretched in circumstances where a number of patients require intensive care. I think two final points might reassure Mr — about this article. Firstly, the consultant geriatricians at the hospital consider the nursing levels on those wards to be adequate although clearly there is always scope for having more hands available at busy times. Secondly, the chief nursing adviser of the Stockport Health Authority has been asked to look into the ability of nurses to give high quality care to patients on the elderly wards at the current staffing levels. If that assessment proves that the current staffing levels are inadequate, clearly the managers will act swiftly to put them right.

From beginning to end I found this letter steeped in inconsistency and misleading comments. While the consultants consider the nursing levels 'adequate', the chief nursing adviser is to see if levels are 'inadequate'. Even if Mr Milnes had 'discussed' and Mr

Richards 'interviewed' (which neither did) how does this improve staffing or remove unsafe practice? All district general hospitals have 24-hour cover at senior nurse manager level. So what? How is this in any way relevant? As already discussed, the consultant geriatricians had no idea what was going on nor, once informed, did they show the slightest concern, so how could they assess the levels as 'adequate'? And to state that 'Very great efforts have been made to discuss the problems that Mr Pink has raised,' must leave anyone who had followed the case speechless.

Although I realised that further correspondence would be futile, it seemed necessary to try to put the Baroness (or more likely the person who wrote the letter for her) right.

23rd July 1990

Dear Baroness,

A copy of your letter to Mr Baxter has been sent to me, and as it would give any recipient a wholly false view of our situation, it is incumbent on me to supply you with precise and accurate information. In paragraph 1 you write: "...Very great efforts have been made...to ensure that nursing levels at night especially were safe..."

We at the bedside are not aware of any "great efforts" having been made and I can assure you that nursing levels are not safe. Please read all the correspondence I have sent and then ask yourself if our nursing levels are safe. Your letter continues: "...aspects of nursing (which) might reasonably be improved through better organisation."

We know of no aspect of nursing which has been improved this last 12 months. On the contrary, changed organisation has led, since February 1st, to a reduction in nurse manpower at night. This I have very precisely explained in my letters to Mr Geraghty of 11.1.90 and to Mr Milnes of 1.2.90. In paragraph

2 you refer to a "senior manager", Mr Geraghty, who "...has written to Mr Pink on seven occasions from 3 October 1989 to 14 March 1990 answering issues raised by Mr Pink."

This sentence is confusing to me and would be most misleading to an outside reader. Of the seven letters referred to, four were to acknowledge a letter of mine and/or arrange a meeting while the other three in no satisfactory way answered the issues. Your first sentence in para. three contains a blatant untruth. There has been a most significant change of nurse staffing levels on the elderly medical wards as I have shown above. You go on to say "...there is a minimum of three nurses available to each ward at night." This is a mischievous falsehood. Never once in the three years that I have been at Stepping Hill Hospital have we had such cover. It is beyond belief that a government spokeswoman, and one of your elevated position and authority, should put her signature to such perversions of the truth. In all I have said and written, honesty and clarity have been paramount. I deprecate concealment, deception, half-truths, duplicity, misinformation and equivocation. In a matter of such gravity, where very elderly people's care, recovery and safety are involved, how can you possibly justify the writing of glaring untruths and distortions to members of the public who must surely consider such assurances from a member of the House of Lords as being no less than ex-cathedra? If I, an obscure member of the populace, take such care over the truth, then surely it behoves a stateswoman, speaking on behalf of Her Majesty's Government, to do no less.

In paragraph 4 you refer to the chief nursing adviser's assessment. To us on the wards, and to all those who have read the correspondence, this has been most visibly a sham, an absurd but shamefully cruel sham. If only management would respond to my many, repeated questions your comments would make more sense and be less disingenuous. To emphasize this lack of response, I enclose a list, far from exhaustive, of unanswered questions, many unanswered for close on a year. You have copies of all the letters referred to.

UNANSWERED QUESTIONS

1. Does management approve of acutely ill, very dependent, patients being left in the care of a nursing auxiliary, an untrained, unqualified support worker? 31.10.89 (G); 25.5.90 (F); 4.7.90 (C).

2. Does management approve of one person left alone with a ward full of patients, when toileting involves moving heavy, listless patients, perhaps debilitated by a stroke, onto and off commodes, alone? 24.8.89 (R); 31.10.89 (G); 13.11.89 (G); 4.7.90 (C).

3. Would the health authority give its absolute support for a member of staff who suffered illness or injury when moving a patient by her/himself? (Back injuries are of special concern here). 24.8.89 (R); 31.10.89 (G); 13.11.90 (G); 4.7.90 (C).

4. Is management prepared to improve the very sparse training available to geriatric night staff? 24.8.89 (R); 9.7.90 (C).

5. Does management fully appreciate the serious yet largely avoidable dangers to which patients are nightly exposed? 13.11.89 (G); 1.3.90 (F); 23.4.90 (M); 25.5.90 (F); 4.7.90 (C).

6. Is management happy with a situation which humiliates and debases patients thus causing them acute distress, loss of dignity and unwarranted suffering? 24.8.89 (R); 13.11.89 (G); 4.1.90 (U); 23.3.90 (M).

7. When is the experiment using geriatric patients at night due to be completed? 4.1.90 (U); 11.1.90 (G); 1.2.90 (M); 1.3.90 (F); 4.7.90 (C).

8. Why have patient dependency figures been collected for some years now?

9. Do the figures for wards A14, A15 and C5 support the nomenclature 'High Dependency Area'? 7.5.90 (F); 9.7.90 (C).

10. Is management satisfied that drug administration at night is safe? 24.8.89 (R); 25.5.90 (F).

11. Why, since February 1st last, has sister cover at night been so inadequate and, at times, non-existent? 24.8.89 (R); 1.2.90 (M); 9.4.90 (F).

12. Is management content to know that on two wards patients can be out of sight and sound of staff for many hours each night? 3.10.89 (G); 4.7.90 (C).

13. Does management intend to correct the patent untruths told to a Member of Parliament?

14. Does the chief nursing officer intend to justify the findings of her 'assessment'? 23.4.90 (M); 7.5.90 (F); 25.5.90 (F).

15. Is management interested in the views and opinions of night ward staff? 11.1.89 (G); 1.2.90 (M); 7.5.90 (F); 9.6.90 (C).

16. Is management prepared to have an independent enquiry, conducted by a recognised body, into staffing? 9.4.90 (F); 24.4.90 (M); 9.6.90 (C).

17. What possible harm could such an enquiry lead to?

18. Will the district general manager produce the 'hard evidence' he uses to refute claims of gross understaffing? 25.5.90 (F); 9.6.90 (C).

19. Has management any plans to improve consultation with and cooperation of bedside staff? 3.10.89 & 11.1.89 (G); 4.1.90 (U); 9.6.90, 4.7.90 & 9.7.90 (C).

20. Would management like to make any expression of regret following the numerous, detailed descriptions

of distressing incidents that have occurred at night in Stepping Hill Hospital? 4.7.90 (C).

21. Can management give the residents of Stockport and its environs an assurance that further such incidents, with our present staff-to-patient ratios, are unlikely? 9.7.90 (C),

22. On 24th May 1990, Mr Caldwell wrote: 'At the health authority the members concluded that the staffing in the geriatric wards at night...is adequate to produce the level of care that we feel is necessary.' To whom does the pronoun "we" refer?

23. Is the night nurse manager, Miss E. Carew, to write a letter withdrawing her inexcusably slanderous and mendacious accusations of December 1st 1989? 1.2.90 (M); 9.7.90 (C).

24. Has Mr J Geraghty, assistant general manager, been reprimanded for his most unprofessional display of unbecoming and objectionable behaviour on 3rd July 1990? 9.7.90 (C).

LETTER REFERENCES
C – Mr D Caldwell   M – Mr P Milnes   G – Mr J Geraghty
F – Mrs J Frederiks   R – Mr F Richards   U – UKCC

The letter and questions were ignored. The secretary of state for health, the under-secretary (Lords) and their staff were, it seems, content to join the lengthening line of those hurrying by on the other side.

◆ ◆ ◆

Thus did all the foregoing flash through my mind like some recurring nightmare on Sunday morning of 15th July 1990, as I attempted to restrain the distraught Mr Kaminski, while Mr Gibb continued to call 'nurse, nurse' every few seconds as loud as his feeble frame would allow. He was in the final stage of cancer of the stomach and had the typically wasted appearance of such a patient. Unable to pass urine lying down, he needed the assistance of one of us every hour or so to hold him upright while he relieved himself, so little for a dying man to ask. His advanced emaciation reminded me of the concentration camp victims of the second world war. I hurried round the partition to Mr Gibb, told him I was not immediately available, would come as soon as possible and went back to try to calm Mr Kaminski. After five or six minutes I was free to help Mr Gibb, whose calling had ominously ceased.

The scene that I faced on return will stay with me for the rest of my life. Mr Gibb had somehow got himself out of bed, was lying on the ward floor in a pool of urine, sobbing. I cannot articulate my abhorrence at this abuse of a fellow human being. Lifting this almost weightless man back onto his bed I carried, it seemed, a much greater burden: an overwhelming sense of shame and revulsion that I, a registered nurse, should be forced to witness, nay inflict, such neglect on a patient only hours away from the grave. And the pitiable gentleman could be forgiven if he imagined that he was in some wartime concentration camp and I was some white-coated guard about to inflict more brutality on him. As I laid down this poor inmate of block A14 my whole being was racked with rage and disgust. I reported the incident to the UKCC:

> It sickens me and offends all I hold most dear, the more so when I know that the managers (both administrative and, to their abiding shame, nursing) appear not to want to know. There seems no point in relating this incident to Mr Geraghty, Mrs Frederiks or Mr Caldwell. Absolutely nothing, I fear, no matter how ghastly or indecent, touches their hearts or reason.
>
> On Sunday Mr Gibb related the incident to his relatives who were rightly upset. They spoke to the day staff who informed

the duty nurse manager. She in turn passed it on to Miss O'Donnell who spoke to me during Sunday night. She told me to make out an accident form and add a comment under "problems" in the nursing Kardex, both retrospectively. This, perhaps unwisely if not unethically, I did. The relatives said they would not make a formal complaint but even if they had it would have served no purpose. Now that my representations of almost a year have achieved nothing (apart from worsening staff-to-patient ratios) and appear unlikely to achieve anything, my continuing presence may appear a contradiction in that by staying I bolster a regime of which I have been so critical. Resignation is an option, of course, and this for me is preferable to another experience similar to that outlined.

Mr Gibb died at midnight two nights later.

My spell of duty finished at 8am on Wednesday 18th July, just hours after Mr Gibb's death. I was in a quandary. How could I possibly continue to work at Stepping Hill with such heartless people as these managers? I had moved heaven and earth for 18 months within, and three months without, the health service to no avail. How could I justify nursing in a system of which I was so critical? But I was resolved never again to allow a patient to be as humiliated and neglected as Mr Gibb. That experience had burnt a deep scar into my soul such that even today, years later, speaking or writing about it is difficult. By Friday morning I had come to the decision not to abandon the patients without one last throw.

I phoned the offices of the local weekly newspaper, the *Stockport Express Advertiser*, and asked if I could come and speak to someone. As it turned out it was the editor, Peter Greenwood, who received me into his office. When asked, as I so often have been since, if I gave this move sufficient thought, if I appreciated the probable outcome, I have to answer 'I really do not know'. What I do know is that the

vision of a living-skeleton lying on the floor would not leave me.
Sadly, I'm sure that both Mr Gibb and his relatives were convinced
that I had hastened his death by my 'neglect', a belief I could well
understand and that I was never in a position to contradict. As it
later turned out, this was very close to the relatives' understanding
of what happened. As I sat down to face Mr Greenwood, my one aim
was to ensure that, whatever the cost to me, Mr Gibb's experience
would not befall another elderly Stepping Hill patient.

I had carefully reread both my terms and conditions of service
and the code of conduct to see if they offered guidance. The first was
quite specific and unequivocal. Under the heading 'confidentiality'
is stated: 'If in the course of duty an employee comes into the possession of information regarding patients and their illness such
information should be regarded as in confidence and as such not
divulged to anyone who does not have the right to this information.
Contravention will result in dismissal.'

Clause 9 of the code states: 'Respect confidential information
obtained in the course of professional practice and refrain from
disclosing such information without the consent of the patient or
a person entitled to act on his/her behalf, except where disclosure
is required by law or by the order of a court or is necessary *in the
public interest*' [my emphasis].

My view was and is that, having done all I could to establish the
facts of the situation, and having failed to improve the standards
of care, then the people of Stockport and surrounding areas who
might become (or be relatives of) patients had every right to the
established and unchallenged information, and it was my duty 'in
the public interest' to let the facts be known.

Mr Greenwood had followed the case with interest. We talked
for an hour-and-a-half. Having had national coverage, I was not
sure whether he would find it of sufficient local interest. He was an
understanding listener. The paper, I was told, had covered several

stories over the previous months (for example the death of three psychiatric patients and the loss of beds at another hospital) and had devoted a long, outspoken leader two months earlier to what it saw as the health authority's lack of concern for proper care and its climate of secrecy. Part of the piece ran:

> The headlong plunge of Stockport's health service into the thrusting techniques of big business accelerates. It means loss-making sectors, like long-stay geriatric wards, being closed and forgotten like the Carlsberg Lager complaints department. The patients, or "consumers" as they are increasingly known in the new Health-speak, are being given greater choice in the marketplace. In plain English, they are abandoned by the health service to the care of relatives or the private sector.
>
> It means short-term expedients to solve cash-flow bottle-necks, like the "temporary" closure two years ago of Stepping Hill's Ward G6. That ward's "consumers", mothers who had just lost babies, did not comprise a viable enough gap in the market to keep the ward open. Still it's only a "temporary" closure.
>
> It means secrecy. Once you get into the swing of running a giant public service like big business you start to believe it's none of the public's business what the hell you do. Where did our recent stories about health workers struggling to cope come from? From health workers themselves. Certainly not from the committee or the managers. They have a business to run and they're damned if outsiders (that means you) are going to find out company secrets.
>
> No, the real stories come from the staff on the ground; the people who became doctors or nurses or midwives or porters because they thought it would be a worthwhile job. They become dispirited, frustrated, depressed, angry because they are unable to do the job as well as they think they should.

They get nowhere with the management, so, in desperation, they risk telling the papers in the hope public pressure will prevail. If a nurse has complained that patients or staff are at risk and nothing is done, that nurse, and the newspaper that is told, have a public duty to alert the public. . . and as quickly as possible.

The paper had for some time been running a series of stories highlighting shortcomings in the local health services, much to the health authority's displeasure. The authority had gone as far as issuing a leaflet to all its workers attacking the *Express Advertiser* and making it plain that 'whistleblowers' should expect dire consequences. 'There are many people who are grateful to you for what you have done,' Mr Greenwood said. 'And there are many who would speak out, as you have, but for the peril of the dole queue.'

What perhaps made my account different from others the paper received was its detail and the fact that I was prepared openly to be credited as the source of the information. In the past, health workers had been unwilling to go public and stories had to be reported anonymously. I showed Mr Greenwood the fruitless correspondence and spoke of the incident with Mr Gibb. As in this account, no real names were used. He was anxious to be sure that I fully accepted the likely consequences of these revelations. I did. Over the weekend he phoned me and read what he proposed to write. At that stage he was prepared to alter anything or withdraw the story entirely. Apart from one or two minor corrections he had it exactly as I described.

◆ ◆ ◆

It was high summer and there were no more letters to write for a while. Time to mow the lawn, visit and write to friends, do some housework, attend a university lecture on 'Crime and illness' by a psychiatrist, continue with my studies (my final year), go out walking and do some reading.

On the Monday I joined my sister, brother-in-law and an old friend visiting from Australia on a delightful day out to the Yorkshire Dales. I had made a point over the previous year of not allowing myself to become so wrapped up in the hospital affair that all else was neglected. With friends and relatives I barely mentioned the case. Although I didn't know it, only four days in a working life of 41 years remained. Had I been faced with that fact in those balmy days before the storm, I very much doubt if it would have altered my resolve. With Edmund Burke I believed that: *'An event has happened, on which it is difficult to speak, and impossible to be silent.'*

NINE
KEEP YOUR MOUTH SHUT

Shoot one and frighten a thousand — **Chinese proverb**

The article in the local paper appeared on Wednesday 25th July. Most of the front page, under the banner heading 'CRUSADER CARPETED' was devoted to the story, as were the two centre pages headed: 'When will they stop degrading patients?' In addition to extracts from the correspondence, the editor Mr Greenwood had added an editorial:

> Graham Pink's lonely crusade for humanitarian standards of care is heading for the conclusion which, with hindsight, was inevitable. One way or another, he will have to go. Mr Pink is 60, an Open University graduate, a charge nurse (the male equivalent of a sister), an indefatigable, caring and courageous campaigner, latterly a national hero among health workers – and a damned nuisance to the health authority.
>
> Since August 24th, 1989, he has written close on one hundred letters. He has suffered condescension, vilification smears, bullying, disdain and what amounts to demotion. He has never cracked. He has long since been disabused of the hope that "something" would be done. Peter Milnes has said that he now believes that the staffing is adequate. Mr Pink is not a member of a trade union, there is no professional body which appears ready to support him and his colleagues

are, understandably, wary of speaking up. If he does face a disciplinary hearing, he goes in there alone. But he carries with him the good wishes of thousands of people inside and outside the health service.

I returned to work on the evening of the following day. Strangely, but not unexpectedly, no mention of the media coverage was made, though the atmosphere was strained. Clearly colleagues had, one way or another, received the message from on high, as before, not to speak to me about it and they were not their usual relaxed, affable selves. What they had been told or understood I do not know, but concern for their own position and continued employment was quite naturally uppermost in their thoughts. Their feeling of apprehension was almost palpable. To be overheard openly discussing with me what must surely have been very much on at their minds was far too risky. As was well known, Miss Carew had one or two informers who made sure she received regular dispatches. The general belief was that little passed between night staff of which she was unaware.

I worked the four nights from 26th to 29th July and was then on holiday until 9th August. A letter from Mr Caldwell told me that he had arranged a meeting of day and night staff for 7.30pm on 8th August. This seemed strange. Why wait for close on a year to have a staff meeting and then arrange it when so many were on holiday? My suspicion was that it was some sort of subterfuge and would not take place. It didn't. As always, I responded to the letter. Here is an extract:

Your reference to "night and day colleagues" is a little puzzling for, as I understand your suggestion, it was night staff's opinions which you were prepared to take note of. Most of our considerable difficulties are particular to nights and result from insufficient staff. Day colleagues' contribution to your meeting would at best be tangential. To include such extraneous staff only heightens my reservations as to the purpose and efficacy of the gathering. These doubts are not assuaged by the date arranged. In my letter of June 9ᵗʰ, I advised midJune as a suitable time. With holidays in full swing, August assures that many of our people will be denied a hearing.

We have, as you know, a complement of 25 staff many of whom would wish to be heard. If management is to be present to speak and comment, and day staff allowed a hearing, the average time per night staff could be, on average, less than a minute. Then the size and structure of the group may inhibit substantial and reliable discussion. Most people do not have our experience of public speaking and are easily overawed. Add to this the inescapable and overriding reality that you have no intention of improving our staffing levels at night and the pointlessness and pretence of the meeting might to many seem transparent. I have elsewhere characterised Mrs Frederick's assessment as "most visibly a sham, an absurd but shamefully cruel sham" – a description that could be applied to so many aspects of Stepping Hill's management. I would prefer not to be part of yet one more sham.

I received no reply, not even an acknowledgement. The 1ˢᵗ August edition of the local paper had a piece on the front page:

Support for crusading charge nurse Graham Pink has been overwhelming since our story last week. This letter is from the son of a geriatric ward patient:

I congratulate you and your paper for publicising the plight of Mr Pink and the hard pressed nursing staff on the geriatric wards in Stepping Hill Hospital. My mother died in Mr Pink's ward at 9.20 in the evening after a month's stay in a state of coma. I visited the ward every day and stayed most nights until around 10pm. I am therefore one of those who has witnessed at first hand the sterling work done by Mr Pink and the other nurses and have nothing but the utmost admiration for their patience, fortitude and calm efficiency in often trying circumstances.

I was profoundly moved when I read of his efforts to try to improve the staffing situation. The case for more staff on the night shift is unchallengeable. What won't be known to those afar is that there are four areas in ward A14 all of which are visually isolated from each other, meaning that with only three staff at least one area is always unmanned. While visiting, I saw a man die alone and had to inform the nurses who were busy elsewhere. At other times I have helped old men to the toilet, drawn the nurses' attention to the plight of an uncomfortable lady, helped patients to reach for the unreachable and chatted to the lonely.

I have seen Mr Pink himself administering the medicine, a task demanding of a great deal of concentration not helped by the knowledge that other patients may be suffering or even dying. Despite these trying circumstances, Mr Pink was always most courteous and comforting during my stressful visits and for this I will always be grateful. The inadequacy of staffing on that ward alone was all too evident to an outside observer and any consideration of reprimanding Mr Pink for his very sincere concern is quite preposterous.

Brian N Collins,
Edgeley, Stockport

It was during my spell of off-duty that I applied to join both the Royal College of Nursing (RCN) and the Confederation of Health Service

Employees (COHSE). Mr Stephen Wright, an RCN council member, had phoned me to say that I really ought to have the support and protection of one of the nursing bodies, preferably the Royal College. I was not altogether convinced. There must have been local RCN nurses in the hospital but I heard nothing from them. The local COHSE representative, Mr Joe Swinnerton, had made contact not so much to enlist me as a member but to offer any assistance or representation I might need. He was most supportive and told me that when Mr Geraghty was ordering me into the night office, he was fully aware that Joe had offered to act either as a conciliator or as a friend – information Mr Geraghty saw fit not to pass on to me.

A letter I received from a nurse in Wigan brought home to me that our plight in Stockport was far from rare.

> I am a state enrolled nurse on night duty on a medical unit for the elderly. The feelings and truths you spoke in your articles must surely be echoed in every unit in the country. We have 128 beds over four wards (two of 30 beds and two of 34 beds). Usually there are two staff per ward per night. If we are lucky we may have an extra auxiliary running between two wards, a complement of ten staff therefore. At meal times as there are two wards per floor it is usual for just two staff (one nurse, one auxiliary) to mind the "floor".
>
> Over the years we have complained and complained as this has been a longstanding problem, but the only reply we get is that if staff did not go sick we would be all right! As I write, there is an auxiliary off with a hysterectomy, an enrolled nurse who has been in hospital and is still quite ill after a violent patient kicked her, and another auxiliary who is off with cervical spondylosis. What the hierarchy tend to forget is that when staff are continually coping shortstaffed it will affect their mental and physical health in the long term.

After reading your article in the *Guardian*, I felt that if I did not speak up on behalf of patients and nurses alike (for I was taught that nurses were the patient's advocate), I would not be doing my duty. So after a particularly terrible night I made a formal complaint on the grounds that I was breaching the UKCC Code of Accountability. I have been supported by some of my colleagues but unfortunately, due to fear of reprisals some staff will not put pen to paper. I hope you continue your crusade on behalf of the patients and even if it only makes a few nurses write like me and finally speak out then, Mr Pink, you have in part been successful. I wish we had a charge nurse like you.

While we were working on a staff-patient ratio of 1:9, this unit had one nurse to 12.8 patients. This sounds an unbelievable state of affairs and makes our staff levels appear generous. I later learnt that the complaint made no progress and the nurse was disciplined for her outspokenness. This is the normal approach of nurse managers: 'If bedside staff do not know their place, we'll soon put them right.' Thus do some nurse managers manage.

On 9th August I returned to work knowing that the disciplinary interview to discuss the incident with Mr Geraghty was arranged for 8.30pm. Sitting in his office with Mr Caldwell was another gentleman whom I had never seen before. He was Mr C Burke, director of personnel. Mr Caldwell announced that because the meeting had been overtaken by events, the agenda had been altered. He said that a complaint had been received from a relative concerning a breach of confidentiality by me – a reference to Mr Gibb, I presumed. Additionally, a failure on my part to correctly administer drugs had been reported to him. I had no idea to what this referred and no details were given. I was to be suspended on full pay pending enquiries. The meeting was soon over. My request for further clarification was disregarded. A letter would be sent in a day or two. Mr Burke did not speak. I returned to the ward, changed and went home.

I was unfamiliar with disciplinary matters but I was perturbed by the fact that Mr Caldwell had made no mention of representation. To meet him alone to discuss the incident with Mr Geraghty was one thing; to be suspended without a representative present was another. Whether the procedure was correct has never been tested but I cannot believe it was either fair or proper not at least to have given me the opportunity to have another person present. The manager's autocratic style, though, will not come as a surprise to those who have read thus far. That a worker has so few rights, or no chance to exercise the rights he or she has, is one of the many disturbing lessons to emerge from this case.

A day or two later, I reported what had occurred to Mr Pyne, believing as I still did that the UKCC would be concerned at my descriptions of patient care and now the treatment of the nurse who had brought it to light. I was mistaken on both counts. I wrote:

> Following publication by the local paper, the editor had a phone call from Mr Gibb's relatives. They were distressed at the paper publishing the account without their prior approval. As I had not given the name, such permission would not have been possible. I realised that the relatives might read anything published and know it was their loved one described but could any nurse have done more than I have these last 12 months to expose what is going on – 40 letters to management alone (comprising more than 2,400 words)?
>
> After a great deal of careful thought I decided to reveal the incident and my own revulsion. The very repetition of it upsets me. When I tell you that very rarely do I display my emotions to anyone you will appreciate my deep torment

and grief at that one incident, which I knew if management's conspicuous unconcern and indifference were anything to go by, would sink into oblivion. In my judgement, as with all the disclosures I have previously made, the continuing and nightly neglect and danger to which patients are exposed, may outweigh other considerations.

Before visiting Mr Greenwood (the editor) I read, line by line, the UKCC's CONFIDENTIALLY booklet. I marked certain passages, for example "...and the expectation of the public that they will not be put at risk because practitioners unreasonably withhold information". The health authority's Conditions of Service make no reference to "public interest".

If this incident was a breach of confidentiality, why have all the previous disclosures been ignored? To be frank, the more I think about it, the bleaker is the outlook. Expert legal advice would be welcome but is, I fear, out of the question. The £700 already spent by me could seem a trifle compared with possible legal costs. Rather than be annoyed with the newspaper, and with me, it would seem more appropriate and just for the relatives to pursue the real culprits, the hospital management.

If, after all my efforts, I am dismissed for "...promoting and safeguarding the well being and interests of patients" (the code's words) who would ever dare speak out again, not just in Stockport, but anywhere in the country? "Just as the practice of nursing involves the practitioner in assisting the patient with those physical activities which he would do for himself were he able, so too the exercise of professional accountability involves the practitioner in assisting the patient by making such representations on his behalf as he would make himself if he were able."

For "able" above read "alive". Distressing as this must be for Mr Gibb's relations and as it was so dreadful for him as he lay sobbing on the floor, I am sure that he would not have wished a similar assault on another patient's dignity, peace of mind and very humanity to be allowed to happen. If that can be assured, the loss of my job is a very small price to pay.

A number of colleagues rang last evening to express their alarm and disbelief at my suspension. All were most supportive and upset. Each, however, felt unable to take any action. As one so perceptively put it: "If I say anything, she'll make my life hell!" And I know from experience that she is not exaggerating.

Light was thrown on the medication charge, known for some time, it seems, by many staff but not communicated to me (which must put a question mark over the propriety of management's handling of the matter). I was told that I stood accused of not giving a patient (Mrs G Hill) her 10 o'clock quinine sulphate tablet. How management could be sure of this I do not know. The drug Kardex may show no signature in the relevant space but that establishes only that my initials are missing, not that the drug was overlooked. However my disquiet at drug administration (on many counts) was well known to management. I cite my letters of 24th August 1989 to Mr Richards; the 9th May 1990 letter to Mrs Frederiks which was a very detailed description of part of a night drug round with its countless interruptions, difficulties and obstacles (six patients given medication in 40 minutes). Then there was my letter of 25th May to Mrs Frederiks where I wrote of: ". . . dangerous drug administration (flouting the health authority's own rules and the UKCC guidelines)."

◆ ◆ ◆

My suspension caused considerable local and national interest and much was written about the case. A leader in the *Guardian*, on 16th August was most unexpected.

IN PRAISE OF MR PINK

Name one institution where conditions are worse, far worse, than prison? No, not the cells in the local police station, though these often are worse than prison. Much worse than this, however, is the ward in your local hospital dealing with grandma. Most people are aware of the appalling state of our prisons; few understand the shocking conditions of many neglected and cashstarved geriatric wards. Geriatric patients do not riot. They do not climb on to rooftops with protest banners. They do not write letters to the press. But four months ago, the *Guardian* printed harrowing descriptions of the geriatric wards of Stepping Hill Hospital, Stockport, drawn from the letters of one of its campaigning charge nurses, Graham Pink. It triggered a national debate which still reverberates in the nursing press. More predictably, Graham Pink has been suspended, and expects dismissal.

What did he say? He described life at night on a ward where there is only one trained nurse and two auxiliaries for 26 highly dependent patients: all over 75, acutely ill, suffering from senile dementia, strokes, pressure sores, incontinence, confusion, disorientation, some needing carrying to commodes, others having bowel movements before they could be got to one, important observations for people on blood being missed by the pressure of work, some patients calling out for long periods, the lack of opportunity to sit and talk to patients – even patients who have just been told they had cancer.

The letters from which these events were drawn were sent to health authority officers, district and unit managers, the nurses' regulatory body, local MPs and the prime minister. They were passed to the Guardian by an MP, not by Mr Pink, but he was contacted and agreed to their publication because the local health authority was still refusing to increase staffing levels on the wards. Stockport health authority did not dispute Mr Pink's accusations, but took issue with his assertion that patients were at risk and the wards needed more staff. He was warned that he should not get involved in further publicity. Two local papers, naturally, have been following the story, one of which wanted to nominate Mr Pink for a national award. A story in one of the local papers has finally lead to Mr Pink's suspension.

Like many whistleblowers, Mr Pink is probably not an easy person to live with. He is strongminded, strongwilled and pernickety. But change is not achieved by the irresolute. Mr Pink has been indefatigable in his campaign to increase staff numbers writing more than 90 letters to people in authority. He has been indivertible from his purpose, despite lengthy replies from his managers. The health authority's game now is to nobble him: to point to the licence he has been given, challenge his assessment of patient risk, question his right to confront the lines of authority in the system. Standards at Stepping Hill, according to a press release yesterday, were "very similar" to acute hospitals throughout the region. Precisely. That is why we need – and must protect – Mr Pink. Too few people are ready to speak out, despite a code of conduct that requires nurses to blow the whistle on poor standards. The local manager insists three nurses are adequate; Mr Pink wants four; the *Nursing Times* commissioned an expert in nursing care who concluded there should be six. The NHS must not be allowed to sack such a resolute defender of patients' rights.

I had not seen the health authority's press release announcing the suspension and knew nothing beforehand of the newspaper piece. Apart from the incorrect 'lengthy replies from his managers', I could not fault it. On 17th August, the authority put out a 28-page press release in defence of my suspension and I spent the best part of a week preparing a response. The report appears to relate almost exclusively to day care and the occasional references to night nursing levels are in error, disingenuous, incomplete or suppositional. A mass of statistics are included but these are partial and inaccurate. I have picked out one or two of the more glaring deceptions.

1. The Health Community Council (HCC) is said to have given a 'positive report' after its one visit to the wards. To suggest that busy staff (the visit was at 9pm when there's just no time to stop and chat to visitors), visited by a phalanx of dignitaries (for so they appeared) with a nurse manager and the general manager in tow, can speak freely and easily and say anything worthwhile, is as illjudged as it is fanciful. Nursing and auxiliary staff feel intimidated by such a 'visitation' and are reluctant to speak openly. The purpose of the visit, and others like it, infrequent, transitory, prearranged, superficial, closely stage-managed and chaperoned as they are, has nothing to do with patient care or staff concerns. It is sad that the HCC members were so gullible.

2. 'We ensure that the patient dies with dignity and respect...' says the report. It is beyond belief that anyone could seriously and honestly write this after the revelations I had made over the previous 12 months. Yes, some die with dignity at night but many do not. The shocking and abhorrent experiences described to managers seem to have rendered them unable to accept, discuss or perhaps even believe that such things happen. This inability to face reality was fundamental to their whole handling of the affair.

3. 'Night activity levels are, as would be expected, much lower than those for days.' This too glib, vague and sweeping statement comes from someone (the chief nursing officer) with little recent bedside nursing experience. Relative to the staff available, I would say that night activity levels were increased by a factor of between 1.5 and 2 over day activity.

4. Without accepting the very complicated and at times unintelligible statistics produced in the report, it is noted that Mrs Frederiks is obliged to accept that the hospital does not provide a good standard of nursing care in its geriatric wards and, for the year 1989/90 the care on ward A14 was found to be *'less than adequate'*. This is quite an amazing admission and surely justifies every line I had written.

Taken overall the report, that must have cost several thousand pounds to produce, but to me it appeared an unconvincing charade. Rather than tackle the problems head on, management funked the real issues. In an introduction to the report Mr Caldwell says that he 'refutes' statements I have made but he has singularly failed to do this. To refute means 'to prove falsity or error of; to rebut or reply by argument'. I can find no rebuttal anywhere in the 28 pages. He speaks of the 'standards we are aiming to provide our patients'. My letters have set down the standards that we *are* providing. I applaud his aims; I denounce much of what is in fact happening on the wards at night.

The dictionary defines 'adequate' as: 'proportionate (to the requirements); satisfactory; barely sufficient'. With the goodwill and support of management, openly accepting the reality of our problems, and the continued devotion and skill of a superb bedside staff, I wish my colleagues well as they work to raise the nursing care to a 'good' standard. How strange that in 1990, the staff on A14 ward should be unable to provide a level of nursing care that four decades ago would have been considered totally unacceptable.

The truly breathtaking aspect of the report, though, is that it was prepared without any reference either to the 25 staff working at night on the wards or to the hundreds of patients involved. How any intelligent adult could deem this to be right beggars belief. Would a head teacher issue a report on the standard of education in the fifth-year classes of the school not having spoken to a single classroom teacher or pupil? Would any head be allowed to get away with it if he or she did? Such was the standard of mismanagement in this authority. And these people have the health, welfare and safety of thousands of citizens in their hands.

Mr Andrew Bennett MP had written to Mr Frank Field MP, chairman of the Select Committee on Health and Social Services, in May suggesting that the committee should take evidence from me and invite the authority to refute the charges. He wrote to me on 19th August with a copy of a second letter to the committee:

> Since May Stockport DHA have done nothing to improve staffing but have suspended Mr Pink from work. I feel it is now even more important for the committee to look at this issue, particularly since it appears that Mr Pink's suspension is aimed at silencing him, stopping the public knowing what is really going on in our hospitals and how the NHS is really under-funded. Please could you put the whole question before the committee again.

Nothing more was ever heard. On 22nd August the *Stockport Express Advertiser* reported on the case. A joint statement from local RCN and NUPE had noted:

> No member of staff is satisfied that the staffing levels on the geriatric unit are sufficiently high. NUPE and RCN feel that in view of the changing needs in the care of the elderly and

the many advances that have been made in medical treat-
ments, enabling many elderly patients to live longer and fuller
lives. . .that staff levels on the unit do need to be reviewed,
both on day and night duty.

The newspaper's editorial commented:

> It is understandable, though dishonourable, that jumpy
> health bosses ask: "Who will free us of this turbulent nurse?"
> The simple answer is no one. If Mr Pink is dismissed, the
> vital and just cause he represents will NOT go away. District
> general manager Peter Milnes and his senior staff have fended
> off attacks over acute elderly care by trotting out statistics
> about staffing levels. That is their job. They carry out policy,
> and it is that policy that is under attack.
>
> Even Mr Pink's colleagues, many of whom had previ-
> ously been cowed into silence, say more nurses are needed.
> So where are the policy makers? Expoliceman Fred Richards,
> an appointed (NOT elected) chairman of the health author-
> ity, has scarcely raised his head above the parapet during Mr
> Pink's letterwriting siege of Stepping Hill.
>
> There won't even be electorally accountable members of
> the health authority after next month. So it is crucial that the
> authority's chairman is seen to be acting PUBLICLY in the
> interests of the people of Stockport. Now that nurses have
> called for more staff, Mr Pink's long, lone crusade can no
> longer be treated as an irritating diversion from the business
> of juggling NHS funds. If Mr Richards won't back his own
> nurses, HE SHOULD RESIGN.

Among the many letters published by the *Guardian* was one from
Stephen Wright (referred to above) from Ashton-under-Lyne:

Like many nurses working with elderly people, I have been reading David Brindle's unfolding saga about the case of Graham Pink. Mr Pink's tenacity, not to say bravery, in pursuing a better deal for his patients and his colleagues has illuminated the dilemmas which thousands of nurses face in all sectors of health care, not just in the care of the elderly. Even when distressed by the conditions which they and their patients experience, many nurses find it immensely difficult to speak out. Not all nurses possess Mr Pink's letter-writing skills, nor are they close enough to retirement to feel unthreatened by the effects on their career.

The history of nursing is littered with the names of those lost to the profession who were unable to pursue and sustain a complaint. People like Mr Pink who hit the headlines are in the minority; thousands more are unable or unwilling to follow this path. This leads to nurses leaving in droves, to higher levels of sickness, absenteeism, and alcoholism in the profession. Worse still, perhaps, are the effects on other nurses who become numbed by the daily grind and who then add to patterns of care that are at best unimaginative, at worst downright cruel.

Our political and managerial paymasters are often far removed from the reality of patients' needs. Sadly, what is happening to Mr Pink is symptomatic of a wider sickness where health care is subsumed in the dubious framework of market forces. While others speak of costs, controls and contracts, it is the nurses who suffer.

The question is: why are nurses so powerless? Despite their huge numbers, more than on two thirds of a million, they appear so often to be little more than glorified handmaidens, seen by the general public – certainly in my day – as dedicated and caring but not necessarily intelligent, responsible decision makers. What happened to me in Stockport highlighted: a) our own impotence and lack of political awareness; we are the disregarded, if willing, lackeys of the health service; b) a complete absence of leaders whom nurses can look up to and who can speak with authority; and c) a lack of professional standing. So many nurses speak about the 'profession' of nursing as if the use of the word confers the attributes.

I leave the last word to a lady who wrote to me from Manchester.

Dear Mr Pink,

I have meant to write to you many times since I first read about you. I simply want to say do not give up. Your action is one of the bravest, most honest, honourable and truly compassionate struggles in Britain today. I imagine it has also been one which causes you terrible stress and heartache. Please believe me, you are speaking out where many of us have stayed silent. You are speaking for us.

I left nursing three months after qualifying as a Registered General Nurse. I, and several of my student colleagues had spent our training constantly appealing and complaining to our tutors and senior nursing staff about the poor and often dangerous standards of patient care which we witnessed (and indeed were unwillingly party to).

Not having your courage and determination I chose to leave the job I loved as I saw no way to change the massive fear, careerism, indifference and 'Keep your mouth shut' mentality which pervades the NHS. For all those without a voice, without power and without money I wish you the strength to continue until your name is cleared and the public understands what is happening to the elderly people we should be caring for.

TEN
I STAND ACCUSED

All truths that are kept silent become poisonous
— **Nietzsche**

Although many of the letters I received were painting a similar picture of deteriorating care, especially due to lack of sufficient staff, all were so supportive that I was buoyed up at this difficult time. Typical are these two published in the *Nursing Times* on 25th July and 29th August respectively:

> After having read the article "Speaking out" about Graham Pink's protests I must congratulate him on the way he has handled his plight. I found his recollections deeply moving and as a sister in an elderly care rehabilitation ward I understand his problems. How I wish more nurses in elderly care settings felt as strongly and reacted as professionally as he has.
>
> *Clare Bennison, Castleford, West Yorks*

> I read with horror of the plight of Graham Pink, who has now been suspended. I would like to express my support for him as a caring and articulate nurse fighting for the rights of patients. It would be a tragedy for the nursing profession if somebody so obviously dedicated to his art is removed. Nurses must support Mr Pink or we may as well all give up now.
>
> *HM Hutchinson, SRN, SCM, Stratford, London*

The leader in *Nursing Times* of 22nd August summed up what many believed:

> Graham Pink, the whistleblowing nurse in Stockport, was once told by his district general manager that something would have to be done about the conditions in his ward. Now it seems something is to be done – Mr Pink has been suspended and expects to be sacked. Stockport looks poised to rid itself of the turbulent priest. His suspension has taken him away from the source of his information about the conditions in the ward and removed him from the very credible position of a charge nurse.
>
> The cynical view will be that someone, somewhere, would have made it their business to try to silence him eventually. He follows the time-honoured tradition of whistleblowers who have either found themselves in trouble or been on the receiving end of some very unpleasant pressure and harassment.
>
> The most amazing thing is that Mr Pink has been asked: 'If the conditions are so bad, why has no one else spoken up?' The answer must be obvious. There are very few nurses who are in a position to take on the pressures of speaking up. They feel they cannot face the misery heaped on them when as a recent *NT* article put it: they are invariably dealt with as deviants "who must be silenced or punished".
>
> Protesters tend to be individuals like Mr Pink, who has the financial security of a pension from his previous job and the confidence to speak up, or students who have few personal responsibilities and a strong sense of idealism. The idea that Mr Pink does not enjoy the support of many other nurses is absurd. He has received dozens of letters of support, and articles about him have been given some of the highest scores

ever recorded by *NT's* readership panel – the group of nurses who systematically read the journal and score articles week by week.

Nurses have traditionally backed off from protesters when the real trouble starts and Mr Pink's case will test their "stickability". It will be a sad day for nursing if he is sacked and sinks into anonymity. Nurses who are concerned about the standards of care for frail elderly people, and about the right to protest in an informal way, will continue to give their support. The immediate call is for Mr Pink to be reinstated. Suspension from duty, surely a crisis measure to protect patients from an incompetent practitioner, seems totally inappropriate in his case.

A letter from management with the detailed charges arrived on the last day of August 1990. The four charges were: (1) Breach of confidentiality (2) Failure to report an accident (3) A drugs error, and (4) Failure to accept instructions. On return from holiday in late September and before preparing my defence, I wrote to the hospital general manager Mr Caldwell.

You are proposing to call as witnesses two managers, Mr Geraghty and Miss Carew, who have written flagrant and intentional untruths that impugn my professional competence and my honesty. Given the opportunity to repudiate these mendacious slanders, you refuse to take the decent and correct action. In any properly-managed organisation such malfeasance by managers would constitute serious misconduct necessitating immediate action.

In your recent letter you refer to the last health authority meeting, held on September 7th, which I attended. With a full and varied agenda, it was interesting to see that of the two hours the meeting lasted, some 90 minutes was spent discussing one item, the care of geriatric patients in Stepping Hill. More than one member was less than satisfied with the chief nursing officer's report. When directly challenged to comment on the incidents that I have detailed, she appeared flummoxed and all but wordless. Here lies, surely, the very genesis of management's predicament. Either you accept the truth of my accounts or you expose me for the charlatan you imagine I am. The choice appears straightforward enough. Mrs Frederiks' defensive and defeatist stratagem was to say that she could not discuss matters under investigation – a specious artifice, for she knows full well that only one such incident is the subject of enquiry.

Sooner or later management must face up to the issue head-on. Evasion, deception and sophistry have a limited life. You may, of course, find what I have detailed shocking and repulsive (I did); but rather than look the other way, why not face the problem openly? I am not alone in deprecating the massive expenditure in time and money that management is employing ("wasting" might be a more precise word) on my suspension and its "Press Release". As the money involved is public money, the general public will, I trust, be entitled to know the full cost of the action. How sad that everyone's exertions are not being harnessed to improve our care of the patients.

If you intend to proceed with the proposed disciplinary meeting, I wish to make my position clear and this will involve bringing into the open matters already known to managers but which have remained unspoken and, until now, I would say rightly so. Staff under pressure can make mistakes, skimp on care, overlook necessary procedures, become lax. We are all guilty. Our shortcomings are most successfully managed with understanding and respect. Nobody becomes a nurse to neglect, offend or hurt. My outstanding regard for all our geriatric staff is known and has been widely broadcast. To work alongside these people has been a pleasure and a privilege, the value and impact of which is inestimable. At the same time I am cognizant of the good name that a hospital can earn in the community. Thus it saddens me to know that some of what is now to be divulged may have an adverse effect. The fact that every incident is true, has been carefully documented and known to managers for years brings no consolation. Nor do I derive any satisfaction to contemplate the additional attention that may ensue. The contempt and condemnation from the length and breadth of this land which Stockport management has had to endure has never received my approval, nor do I now seek to exacerbate the situation.

Over two years ago I brought to nurse managers' attention serious concerns regarding patients' identification, care and treatment. For example, widespread and dangerous intravenous infusion neglect; failure to administer prescribed drugs in accordance with the authority's Rules for Prescribing, Administration and Storage of Drugs and negligence in correct patient identification. Let me quote from my letter of July 12th, 1988 to Mrs A Matthews, clinical nurse specialist for the elderly: *"No experienced nurse can be unaware of the many problems that have arisen in hospitals because of errors in drug administration. Such errors can prolong a patient's stay and may cause much distress and suffering. Anything which reduces the risk of a mistake must be employed."*

If the presumed failure to sign for/administer quinine sulphate is serious enough to warrant inclusion in a disciplinary interview, why did not the improper administration of 1) PETHIDINE and 2) MORPHINE SULPHATE lead to similar action? My letter of July 12th continues: "The vital importance which our authority, and every health authority throughout the land, places on unit numbers and the Identiband is well-founded on experience. It would be difficult to suggest a more essential part of a patient's admission. It is not only in the area of drug administration that unidentified (or misidentified) patients are at risk. Errors are not unknown in surgery (we do send patients to theatre) or in blood transfusion. Two quite dreadful mishaps have occurred (one only this year) in this region. The possibility, slight though it may be, is always there, especially where two or more patients have the same surname, as was the case on one ward last week (one had no Identiband)."

There followed details of one ward where 60 per cent of the patients, despite many previous mentions of the importance of the rule, were not properly identified. Following a meeting held on July 22nd, 1988 to discuss the situation, at which two nurse managers spoke, I submitted a further list of disturbing negligence, including another maladministration of morphine Sulphate. Twelve months later more details of neglect, all of a most worrying nature, were reported. The alleged actions/lack of action that constitute the four charges put against me would in no way have threatened patients' recovery; would in no way reflect serious neglect; would not have placed patients in any danger. Yet a disciplinary interview is considered appropriate, and this I am not questioning. Why then have much more serious matters, well-known to management, not resulted in similar action? If my continuation on duty was "clearly undesirable" (your reason for suspension) perhaps you will explain how one nurse continued on duty after he:

1. Failed to report a patient's pyrexia (39°C) at handover,
2. Allowed an infusion for a patient (permitted nil by mouth)

to run six hours behind regime,

3. Failed to enter a blood transfusion on the chart of a patient with leukemia, nor refer to the transfusion at handover,
4. Failed to care for a urinary catheter, found in a dirty, encrusted condition, thus exposing Mr A (who was already very ill) to a high possibility of urinary tract infection,
5. Allowed a gastric feed for a very sick 88-year-old patient with cancer to be up to seven hours behind schedule and
6. Made no mention of 2, 3 or 4 at handover time?

Much of the malpractice relates to one ward where serious omissions and carelessness were routine and regularly brought to management's attention. For example, a patient whose documentation showed FIVE DIFFERENT surnames; a patient's mouth described as filthy, a patient's urinary catheter described as disgusting, both observations made by a visiting staff nurse sent to help from another ward; massive and repeated slackness over patient identification; unreadable nursing Kardex entries; unwashed patients, etc, etc (I can only mention a few of the matters here).

I need not tell you, Mr Caldwell, that fatalities have occurred in hospitals because of, and for no other reason than, incorrect identification of patients. Yet, while such lack of proper identification has been widespread in our geriatric area, and known to be so by managers, to the best of my knowledge, no reprimands, let alone disciplinary actions, have been issued. It is obscure and paradoxical to me that my actions which put no one at risk (and in fact were aimed at improving patient care and safety) necessitate suspension, while action by other nurses, that placed patients in consider-able potential danger, and has been known to lead to death of a patient, is not only overlooked but acquiesced in. Can you please explain? In your letter you refer to "...nurses, trained and untrained..." May I point out that there is no such person as an 'untrained nurse' – the expression is a contradiction. Perhaps you mean student nurses, who do not work at night on our wards. Your next sentence appears to be at odds with Mrs Frederiks' findings, which show (page 21) "shortfalls' at the "Good" standard of nursing (1988/89 and 1989/90) on all three wards, and, most significantly, a negative figure (-0.16) for A14 (1989/90) on the "Adequate" scale. Thus, by your own admission, Stepping Hill was NOT PROVIDING A GOOD STANDARD OF NURSING CARE on its geriatric wards, a refreshing if disturbing disclosure. In the year 1989/90 the care on ward A14 was NOT EVEN ADEQUATE, clearly contradicting your statement.

If having considered this letter, you believe a quiet, face-to-face discussion would be useful (not, I suggest, at the hospital), please let me know. You are most welcome here anytime. You have my phone number.

Mr Caldwell's reply ignored all the points made. He was obviously happy to call as witnesses against me managers who had tried to discredit me and ignored the most negligent and alarming practices by day staff that I had documented. At the same time, I made it clear that even at this stage I was prepared to seek out some way of avoiding a damaging period of further unsavoury revelations and hostile publicity for the hospital. He must have realised that all this might be avoided from my last sentence that was a genuine offer to seek out mutual solutions. If he really had the good name of the hospital at heart, do not you think he would have at least explored my offer of a meeting? If the health authority really put patients first, surely it would have seriously considered a way out of the mess. I can only deduce that they were all so hell-bent on removing me, that the additional damage to the authority's and their personal reputation, the possible loss of public confidence, more national condemnation, and above all else the worry and distress likely to fall on future patients and relatives, all of which they must have foreseen, counted for nothing. Whether others above and beyond were pulling the strings I do not know. Either way, it suggests a failure of management, of public relations, of understanding human nature and of concern for sick people on a monumental scale. In his response Mr Caldwell wrote:

> At the meeting I have arranged for October 12th, 1990, I will require you to give an explanation of the four incidents detailed in my letter dated 31st August, 1990. I have no doubt that you will wish to raise at this meeting a number of the points you have raised in your letter dated 25th September, 1990, and this you will be able to do. However, I will not, at this meeting, be discussing the general issues of the adequacy of staffing at night on the Geriatric Wards at Stepping Hill Hospital, as the District Health Authority considered this issue at length in September, 1990.

How a disciplinary hearing could be fairly conducted without reference to the adequacy of staffing, I find it impossible to conceive. The staffing position related so seminally to the charges brought against me that any fair enquiry into my behaviour would have to discuss it. Before the hearing started, it seemed, Big Brother had decided that I would have both hands tied behind my back. This display of implacable resolve to have no truck with a conciliated outcome, to sort me out once and for all, is well illustrated by Dr. David's attempted intervention. Dr TJ David, PhD, MD, FRCP, DCH, was senior lecturer in child health at the University of Manchester and consultant paediatrician at the Booth Hall Children's Hospital in the city. He wrote to me late in 1990 after seeing a television programme. He offered to mediate. I sent him the full file of correspondence so that he would have as comprehensive a picture as possible of events and welcomed his intervention. He wrote to Mr Richards, the health authority chairman, on 24th January 1991.

> I happened to be watching the programme World in Action recently, and I was surprised to learn of the difficulties faced by Mr Pink. As a result of seeing the programme I was moved to write to Mr Pink to express general support. In response to this, he has allowed me sight of the extensive correspondence which has taken place between himself and various members of the hospital staff, members of parliament, the DHSS and colleagues in the nursing profession.
>
> I hesitated to speak out, as having been a member of a Health Authority (Oldham) myself until recently it was clear to me from the television programme that only one side of the argument was being portrayed. Having seen the correspondence, and the responses from various members of the nursing management team, I now feel slightly better informed.
>
> I must confess that I do feel some sympathy with Mr Pink's plight, and as an outside observer I do not get the impression that he has been dealt with fairly. I do believe that the NHS is currently under-funded, and my observations are that there are nursing shortages across the hospital spectrum and not just in geriatrics; we too have had our problems with nursing shortages, not least at night. I realise that this is a late stage, and that to some extent the two sides have become rather entrenched, but I am writing in the hope that the disciplinary action (which I get the impression has been constructed rather artificially) could be dropped in favour of a more constructive approach.

I wondered, for example, whether Mr Pink's abundant energies could not be more usefully channelled by reinstating him to his hospital-based post, and engaging him part-time in a prospective study of nurse dependency and nurse staffing in his speciality, comparing the needs and demands in several different geriatric units in other districts. Such a study, if it were to be meaningful, would have to be carefully planned, but I am sure that Professor Butterworth (one of the two Professors of Nursing at the Medical School) and his department could provide guidance on research methodology and general support.

Please forgive this unsolicited letter.

Before seeing a copy of the doctor's letter I had spoken to him on the phone and welcomed his attempted mediation. His suggestion had the basis for a common sense and practical settlement and I promised to meet the authority more than half way if it showed an interest. Apparently, though, it dismissed his unsolicited letter as just that and nothing came of his attempt to arbitrate. No clearer testimony, I suggest, could be evinced of the management's hostility to any outcome other than my removal which it seemed set on from the start. If the Queen Mother had arrived at the hospital to offer to intervene, she would have been sent packing with a flea in her ear. In the face of such overbearing intolerance, my chances of survival seemed remote indeed. Nevertheless, I now devoted all my time to preparing a rebuttal to the charges.

I.   BREACH OF CONFIDENTIALITY

There were three questions put by Mr Caldwell under this heading:

1. Why, despite our meeting on 17th May, 1990, at which I gave you a clear indication, subsequently confirmed in writing, that your media activities were causing unnecessary

anxiety to patients, relatives and friends, did you continue with this course of action?

2. Why, despite an explicit instruction "that you should not
   become involved in any further publicity" did you choose
   to report in detail an incident that happened on 15th July,
   1990 to a patient in your care to a local newspaper? Because
   of the amount of information you supplied, it was obvious
   that a specific patient's details had been identified.

3. Why you did this in clear breach of the confidentiality
   clause stated in your terms and conditions of employment and in direct contravention to the confidentiality
   guidance given to all nursing staff in Stockport Health
   Authority. You should be aware that this action resulted
   in a complaint being received from a relative of a patient
   about information appearing in a newspaper without
   direct permission being given which caused distress and
   grief to the family.

Management never produced any evidence to support the claim
that my activities were causing 'unnecessary anxieties'. When I
pressed Mr Caldwell at the hearing, he said vaguely that he thought
one or two letters had been received. I twice requested that these be
produced in evidence. They were never seen. No attempt was made
to establish that any breach had occurred. It was taken as read, and
my request that management both define 'breach of confidentiality'
and establish it had happened was brushed aside.

Many people, far more experienced in employment matters than
am I, have suggested that in a court of law the health authority's
confidentiality clause would be found unsustainable. Interestingly,
the clause is flouted daily by nursing staff. The phone rings and
someone enquires about 'my auntie, Mrs Blades'. Without any
way of knowing if the caller is who he says he is, staff give out a

great deal of information. So what is 'information', to whom does it belong, who has the right to it, who decides who has the right to it? are but some unresolved questions I would have wished the managers to answer. Did Mr Gibb's relatives have the right to know what had happened to him? When they read of the incident in the paper surely they above all had a right to the information, which in fact they already had, while those it might be argued did not, the mass of readers of the paper, would not be in a position to identify Mr Gibb. None of this was of interest to the hearing nor was discussion along these lines allowed.

The whole question of confidentiality is a minefield and staff are presented with dilemmas daily. I recall one Saturday afternoon some years ago when I was working in casualty at Withington Hospital, Manchester. A young man came in with a badly lacerated hand. Another youth was with him. I took all the details. The accident, they said, had happened at home with a woodworking tool. Five or ten minutes later, as the young man waited for his turn to see the doctor, I was sitting just behind him taking details from a newly arrived patient. Not realising I was there, the men were discussing the 'accident'. From what I overheard, the injury had occurred as they were committing a house burglary. I reported this to the sister in charge. She said that how or why the injury happened was of no concern to us and I must put what I had heard out of my mind. This disturbed me and to this day I believe her advice was wrong. The logic of her ruling is that even if, for example, the householder had been injured, perhaps lying alone on the floor of the house, the nurse must keep quiet and protect those possibly guilty. On the way home I called into the local police station and, under some pretence, discovered that there had been an attempted burglary in Chorltonville that afternoon. My impression is generally that nurses do not accept that they bear any responsibility to protect the public whether it is from burglars or negligent colleagues or managers, a very strange and misguided belief. 'It has nothing to do with me' seems to be the motto. What the confidentiality clause in question amounts to is not so much a protection for Stockport's patients as an iron curtain for managers. It was not privacy that was at stake but *secrecy*; for NHS Stockport read GCHQ Cheltenham. The catch-all clause taken literally means that no one may report anything to anyone outside the hospital. No wonder managers were not prepared to have Dr David step in. Of course, the correct procedure is always to seek remedies within the organisation, as I had done ad nauseam, but should that fail or where those complained about are the very people to whom one must take a grievance, outside disclosure should not automatically lead directly to the sack, as it did in Stockport.

I was prepared to quote from the code of conduct ('. . .to serve the interests of society, and above all to safeguard the interests of individual patients') and make other references to my duty as a nurse. If management places me in an intolerable position in which I am forced to neglect patients' wellbeing, dignity and safety, and if management repeatedly states that we are sufficiently staffed, it is difficult to see what other action to uphold the code, and my personal ethic, was available. It may not be illegal for management to fail to staff our wards adequately, but I believe it to be unprincipled and inexcusably reprehensible.

II.   FAILURE TO COMPLY WITH THE ACCIDENT POLICY

1. Why was the incident (with Mr Gibb) not reported to the night nurse manager? Why you failed to ask for assistance to help deal with the ward despite being told explicitly to do this if you were experiencing difficulties (instructions which were put in writing to you in a letter dated 9th January, 1990, from Miss EM Carew).

2. Why there is no record of a medical officer being called to

examine the patient to exclude injury?

3. Why was no accident report form completed until you were requested to do this by Miss O'Donnell, night nurse manager, the next evening, after she had been informed that the relatives of the patient had complained about the accident to staff?

4. Why you failed to report the incident in the Kardex?

5. Why you record the patient as having 'a quiet, restful night' in the Kardex.

6. Why you did not mention the difficulty you had had with the patient in the handover to day staff.

7. Why, instead of following any of the above standard nursing practices to report and record the incident, instead gave a full outline of these incidents to the press?

The health authority required all 'untoward incidents' to be reported to the nurse manager. The fact that she will do nothing to try to prevent such events from happening again is by the way. But surely staff must clearly understand what 'untoward' means. At no stage during the hearing was I able to get anyone to define an untoward incident. When I directly asked Mrs Frederiks to tell me, Mr Caldwell sharply intervened to say that the panel was not there to answer questions; *I was.*

I prepared for the hearing a list of 24 incidents:

1. One patient climbing into another patient's bed.

2. An intravenous infusion found to be 24 hours behind schedule.

3. A patient left alone to die.

4. A patient obliged to defecate into the bed and lie in her own excrement.

5. Very sick and paralysed ladies manhandled onto and off commodes by one person alone, subjecting both patients and staff to massive risk.

6. Reports in the nursing Kardex which are all but unreadable.

7. Controlled (dangerous) drugs improperly given.

8. A new patient, a feeble and poorly lady, pushed into the dayroom and left there for an hour because a corpse was in the bed she was to occupy.

9. Vital observations (for a patient on a blood transfusion, for example) not carried out.

10. Patients unwashed for 24 hours.

11. More than half the patients in a ward not properly identified.

12. A student nurse blamed by a senior sister for an IV infusion eight hours in advance of the regime.

13. An unidentified body sent to the mortuary.

14. One patient with five different surnames recorded on his documentation.

15. A patient shouting out for much of the night/ keeping most of ward awake.

16. Dangerous drug rounds.

17. A patient dying as a auxiliary (left alone to care for 20 acutely ill patients) helplessly looks on.

18. Half the ward (13 patients) repeatedly left alone, out of sight/ earshot of staff.

19. A 90-year-old patient (almost totally deaf) walking out of the ward unnoticed at 4.45am.

20. An experienced nurse reduced to tears because grinding stress made it impossible to care for patients and comfort bereaved relatives decently.

21. A confused lady in her eighties having to be dragged back into the ward.

22. A ward full of patients abandoned during the above incident.

23. A patient distressed and unable to sleep because of cats wandering among the beds at night.

24. Inadequate/non-existent sister-cover.

My intention was to ask the members of the disciplinary panel if these occurrences were 'untoward'. Most were more serious and untoward (defined as: 'perverse, awkward, unlucky, inconvenient') than the event under consideration with Mr G. Yet despite all these incidents being made known to managers, not one was set down on an accident report form and no disciplinary interviews ensued. If these incidents were not regarded as untoward, why should the event of 15th July be so construed? If managers are happy to leave someone (whether nurse or untrained helper) in charge of a ward or area of a ward it must allow that person to exercise discretion as to what is reported to managers, especially when no guidance as to what is and what is not 'untoward' has been provided. Compared with previous, nightly experiences on our geriatric wards, this one episode was far from untoward. When, at the hearing, I attempted to put these observations to the panel I got no further than question number 4. Mr Caldwell, in the chair, would not allow me to continue, saying that he did not wish to hear any more.

It is the height of cynicism for management to dismiss my claims for extra staff and state for a year that we were not understaffed and then ask, when it suited them, why I failed to request more staff. If the wards were sufficiently staffed, it seems illogical and devious to ask why I 'failed to ask for assistance'. An 'accident' by definition is an 'unforeseen or unexpected event; an event that is without apparent cause'. The incident under scrutiny was neither unforeseen nor unexpected and high on the list of causes must come insufficient staff to protect so many dependent people. No accident occurred; neglect occurred. We did not have a neglect report form. As I wrote at the time:

> The episode with Mr Gibb was loathsome and beyond all human decency. As just about everything written in 17 letters (56 pages) over the previous 11 months had been ignored,

further reporting of incidents would clearly be treated to similar disregard and disdain. *When I report bedside incidents to management, I am ignored. When I do not, I am disciplined.* The irony of the situation, a form of management-imposed Russian roulette, will not be lost on a discerning public, which already sees Stockport's managers as inept and unfeeling; in short – out of order, out of touch and out of excuses.

III. FAILURE TO FOLLOW THE RULES FOR ADMINISTERING OF DRUGS

1. Why, on four consecutive nights of 26th to 29th July, 1990, when you were on duty in charge of Ward 14, the above regulations were not complied with as there are no entries against the prescribed medication of quinine sulphate for a patient, Mrs H. It should be noted that the patient complained of severe cramps conducive with not having received the appropriate medication.

2. According to Sister Field, there have been previous occasions when omissions of this nature were brought to your attention, notably with regard to two patients, namely Mr H and Mrs S on occasions in May and June of this year after these had been spotted by the medical and paramedical staff.

Not until 31st August, some five weeks after the dates of the alleged errors, was I informed of the details of this charge that could, and ought in fairness, to have been provided on suspension on 9th August. I did request the details that evening but my request was refused. This plainly put me at a grave disadvantage when it came to recalling the nights in question. Most people would have difficulty recollecting in detail their actions of a week previously, especially on an incident-packed day or night. There was no way that I could be expected to remember incidents 33 or more nights old, and to imagine otherwise would have been dishonest and irresponsible. The fact that the charge was withheld from me, maximally undermined my defence. Meanwhile, the missing signature charge was known to and openly discussed by both day and night staff immediately following suspension. Was this just? Was it ethical?

Mr Caldwell never justified why it was necessary to suspend me. The health authority's disciplinary procedure states that suspension 'should only be implemented. . . when it is clearly undesirable for the employee to remain on duty'. Management did not attempt to establish how my continued presence on duty could be considered as clearly undesirable for patients or colleagues. Nevertheless, it was evidently undesirable for managers if I was able to speak to colleagues and consult relevant documents and records in the preparation of my defence. If the answer is that I was a risk to patient care, then why had other nurses, who undoubtedly placed patients at risk by their indifferent and dangerous practices, been allowed to continue working on the wards?

Not infrequently nurses slip up by failing to sign a drug Kardex. When this is spotted it is mentioned at handover (or the next drug round) and the oversight rectified. Neither I nor any other nurses whom I have consulted has ever heard of such a comparatively minor mistake forming the basis of a disciplinary charge.

For more than two years I had brought to managers' attention 1) serious carelessness regarding drug administration by day staff and 2) the inevitable probability of error when one nurse only has to run the ward. On any busy ward mistakes can and do occur. Allowances are made. The number of mistakes, though, in the geriatric area during the day suggested massive and increasing carelessness. Some of the maladministration was of a serious nature, putting patients at obvious risk; yet no action against any nurses had been taken. With my first letter to the senior hospital nurse, Mr Geraghty, on 3rd October 1989, I sent 18 pages of detailed descriptions of careless/negligent practices relating to drug administration. No attention was given to these. Repeatedly I had reported both actual errors (by day staff) and potential errors (unsafe drug rounds at night) to Mr Richards, Mr Geraghty and Mrs Frederiks only to be ignored.

When it came to the charges, no evidence was produced from Sister Field to support her claim that she had brought to my attention previous omissions. And at the hearing my attempts to highlight the failings of others and to discuss the general negligence in drug administration in the geriatric area for more than two years was hindered and eventually dismissed as irrelevant. The drug Kardex did suggest that Mrs H had not received her tablet for four nights (on one of which I did not dispense the drugs) and if this was so I very much regret the distress she had been caused by my carelessness. But to call such lack of care gross misconduct is an incredible distortion of language. If the non-administration of this drug amounts to gross misconduct, as the panel decreed, there can hardly be an experienced nurse in the land who is not similarly branded.

IV.   FAILURE TO COMPLY WITH A LEGITIMATE INSTRUCTION

1. At 10.30pm on 3rd July, 1990, you were required to attend a meeting with Mr J Geraghty, assistant general manager, and the two night nurse managers. It is alleged that you refused to attend the meeting despite being repeatedly requested to do so.

2. I will also be investigating your serious allegations that Mr Geraghty behaved in a bullying and menacing way and shouted in an aggressive and ill-mannered voice after you on 3rd July, 1990, which appears in direct contradiction to statements received from the two night nurse managers present.

3. In addition, I will be seeking an explanation as to your
    conduct on 9th August 1990, when despite receiving a
    written instruction to attend my office you failed to arrive.
    This necessitated you being sent for, first by the night
    nurse manager and finally by me having to telephone you
    directly to further instruct you to attend.

There is little to add here about these accusations. I never refused
to attend a properly-arranged, unbiased meeting at which representation was granted. While Mr Geraghty and I met ALONE on the
corridor, the two nurse managers were some 20 yards away out of
earshot in the office with the door closed. This in 'manager-speak'
equals 'present'. It is based on the same logic that states that sister
cover is 'readily available' when the sister concerned is a quarter of
a mile away.

ELEVEN
A TRAUMATIC AND DISTURBING ORDEAL

No! No! Sentence first – verdict afterwards
— **Lewis Carroll**

The Royal College of Nursing put out this press release on 3rd October 1990.

> Graham Pink, the nurse from Stockport who has been campaigning to get more staff for his ward of elderly patients, has joined the Royal College of Nursing. Mr Pink's tireless letter-writing campaign to secure more resources has been widely reported in the press. His efforts have met with the traditional establishment response to a whistleblower, suspension from duty.
>
> The RCN's general secretary, Christine Hancock, is already on record as supporting Mr Pink. The council of the RCN has now considered Mr Pink's position and has stated that his stand in defence of patient care will be vigorously supported by the college. The RCN believes that Mr Pink's case highlights the severe problems faced by health care staff if they attempt to blow the whistle on poor standards of care. Instead of managerial support to increase resources, nurses too often find themselves branded as troublemakers and may be victimised.
>
> The nurses' code of professional conduct requires them to act in the best interests of patients at all times. The RCN

council warned over a decade ago, that the requirement to protect confidentiality should not be misused by managers to prevent nurses from speaking out on poor practice or to defend the quality of patient care.

The RCN believes that Mr Pink's case exposes a fundamental problem about standards of care in the health service. In the context of the government's NHS reforms, quality has become part of the rhetoric of every NHS manager. However the college fears that managers are often not listening to the views of experienced nursing staff when assessing the staffing complements needed to care for highly dependent patients. Rigid staffing formulae are no substitute for the judgement of the experienced ward sister, the college argues.

The college warns that attempts to improve the quality of patient care must be built on the commitment of staff toward improving their own standards. However, unless their efforts are supported by managers, and resources released to remedy problems identified by staff, their commitment will peter out in frustration and demoralisation. Commenting on Mr Pink's position, RCN general secretary, Christine Hancock says:

"I am delighted that Mr Pink has joined the Royal College of Nursing and that we now have the opportunity to represent him formally in his difficulties with the health authority. Mr Pink is the kind of nurse who inspires other would-be whistleblowers to speak out. In the interest of patients, he and they must not be silenced."

The general secretary had seen the correspondence prior to the council discussing the case and issuing this trenchant and promissory statement. I was not involved in its publication. A second complete set of the correspondence was sent to Mr Paul

Mullany (at the RCN North West offices in Preston) who was to represent me at the disciplinary hearing. Two meetings were held in October with Mr Mullany and another full-time college officer, Mr Trevor Ride, to discuss our approach to the case.

The first day of hearing was Friday 12th October. I was disturbed to discover that the panel was to consist of the director of personnel, Mr Burke, plus Mr Caldwell and Mrs Frederiks. Immediately this became apparent, I indicated my considerable disquiet but to no avail. However, the more one considers the set-up, the more objectionable and insidious it appears.

As I understand British justice, it is essential that one be tried by jurors (in the criminal courts) or magistrates who are completely unknown to the defendant and who are thus as unbiased and fair as human nature allows. In other arenas (the civil courts, for example) this principle is strictly adhered to. When I was sitting as a magistrate on a case, I must not know, even remotely, the accused or any of the witnesses.

Yet here we had a tribunal considering my guilt/innocence and sitting on it were the hospital general manager and the chief nursing officer, both of whom had been intimately involved in the case and concerning whose behaviour I had been critical. In an organisation the size of Stockport health authority there must be many senior managers from whom to draw a panel of people to hear the case who would have been unknown to me and uninvolved in what had been going on. This then might have been an impartial and legitimate group, but as constituted there was no way that these people could be seen as disinterested parties. It was contrary to all standards of natural justice in this country to have such a triumvirate.

It is not possible to give more than a glimpse of the three days of hearing (12th and 29th October and 26th November) but I shall try to present a fair overall picture. Mr Gibbs's daughter attended as a

witness to say that she and the family could identify their father
from the article in the paper and they were 'angry and distressed'
at the way the incident was described. When asked by Mr Mullany
if they were not distressed at the fact that their father ended up on
the floor in the first place, and the reason for this, she seemed not to
grasp the inference. There were some questions that I would have
liked to put, one or two facts made clear, but I declined. It would, I
believed, have been too insensitive so soon after the bereavement.
Miss Gibb left, as she arrived, convinced that I had been unkind to,
and had neglected, her father.

My colleague Nurse Peel came as a witness. She was obviously
nervous and who could blame her? When asked why she wished to
appear she replied:

> Basically because I believed all along in what Mr Pink has
> been trying to achieve; we are short staffed and he has been
> most sincere in his efforts. I feel that he has an awful lot
> of support and felt duty-bound to come along and give my
> support, and I feel I speak for my colleagues, I know I do.
> They won't come to speak because they are intimidated.

And later:

> As a professional nurse I feel it is a great shame that the situ-
> ation ever got to the press but I feel it is totally the authority's
> responsibility. Unfortunately, I do not think they took his
> claims seriously; if they had it would never have got this far.
> It is the authority's responsibility that it got to the press. She
> added that she had been called a "silly girl" for coming to the
> hearing. "Who called you that?" asked Mr Mullany. "Miss
> Carew," she answered.

Throughout the hearing there was an ominous sense of futility and inevitability. The atmosphere was hostile with hour after hour of leading questions, harassment, intolerant assumptions and minute examination of my every move, motive and thought. Whereas to start with I saw Mr Burke, the director of personnel, as perhaps the only unbiased member of the panel, I was soon to learn that he was a most unpleasant individual.

Two conclusions soon emerged. First, Mr Caldwell was not in charge of the hearing; his weak, indecisive chairing allowed Mr Burke free rein. If Mr Caldwell was as weak-kneed in running the hospital as he was in curbing Mr Burke, no wonder the situation had been allowed to deteriorate so badly. Second, though Mr Mullany may have done his best, we were walked over and trodden into the ground by these people. After enduring a prolonged spell of Mr Burke's attacks, I eventually said to Mr Caldwell that unless Mr Burke quietened down and behaved in a more civilised fashion, I would either ignore him or leave the room.

Two days into this ordeal, on 8th November, I wrote to the chairman Mr Caldwell. The letter read in part:

> The whole proceedings reek of prejudice and injustice. You must yourselves know that there is no way that you can come to an unbiased conclusion. These proceedings are a mockery of all that British justice and fair play stand for, a grotesque deception which deceives no one. But for the advice of my Royal College representative and my respect for him, I would have nothing to do with your "kangaroo court". I am informed that Tuesday 20th November is now the rearranged date for DAY 3 so, despite my serious misgivings and undisguised objection to further association with this clumsy charade, I shall attend prepared to speak to Charge 3. [Breach of drug administration]

THE FUTURE

The final section of this letter is beyond doubt the most important. In the light of what has been said, but more to the point, foreseeing what lies ahead, I ask you, Mr Caldwell, to stop these farcical proceedings before more distress and harm result. Have you any idea of the consequences which await us all if you insist on a continuation? What happens to me is of little concern, but do please consider the effect on staff, both individually and as a body, on whatever good name Stockport enjoys in the community, on our geriatric department in particular, on a number of named senior staff and, surely of overriding consideration, on our present and future patients and their loved ones. I see nothing but trouble with lasting and incalculable harm ahead unless you change course now.

After a great deal of thought, I make bold to suggest how what appears to be an intractable situation might be retrieved. Please do not dismiss these suggestions out of hand.

RECOMMENDED ACTION

1. Provide immediately more nurses to the geriatric area at night – a minimum of six nurses and five nursing auxiliaries to cover the three wards every night.
2. Miss Carew to be suspended forthwith and an enquiry into her conduct established. Once this is done a great deal of information/evidence, at present withheld, is likely to emerge.
3. Invite an independent, respected, outside body, the University, ACAS, a group of local people of standing with legal advice, a judge, the UKCC etc, to carry out a wide-ranging enquiry.
4. Ask Mr Geraghty to reconsider his testimony.

5. Request an appearance by or statement from Mr Milnes regarding my letter to him of 1.2.90.
6. Withdraw charge No. 4. [failure to comply with a legitimate instruction]
7. Charge Nurse Pink to be returned to his appointed post as geriatric block charge nurse.
8. Discontinue the present hearing.

To emphasise (a) how serious I consider our present situation to be, and (b) my wish to help in a positive modus vivendi, let me tell you that I have discussed the matter at length with ACAS (the Service is prepared to assist) and shall now approach the UKCC. As matters stand, Mr Caldwell, you are driving us all, Gadarene-like, towards the precipice. If we go over, the harm could be enduring and widespread.

I BEG YOU TO PAUSE AND PONDER.

The letter and enclosures to Mr Caldwell ran to 11 pages (some 5,000 words). His reply was longer than was usual from management, 24 words. All my points were ignored.

♦ ♦ ♦

And so I began preparation for the third and final day, set for 26th November, of the farce that my hearing had become. A few days earlier, on 18th November, I had written to Miss Christine Hancock, RCN general secretary. The letter read in part:

We have now spent some four hours discussing the case of the 83-year-old patient who was found on the floor. Every minute aspect of why I failed to do this or report that and, most heinous of all, why I had the audacity to report the incident to the local paper, is being pored over inch by snail-like inch. As to why the poor man was on the floor in the first place appears of no concern whatsoever! That is totally insignificant and subsidiary, as if a dying, emaciated, elderly cancer patient lying on the floor in a pool of his own urine was a trivial and quite irrelevant episode. Words fail me to describe my repugnance at such an attitude by management. They seem so inhuman, so uncompassionate. How such people come to be working in a hospital, I shall never understand. The man in charge of the inquisition, Mr Burke, appears to be enjoying himself enormously. So non-judicial is the procedure, so jaundiced the panel and so unreliable and inadmissible much of the "evidence", that I shall not be surprised to hear on November 26th that the decision includes kneecapping...

...I sincerely trust that this is not a typical disciplinary hearing in the health service for it affronts all the norms of fairness which a citizen has the right to expect. For example, is it usual for management to put forward the charges, gather 'evidence' (whilst preventing the suspended nurse from meeting colleagues or seeing documents), summon witnesses, interrogate and badger the defendant for hours on end with virtually no let or hindrance, lay down the rules of procedure and evidence, refuse to accept, let alone respond to, questions directly relevant to a proper defence, allow the hearing to drag on for weeks, prevent any outside, independent observers from attending, allow a charge based on demonstrated untruth to stand, and finally to decide the outcome? This is my situation and it is a stark travesty of all that is right, moral and just.

During October, Granada Television made a film in the *World in Action* series about the case. It was shown on the evening of 5th

November and generated considerable interest. This letter appeared in *Nursing Times* a month later:

> I watched the *World in Action* programme about Graham Pink with sad personal memories. I was a nursing auxiliary in a geriatric ward in East Suffolk Health Authority. I, too, remember night duty with only me and a staff nurse in a 26-bed ward.
>
> I remember the many nights when patients injured themselves because we were unable to cope, or ended up lying in their own filth because we were too busy and therefore unable to help them with a commode.
>
> The main problem with this situation is that most staff are frightened to complain because of the fear of losing their jobs on trumped-up charges or of being branded as troublemakers. Qualified nurses are taught not to question or complain to their elders and betters. Until they conquer this fear, things will not change.

On 26th November the result of the hearing was announced. I was found guilty of gross misconduct on each of the four counts. In a letter the following day Mr Caldwell wrote:

> Looking at all four allegations I am presented with a collection of problems, omissions and inappropriate behaviour that require the severest of disciplinary actions being taken against you on the grounds of both conduct and/or capability. There is no doubt in my mind that the events that have been investigated justify your dismissal from employment with Stockport Health Authority because of gross misconduct.
>
> However I am conscious of how some of these events began and the circumstances which preceded the disciplinary

investigation. Your original motives were, I feel, sincere in seeking to internally redress what you felt to be unsafe staffing levels on the geriatric wards at night. I am also mindful of the statement of mitigation made by Mr Mullany on your behalf. It is my feeling that you have most recently become overtaken by the media's activities in seeking publicity for their own ends.

These mitigating circumstances need, however, to be tempered by the fact that, it is apparent to me that there has been a breakdown in confidence between yourself and the line managers within nursing. I believe that this has resulted in a situation where it would be impossible for you to return to your previous duties as a charge nurse in the geriatric area.

As an alternative to dismissal, and to enable you to continue in nursing, it is my decision that you should be transferred to a position on night duty within the community nursing service, providing one-to-one respite care within the patients' homes. Your grade and pay and conditions of service will be unaffected and you will work to your existing rota pattern. I am also issuing you with a final written warning in respect of the four allegations that were heard.

This warning will remain on your file for a period of 12 months and will be taken into account should you commit offences during the period which could lead to disciplinary action.

In connection with the allegation relating to the Breach of Confidentiality and the Rules for Prescribing, Administering and Storing of Drugs, it will be necessary for me to report the facts to the UKCC. You have the right to appeal against this decision and any such appeal should be made in writing to the district general manager and received within 21 days of receipt of my letter.

On 18th December Mr Andrew Bennett MP had two questions answered in the House Of Commons by Mr Stephen Dorrell, the junior health minister:

— Mr Bennett MP: To ask the secretary of state for health if he will visit Stepping Hill hospital, Stockport to discuss staffing levels.

— Mr Dorrell: I have no plans to visit Stepping Hill hospital. Staffing levels in hospitals are a matter for local decision.

— Mr Bennett MP: Will the minister join me in congratulating Mr Graham Pink on having the courage to describe so movingly in the *Guardian* and on television the major problems faced in Stepping Hill on the night shift on geriatric wards? Will the hon. gentleman condemn the district health authority for suspending Mr Pink for his whistle-blowing activities rather than solving the problems at that hospital? Does he agree that that is deplorable?

— Mr Dorrell: No, Sir. I shall not join the hon. gentleman in congratulating Mr Pink. The trouble with his allegations is that he does not have the support of his colleagues, the clinicians in the hospital or the health authority's chief nursing officer; nor can it be established on any of the published criteria that his allegations are justified.

TWELVE
A BREACH OF
NATURAL JUSTICE

Is it possible to succeed without any act of betrayal
— **Jean Renoir**

Mr Mullany had discussed with me during the hearing the possibility of going to appeal and we were agreed on that move. While the suggestion of a community post came out of the blue to me, he did not appear surprised. After the announcement, and notwithstanding the suggested post, the need to appeal was not in question. There were many matters arising from the hearing which needed scrutiny and discussion.

The code of conduct is an example. The relevance of the code was cardinal to the whole case. One paragraph in Mr Caldwell's findings was particularly worrying and called for rebuttal at the appeal if not before. It stated:

> I further disagree with Mr Pink's contention that the United Kingdom Central Council's code of professional conduct and its Advisory Paper on Confidentiality, supports his action in breaching confidentiality. The explanation offered that the breach of confidentiality was in the public interest, is not accepted.
>
> Mr Pink's interpretation of Clause 9 of the code of professional conduct is not shared by management, nor by the chief nursing officer, whose advice I sought.

Disregarding for the moment that a) management's definition of breach of confidentiality may not be legally tenable and b) that I have never accepted that a breach, even by management's standard, took place, we are left to consider the role of the code in such a situation. This will be looked at in some detail later, but as it stood Mr Caldwell's decision needed to be challenged.

After the announcement of the outcome I lodged my appeal and a date was set for the 3rd and 4th of January 1991. The UKCC's Mr Pyne had told me that should I be found guilty at the hearing, he would very much like to come to the appeal to speak on my behalf (a promise on which I placed much store) though I was later told that this had been vetoed by his superiors.

During the next week I was to learn that the RCN was recommending not going to appeal and wanted me to accept the job in the community. It seemed to accept management's opinion that there had been a 'breakdown in confidence' between myself and the staff and managers and that this in itself would be sufficient grounds for dismissal. I pointed out that no evidence was produced at the hearing to support this statement by Mr Caldwell; that there had been no breakdown of confidence between myself and the staff (76 per cent supported me).

As for accepting the community post, I and every person with whom I discussed this offer, found management's proposal staggeringly ham-fisted and irresponsible. A nurse found guilty on four counts of gross misconduct and who has been reported to his professional body with a view to being struck off the register, is then offered a position working alone and unsupervised 'providing one-to-one respite care in patients' homes' (management's words). A more ill-considered and improper suggestion it would be difficult to imagine. So, to cut a long story short, the RCN and I parted company.

In preparation for my appeal and in response to a request from the UKCC solicitor who was making enquiries, I wrote to some of the staff with whom I had worked. The letter went to the few whose home addresses I had. I would have preferred it to have gone to all 24 ex-colleagues. The only way to achieve that would have been to write via the hospital and I was certain that such a move would have been sabotaged. I wrote:

> It is with some trepidation that I write to you. Throughout all my efforts to gain more nursing staff for the care of the elderly wards I have never asked any of my colleagues to become involved, knowing as I do the problems and difficulties staff face. But now that my good name and integrity are at stake, not to mention my continuance as a nurse, I must try to enlist some support, not so much for myself as for the patients.
>
> As you will know, after a long, unpleasant and I believe very hostile disciplinary hearing I was found guilty of "gross misconduct"; I have been removed from my post; will almost certainly be dismissed within weeks and have been reported to the council, a harsh and grossly unfair outcome, you might think, for someone whose only aim was to improve patient care and ease the burden on a truly devoted and magnificent staff. Of course I have made mistakes and perhaps acted unwisely but have never told an untruth, behaved unprofessionally, or intentionally put a patient at risk. My crime has been to speak no more than the truth and, whatever the outcome, that I do not regret.
>
> The UKCC (through the English National Board) has now to make an enquiry to establish the facts and a solicitor, Miss Katrina Wingfield, has been asked to look into the whole situation. As I understand the position, Mrs Frederiks, Mr Geraghty, Miss Carew (each of whom I have, some months ago, reported to the UKCC), Mr Caldwell and perhaps others are prepared to speak out against me whereas not one person

from the hospital has so far officially spoken out on my behalf. I say "officially" because as you may know, Mrs Peel, against enormous odds, was prepared to face the tribunal and support me. Hers, though, was a lone voice. Miss Wingfield has seen all the correspondence (which you are most welcome to have if you wish) but now needs to speak in confidence to as many bedside staff as she can. Quite rightly she is not able to accept the testimony of a single person. No one else needs to know that you have been involved. Your comments will be known to Miss Wingfield alone. She is prepared to write to you or phone at a time suitable to you.

To be found guilty of gross misconduct and treated as I have after a working life of 42 years (17 in nursing) is a distressing business and, I believe, a monstrous injustice, especially when my former colleagues have not had an opportunity, fairly and without fear to voice any opinion. That opportunity is now provided and I beg you as a colleague and a friend to take it. Should you want me to bring round the folder of letters or to speak to me about anything do ring. Do please let your voice be heard. But whatever you decide, my regard and respect for you will remain undiminished. You will act I am sure as I have tried to do, according to your conscience. I can ask no more.

Most faithfully,
FG Pink

Miss Wingfield's address and phone number were given. None of the staff to whom I wrote contacted me. While fear is usually cited as the reason why my colleagues were (and nurses generally are) unwilling to back a fellow nurse who discloses unacceptable standards, it saddened me nevertheless.

Among the many offers of support and help that came in during late 1990 was one from a local solicitor, Mr Brian Hamilton. He was anxious to start a campaign for my reinstatement and as part of this he prepared a petition which read:

> We the undersigned are concerned at the disciplinary measures taken against charge nurse Pink who has criticised staffing levels in Stepping Hill Hospital, Stockport. We call on Stockport Health Authority to rescind the steps taken against Mr Pink and to reinstate him.

Sheets with spaces for ten signatures were prepared. The first completed set to arrive back came from Mr Andrew Bennett MP at the House of Commons with the signatures of 28 MPs. To give local people the opportunity to sign if they so wished, Mr Hamilton, one or two other volunteers and I went into the centre of Stockport each Saturday morning during February, March and April. We stood outside Marks and Spencer with two large posters reading 'SUPPORT NURSE PINK'S CAMPAIGN'.

At first I was acutely embarrassed to stand out in public like this and while the others accosted passers-by, I hovered in the background waiting for shoppers to approach me. They soon did, recognising me from the photos in the local papers and the *World in Action* programme. At times we had small queues waiting to sign and it really was most encouraging. Many stopped to chat, often to say they had had a father, mother or partner looked after by me (among other staff) and to make the most generous and embarrassing comments. One form found its way to Dr Wendy Savage, senior lecturer in obstetrics and gynaecology at the Royal London Hospital, who had herself been through a similar ordeal. In sending the signatures she had collected she added a most significant comment: 'Much apathy from nurses I'm afraid'. My experience led me to the conclusion that the one quality most nurses possessed, and in abundance, was apathy. Dr Savage included a copy of a letter which she had sent to the chairman of Stockport health authority:

> I understand that Mr Pink is appealing against the decision of a disciplinary enquiry held last year, to move him from his position on the geriatric wards to the community. From the reports I have read in the Press including the independent evidence about inadequate staffing levels, this seems to be unjust. It also smacks of expediency and an attempt to silence a nurse who is genuinely anxious about patient care.
>
> If Mr Pink is transferred in this way, Stockport Health Authority will be continuing the recent tradition of health authorities of secrecy and upholding management decisions, however poor these are, and to punish the bearer of unwelcome bad news. Free speech is supposed to be part of a democracy but in the NHS it appears that some managers consider this a crime and worthy of disciplinary action.

Another petition form was sent through the post to the solicitor Brian Hamilton. It had nine signatures on it and at the bottom was written:

> Dear Mr Pink,
> The above names are the family of Mr Whitelegg. The ninth name is his widow. You were wonderful when my dad was dying and we'll never forget your kindness. If you need anyone to speak for you please do not hesitate to contact me. We do all hope you are successful in your plight; you deserve to be!

Those words mean more than I can express and even now, writing them brings a lump to my throat. What a privilege to be told so directly what one's meagre efforts have meant to others. These few lines I shall cherish long after the hurt and disappointment have been forgotten. They brought, and still bring me, the deepest satisfaction and fulfilment imaginable.

When one is closely involved in a given situation it is, of course, very difficult to stand back and take an objective view. I would be the first to admit that my proximity to the events might cause some people to hesitate before accepting my assessments, a sensible precaution. The thoughts of an impartial and knowledgeable observer, however, can be seen as unbiased and reliable. One of the first to comment publicly on my treatment by the health authority following the disciplinary hearing was the *Guardian*'s highly-respected columnist at the time, Melanie Phillips. I had never met, spoken to or corresponded with her. Under the heading 'A sick system of secrecy and persecution' this is what she wrote on 30ᵗʰ November 1990:

> Meanwhile, in the real world of everyday folk it's a contin-
> uing story of secrecy, abuse of power and the persecution
> of those who stand up to be counted. While everyone is
> jumping up and down this week over the dawning of the
> open society and the age of equal opportunity, Graham Pink
> was being sold down the river for telling the truth about the
> opportunity his geriatric patients in Stockport have to enjoy
> the essential decencies of life. Over in Swansea, meanwhile,
> a university lecturer, Anne Maclean, alleged poor standards
> in her department and was then promptly suspended. So
> much for the open society of academic life.
>
> Mr Pink and Mrs Maclean have much in common, not
> least because they each blew their respective whistles to
> the *Guardian*. Mr Pink's story, however, has now reached
> bizarre and utterly scandalous proportions. His crime was
> to come to the *Guardian* with correspondence, which we

printed, between himself and his health authority in which
he argued fruitlessly for more nursing staff. Stockport health
authority was digging in its heels and refusing to provide
additional cover, despite the distressing and utterly unacceptable conditions described by Mr Pink, sticking to a
calculation of nurse ratios based on simple numbers rather
than dependency levels used in other health authorities.
Since Mr Pink's patients were all aged over 75 and seriously
ill or dying, the health authority's attitude seemed to be a
typical bureaucratic response to a human problem it could
not or wouldn't deal with properly.

The publication of Mr Pink's correspondence drew a spec-
tacular response from the public and other media. The health
authority was severely embarrassed. Lo and behold, Mr Pink
was shortly afterwards suspended from duty pending a disciplinary hearing which finally reached its judgment this week.
He was arraigned on four charges, the fourth of which was
landed on him as an afterthought shortly before the hearing:
breach of confidentiality, failure to attend a meeting with
managers, a drug administration error and failure to fill in
an accident report form.

The nursing world quite rightly takes reported failures
extremely seriously, particularly breach of confidentiality
and errors in administering drugs. But such faults more
frequently occur without action being taken; if the record
of the most efficient nurse or any other professional is
trawled through with sufficient zeal, some errors will
almost inevitably show up. Normally, though, such a trawl
does not take place.

The question in Mr Pink's case is why he was pursued with
such zeal; and if those charges are examined more carefully,
the case against him stinks.

Take the most serious, the failure to administer a drug. Mr Pink admits this. He made a genuine error. But one of the devastating points brought out in his correspondence was that the pressure on the wards was such that nurses were making errors all the time. Rather than correct the cause of the problem and increase the safety of the patients, therefore, the health authority chose to throw the book at him instead.

Failure to attend a meeting is a petty charge that hardly merits third degree treatment. Breaching patient confidentiality is a serious charge, but just consider what it meant in this case. Mr Pink published in a local newspaper an incident in which to his intense distress an elderly patient had fallen and lain crying in a pool of urine while Mr Pink was struggling to cope with another patient. Although the patient's name was not given, his family complained that they had recognised him and this had caused them great distress – although whether the distress was actually caused by his identification or by the appalling circumstances described by Mr Pink would be hard to say.

But although nurses have a duty to keep their patient's identity confidential, their profession confers on them another important duty to speak out over patient care. Clearly the two duties may from time to time come into conflict, yet such a conflict cut no ice with Stockport health authority.

There was yet worse. The fourth charge related to that same incident. Having strung up Mr Pink for making it public, the inquiry then had the gall to say that since it accepted Mr Pink's account of that incident in the press, it was going to punish him for failing to record the fall on an accident form – even though the whole point of his account was that Mr Pink had been unable to deal with this fall because he was occupied with another patient.

The idea that Mr Pink may actually have been discharging his duty and performing a public service in disclosing the details of this and other incidents did not impress the disciplinary panel, perhaps unsurprisingly since it was the very same health authority, to whom and about which Mr Pink had complained, that was hearing the case against him. If ever there was a clear case of conflict of interest and breach of natural justice, this was it. The panel found him guilty of gross misconduct, transferred him to community nursing respite care and reported him to the UK nursing council which can strike him off.

This shows up the whole hearing for the farce it was. If the charges were so serious, why has he been transferred to a nursing role which, because it is unsupervised, requires a very high standard of nurse? If he is to be trusted with such a demanding role, why has he been reported to the nursing council? If he was so unprofessional, why did the hospital's general manager, Derek Caldwell, single out instead the breakdown in confidence between Mr Pink and hospital staff and the "unwarranted criticism" of Stockport's care of the elderly in his statement about the case?

Mrs Maclean's complaint was in a different arena but the underlying issue is the same. She and some other lecturers in Swansea university's department of philosophy and health care claimed that pressure to recruit as many students as possible led to lowered standards in checking, with some students being awarded degrees for inadequate work. Mrs Maclean, who was more outspoken than her colleagues, said what was going on was outrageous and made it impossible for anyone with academic integrity to stay on in academic life. She has now been suspended, with the college principal, Professor Brian Clarkson, using language reminiscent of Mr Caldwell of Stepping Hill hospital. If her statement did represent Mrs Maclean's views, said Professor Clarkson, it was not possible for her to work with colleagues "in a normal academic relationship of trust and respect".

The real issue here, as with Mr Pink, is not the relationship with colleagues but the embarrassment to the authorities caused by employees who speak the truth. They have blown the whistle and are being punished for it. Some might conclude from their experiences that the opprobrium being dished out should be directed elsewhere!

THIRTEEN
FAIRLY AND CONSISTENTLY APPLIED

Yet the first bringer of unwelcome news
Hath but a losing office... — **(Henry IV, *Part 2*)**

The appeal was set for the end of January and Mr Joe Swinnerton of COHSE, who had taken a close interest since the summer of 1990, told me that the confederation would gladly take me through the appeal. A full-time regional officer, Mr Tony Clarke, was allocated to my case. He was unavailable at such short notice so the appeal was postponed. Because many people were involved, all of whom I presume were booked up, the rescheduled dates went to late March. This gave us time to prepare an intelligent and comprehensive approach to the appeal. Meanwhile, for what reason I have never discovered, the UKCC continued to ignore my many requests for a response.

All my letters to the council were formal and polite. One would think that an organisation with as many staff as the council would have the resources, not to say the basic courtesy, to at least acknowledge letters.

In response to a letter from Brian Hamilton the solicitor, Mr Nicholas Winterton MP wrote to the chairman of the health authority, Mr Richards, on 20th March 1991. Mr Richards' reply was mostly the stock authority letter but with one or two significant additions. Mr Richards stated that he visited the ward 'within a few days' of my letter of 24th August. In fact his visit was on 16th September – 23 days later. It may seem unimportant that 23 days becomes in the chairman's words 'a few days' but, as I wrote to Mr Winterton, 'such disregard for accuracy is symptomatic of the authority's approach. While I have been at pains to be accurate and specific, management's response has been equivocal, evasive and disingenuous.' Mr Richards wrote that 'Mr Pink returned to nursing some four years ago...' Incorrect. I returned to nursing in 1977 but the fact that he was just ten years out would be of no concern to the chairman. 'I believe he is genuine and conscientious but the ability of people to cope under pressure varies in us all and I really think he has found a substantial difference since his return to nursing compared with the situation years ago and does have difficulty in organising himself and coping as he should.'

Regarding this sentence I wrote to Mr Winterton:

If this is a fair and accurate comment – not based, of course, on any first-hand observation or knowledge, why one asks is this the first time ever it has been mentioned. At no time since 1987 when I took up my post has the slightest doubt been cast on my capabilities in organising myself or anyone else.

If such a difficulty existed and had been noted by managers, should not the matter have been properly brought to my attention and advice/counselling offered. Is this not one of managers' most important responsibilities? Yet over a period of three years no mention, no hint of any problem was made to me. Had it been, I would have gladly accepted any comments and guidance to put matters right and improve patient care. Mr Richards must have been given this "information" by a nurse manager. It seems unethical to pass on comments regarding a nurse's competence without first making the person concerned aware of the situation and giving him the opportunity to speak.

A more disturbing aspect is that someone in Mr Richards' high office with its attendant responsibilities, should reveal confidential information (whether substantiated or not) relating to an employee of the health authority to a person "who does not have the right to this information". Can the chairman of the health authority so breach confidentiality? Of course, most fair-minded people will see Mr Richards' references to coping under pressure and organising himself as a shoddy and barely-disguised ploy to discredit me, and illustrates far better than anything I can say how exposed and barren is management's case.

On Friday 19th April Mr Andrew Bennett MP handed in the petition (we had collected just over 8,000 signatures) at the health authority offices. Mr Richards or Mr Milnes had been invited to attend to accept, but instead an unnamed official came out to receive the pile of forms. I was amazed that in so little time we could gather that many names. To thank all concerned the local paper printed my letter to the editor:

> For the past three months, one or two friends and I have been seeking the support of local people for the petition calling for my reinstatement as a nurse at Stepping Hill Hospital. The response has been quite overwhelming and we would like to say a huge "thank you" to the citizens of Stockport and surrounding areas for their wonderful backing and encouragement. Countless people have come up to me and made the most generous remarks. Especially appreciated have been the words of former patients or relatives who recall my care of a loved one who had died. Whatever the outcome

of next week's appeal, the opportunity to speak to so many kind people – an uplifting and humbling experience – is something that will remain with me for years to come.

My only regret is that during these last nine months I have been prevented from nursing alongside the outstanding team of devoted staff who so tirelessly and so cheerfully care at night for the elderly patients. If the opinions of the people of Stockport count for anything, I should soon be back on duty. Thank you for your massive vote of confidence.

Before the appeal a number of ex-patients and relatives wrote to management with their views. One was from a Mrs Howard from the Adswood district of Stockport. It read:

May I take this opportunity to express my deep gratitude to Mr Pink and I may add, to all the other nurses and medical staff, who so wonderfully nursed my mother. The occasion was February/March 1988. The ward was A14, Stepping Hill Hospital. Unfortunately my mother lost her fight and died on March 5th. I and the rest of my family took turns so my mother had someone with her at the hospital 24 hours a day.

I therefore was there up to midnight each day for two weeks. During this time I saw Mr Pink and what was required of the doctors and nurses during the night-time duties. How they did and still do it, I'll never know. Mr Pink was kindness itself and somehow found a comforting word for all the patients, no matter what.

I find it very difficult to understand why Mr Pink has been suspended from his duties for all this time when indeed he would be more valuable spending his time doing what he is best at – "NURSING". This gentleman seems to be speaking his mind about the state of our hospitals only to be penalised for doing so. I thought it was a policy in this country to be able to speak one's mind! I hereby ask the Medical Board to think again about Mr Pink and re-install him into his proper professional job.

Early in May I received a letter from the English National Board For Nursing (ENB) to say that I had been reported to the professional body on two charges of breach of confidentiality and failure to record or administer quinine sulphate (300mg). That Mr Caldwell had not included the other two 'proven' charges of failure to attend a meeting and report an untoward incident was unexpected.

> "According to the Nurses, Midwives and Health Visitors (Professional Conduct) Rules 1987, Rule 4," stated the letter, "the board is required to carry out investigations of cases of alleged misconduct by practitioners." The definition of misconduct as laid down is as follows: Misconduct means conduct unworthy of a nurse, midwife or health visitor as the case may be, and includes obtaining registration by fraud. In order that the investigating committee may consider the matter, you are invited to make a written statement or explanation of the incidents. The committee will consider all the documentary evidence at the earliest opportunity which in your case will be in June.

As I had already sent to the council a complete set of papers there was little else to submit. In a letter to the Board on 30th May I wrote:

> Over three quarters of the nursing staff with whom I work have privately expressed support. They could confirm that every account I have written is true, that there is a need for more night staff, that neglect does occur and that patients'

lives are put at risk, that management's treatment of me appals most of them, that none of the regular, geriatric, bedside night staff has been asked in a fair and open manner to express an opinion on staffing, on levels of care, on anything. But such is the concern at possible reprisal, harassment and victimisation (a very real fear apart from the example management has made of me), that none of the staff still employed feels able to speak – and knowing what they face, it would be unreasonable to expect them to. You do not have to look to Eastern Europe, or to have lived through the second world war, as I did, to find examples of people knowing that what they were part of was oppressive or immoral – even illegal, yet unable to speak out. Nursing staff generally think twice before "standing up" as I have done, but at Stepping Hill Hospital at night one nurse manager holds such pervasive and omnipotent control, and uses it to brook no questioning of her reign, that no nurse, still less nursing auxiliary, dares to step out of line. Were one foolhardy enough to consider doing so, the humiliation, vilification and distress which I have been subjected to would have their intended effect.

I notice that management has not included charges 2 and 4 of which I have been found guilty. Why this is so, I have not been told. It is difficult to avoid the conclusion that it is a shrewd and cynical ploy to try and avoid exposing much disturbing evidence regarding management's deceptions and concealments, and the hospital's dubious record of geriatric care. As you may be aware, my appeal before the health authority stands adjourned at the moment. Of the 36 hours of hearing to date, at least 20 hours, perhaps more, have been spent addressing charges 2 and 4 and in the case of charge 2, "Failure to comply with the Accident and Untoward Occurrence Policy", much has been made of the danger in which my deemed failure placed patients. If charge 1 (breach of confidentiality) which put no one in danger nor reflects lack of care (on the contrary it vividly demonstrates my concern for patients), is serious enough to warrant reporting me to the Board, then why omit a charge which management believes reflects lack of care, lack of judgment and involves endangering very sick and dying old people? I see it, for what it is, another shabby and contemptible sham which places managers' skins above patients' wellbeing.

As you will have gathered, I would very much welcome a hearing on these allegations and hope that the Board will see the necessity to hear and know the truth of what has been going on. The chance to clear my name, and more importantly to have the truth accepted in public, I approach with open arms.

◆ ◆ ◆

The appeal ran for four days at the end of April 1991 and was completed in the late afternoon of the fifth day, 8th June. The panel comprised three members of the health authority – Mr D Higginbottom, a solicitor, as chairman sitting with a Mrs J Murphy and a Mr P Allen. Joining these three was Miss Farrington-Wood, a nurse manager from the Merseyside regional health authority. She was to act as nurse advisor to the panel. The management case was presented by hospital general manager Mr Caldwell with personnel director Mr Burke at his side. I was represented by Mr Clarke with Mr Swinnerton in attendance. It is possible here to touch on only one or two of the significant discussions.

The proceedings were opened by the chairman who straight away made a quite extraordinary statement. With reference to recent press coverage of the case, he announced that he had before him a document that stated that charge nurse Pink was 'incompetent' and this assessment he accepted. When asked by Mr Clarke for a copy, Mr Higginbottom prevaricated. When asked again later in the morning if we could be shown this document, he said that it could not be located. That the chairman, himself a solicitor, could open the appeal hearing with this statement was so breathtaking as to leave our side of the room all but speechless. Mr Clarke protested, adding that he believed that his client could not now receive a fair hearing. This was ignored. So unexpected was Mr Higginbottom's comment, that we ought to have withdrawn at once from the room and declined to continue with this man on the panel. We were, though, so taken aback by his comment that our senses were numbed for a while.

Just before lunch Mr Clarke made a third request to see the 'evidence' but it never materialised. The chairman made it quite clear early on, that he and he alone, would decide what was to be classed as relevant, how long the defence was to speak for, and what questions or statements would be allowed. It was a display that defies description.

One of the first witnesses was chief nursing officer Mrs Frederiks. She contended that by going to the local paper with the account of Mr Gibb's last days 'Mr Pink was acting out of self-interest'. When asked to prove this she could do no more than repeat her opinion. She agreed that at no time had she visited the Care of the Elderly wards during my spells on duty nor met me to discuss care, nor would she have seen that as appropriate. In answer to the panel's nurse adviser Miss Farrington-Wood's question: 'Are there written standards of care for the elderly?' she spoke about 'work in progress'. Had she ever visited the geriatric wards at night? Another vague and evasive answer.

The assistant night nurse manager, Miss O'Donnell, was asked to give her impression of the general standard of care on ward A14.

She thought that it was very good and a tribute to the staff. She was asked by Mr Clarke about the lifting of patients at night. 'Nurses must not lift on their own; they have strict instructions about this,' she answered. 'This is the written hospital policy.' It is surely a measure of the obtuseness of the managers that she could sit there and make such a cynical statement, when she knew that nightly staff were left alone to move and lift without any assistance. After hearing her answer whatever respect I might have had previously for her was forfeited then and there.

Nurse Peel appeared and stood up well under questioning. She stated that she found the night nurse manager Miss Carew 'completely unapproachable, very rude at times, had me in tears on occasions'. She explained how it was so often necessary to lift alone, despite the danger to patient and oneself and replied, in response to a direct question, 'Mr Pink's care of patients was outstanding'.

An additional handicap for us was the lack of a proper transcript of the earlier disciplinary hearing. As we were appealing against the conduct and findings of that body, reference was often made at the appeal to what had been said during the hearing. Management had its own transcript which we gathered was a reasonable record. Mr Clarke explained our difficulty and asked to be provided with a copy. This Mr Higginbottom flatly refused. Later Mr Clarke made it clear that he could not properly conduct his case without access to the transcript. He asked to be allowed at least to see it and be given time to read it. The chairman was adamant. He had no intention of letting us see management's copy. No reason for this stance was offered. To me it seemed utterly unreasonable and simple obduracy.

Mr Geraghty's appearance as a witness was most revealing. He soon found that the sort of incomplete or equivocal answers provided at the disciplinary hearing were not acceptable this time round. For example, at the end of some incisive questioning by Mr

Clarke on the need for proper patient identification, he rather testily, and so revealingly, announced "Identibands are not important." He agreed that he went onto ward A14 soon after I had finished my last spell of duty to examine the drug records. It is beyond strange that Mr Geraghty should take no interest in the countless errors and negligent administration of drugs by other nurses for two years, then visit ward A14 only (he admitted he went nowhere else) to discover errors attributed to just one nurse.

In answer to a question from Mr Clarke, he stated that his inspection was a general one, not targeted towards anyone in particular. When pressed, he insisted that he was not just on the lookout for errors attributable to me. It should be pointed out that Mr Geraghty was the assistant manager and the hospital's most senior nurse with at least two layers of nurse management between him and the bedside staff. It was unheard of for a person of his status to do so routine a job as check drugs and I suspect it was a unique task he undertook that morning.

At the panel's request, photocopies of the records in question were made over the lunch break and Mr Geraghty was recalled. Miss Farrington-Wood seemed particularly troubled by what the Kardexes (drug records) revealed and again questioned Mr Geraghty. The exchange went something like this:

Miss F-W: 'Mr Geraghty, this morning you assured us that when you visited A14 to undertake a drugs' check, you were carrying out a general, routine audit.'
Mr G: 'That is correct.'
Miss F-W: 'May I ask you again if you were not just checking up on charge nurse Pink?'
Mr G: 'Certainly not.'
Miss F-W: 'Did you find any errors by other nurses?'
Mr G: 'No, none.'

Miss F-W: 'Then can you explain the many other discrepancies and errors which the records contain?'

Mr G: 'No. I can't.' (Long examination, directed by Miss F-W, of records; see below.)

Miss F-W: 'But you have told this enquiry that your visit to A14 was to check on drug administration generally.'

Mr G: 'That is so.'

Miss F-W: 'Why, then, did you discover and report on the errors of one nurse only?'

Mr Geraghty mumbled something, looked acutely uneasy, and shook his head to indicate no explanation.

Miss Farrington-Wood was unearthing what I had known and reported on for some years. She was obviously amazed at what was coming to light and a close look at the records showed that she had every right to be. Excluding the errors that Mr Geraghty attributed to me, there were an additional 32 errors/discrepancies (the word 'discrepancy' is used to include no initials in the required box to show the drug has been taken by the patient, scored-through initials, an incorrect mark [such as a cross], initials of a nurse not on duty or any other irregularity). These related to all drug round times (9am, 1pm, 5pm and 10pm.) covering 14 days between 7th May and 28th July 1990. Keep in mind that only three patients' Kardexes were being examined.

As I had pointed out so often, in writing and with difficulty at the first hearing, if the assumed failure to give quinine sulphate was so serious as to necessitate a charge of neglect against one nurse, then the failure by other nurses to correctly administer digoxin and isosorbide mononitrate (two vital drugs used in the control of heart failure and angina) and frusemide (prescribed for renal failure) should have caused someone the utmost concern; and at last, to an independent observer, it did.

Under further cross examination, Mr Geraghty had openly to admit that he had not carried out a 'normal, routine' drugs' check on any other wards in the hospital and that no action had been taken against other nurses involved nor was any envisaged. The three drug Kardexes show 40 errors of which six were made by me; a patient had appeared to refuse medication in two instances, leaving 32 errors due to other nurses. That is, 80 per cent did not involve me. At least eight nurses can be identified from the initials, one responsible for 12 of the errors. The sister who had testified to both hearings of my mistakes, appeared to have made eight errors herself. Yet after all this Mr Geraghty yet again stated that (a) no, he was not trawling for one person's mistakes; (b) he had not found other nurses' errors; (c) he could not explain how he had managed to miss these and (d) only Mr Pink had been disciplined.

The discerning observer will appreciate the magnitude of these facts. If three drug records chosen, in a sense, at random, are found to contain 40 faults, then the full set of 26 for the ward could show, at any one time, in excess of *300* such errors on one ward and close to *1,000* over the whole department. The enormity of this possibility and the attendant dangers need no embellishment from me. Those who have followed the case were not in the least surprised at these findings. My reportage of the dangerous state of drug administration (backed up with very detailed and prolific documentation) had been ignored since 1988.

When the matter of unsafe/reckless drug administration was raised at the disciplinary hearing, I pointed out that in my letter to Mr Geraghty of 3rd October 1989, I had written: 'Please find enclosed some notes made prior to a meeting held in our unit in July 1988 and some made subsequently. Though peripheral to the immediate problem, they may cause you as they do me serious unease and dismay.' Enclosed with the letter were 18 pages of detailed notes, reports, letters, descriptions of numerous IVI and drug errors. I assumed that Mr Geraghty, as the most senior nurse in the hospital, would have been made fully aware of such a serious problem 15 months earlier. When I referred to these 18 pages at the earlier disciplinary hearing, Mr Geraghty denied all knowledge of them, and insisted that he had never received them. I expressed disbelief, whereon he rummaged through the thick file of papers before him, then repeated that: a) he did not have the papers in question and b) he had *never* received them.

At this point I had been able to produce the originals, and on my insistence that I would not accept Mr Geraghty's denial, he was prevailed on to leave the hearing, go to his office and check through all his papers. I expressed concern because my case was that the state of drug administration was perfunctory and often hazardous and that, despite this being well known to management, no action had been taken against any other nurse. If Mr Geraghty had received the papers in early October 1989, as I knew he had, why had he not sought to discuss the situation with me or taken steps to put matters right and tackle those responsible. He had done neither.

After a wait of some five minutes, Mr Geraghty had returned to the disciplinary carrying the papers which he had 'never received'. He offered no explanation or apology, nor did the chairman or anyone else seem to consider that either was necessary. The hearing was suspended again while copies were made and distributed. On resumption, Mrs Frederiks and Mr Caldwell seemed at pains to distance themselves from Mr Geraghty, stating that they had no knowledge of the papers or their contents.

At the appeal, from the evidence and cross-examination of assistant night nurse manager Miss Carew and nurse Peel, additional disturbing information emerged. Miss Carew had previously stated that she could complete the 10pm drug round in half-an-hour, implicitly questioning my description of the time and difficulties involved. Of course, I was well aware how she achieved this lightning feat. When Miss Carew or one of the sisters undertook the round, her presence on the ward was supernumerary, making four staff and leaving her to work uninterrupted. But the real time-saver was her method. With very elderly people the time is taken up more often than not coaxing and helping them to swallow the tablets or medicine; and the initialling of the Kardex is to verify NOT that one has put out the drug but to attest that the patient has taken it. The practice of Miss Carew and others was not always to stay and see that each patient actually took the medicine, but to leave many standing on the patients' lockers to be given later by the ward staff when they arrived in the course of the bed round.

Not only were Miss Farrington-Wood and Mr Clarke alarmed by this practice (one employed for years) but so were others in the room. Such elderly ladies and gentlemen, many in a confused or demented state of mind, will hide tablets, throw them away, appear to swallow but secrete in the mouth to remove later, refuse to take, forget that they have taken them or swallow them and a moment or two later deny having done so. A wandering patient may pick up another's medicine glass or drop his/her tablets into a neighbour's glass. The possibilities for error and serious mishaps are endless.

While little reference was made to standards of care at the first hearing (and discussion of the countless dangerous and unacceptable incidents highlighted by me was disallowed by Mr Caldwell), the subject was raised at the appeal. Miss Farrington-Wood questioned Mr Geraghty closely regarding the nursing care on the geriatric wards but he seemed out of his depth in the face of her expert and up-to-date knowledge and experience. She asked him to provide the panel members with a copy of the 'Standards of Care' statement used on the care of the elderly wards. He was visibly embarrassed by this request and for a moment or two appeared quite nonplussed. He waffled for a while but his interrogator would not be deflected. She stated that it was essential for each member of the appeal panel to read the hospital's written standards. At this, Mr Geraghty said that they were in preparation but he thought that they were not quite finished.

'No,' replied Miss Farrington-Wood. 'You perhaps misunderstand me. May we see the standards of care in use a year ago at the time of Mr Pink's suspension?' Mr Geraghty was again flummoxed. There was a long pause before he admitted that there were no proper, written standards either then or 'now'.

'How then were you in a position to assess the quality of care on the geriatric wards without such necessary guidelines?' persisted Miss Farrington-Wood. Mr Geraghty mumbled something but was unable to provide an answer. Asked if there was any system for reliably judging patients' and relatives' views of care, he provided a vague response that did not satisfy his questioner.

Quietly but pointedly Miss Farrington-Wood delivered her coup de grace: 'But if you had no validated, approved standards of care how could you possibly disprove Mr Pink's claims of neglect and danger?' Mr Geraghty remained silent.

Another concern of mine was that there appeared to be no system whereby a nurse was moved to lighter duties once her pregnancy reached a certain stage. There were wards where the pressures of work at night were much less and where seldom, if ever, did heavy, immobile patients need lifting and toileting. The impression of staff with whom I discussed this situation was that becoming pregnant was frowned on by management and if a member of staff chose to get herself into this condition it was no concern of theirs.

There was multiple risk of danger, to mother, patients, future child and colleagues by insisting that she carry on as normal. We always tried to prevent a pregnant member of staff from being put in danger, but this was just not possible when only two or one staff remained on the ward. In view of the glaring danger that we were nightly placed in when lifting alone, perhaps I ought not to have been surprised at this shameless disregard for expectant mothers.

It has been possible here to give only one or two extracts from the 35 or 36 hours over five days of the appeal hearing. We on our side were constantly harassed by an impatient, tetchy chairman who missed no opportunity to interrupt or curtail our presentation. It amazes me that the three people who were sitting alongside Mr Higginbottom did not feel able to distance themselves from his unpleasant behaviour and attitude. Perhaps he dominated them as he did the whole appeal.

The management side was permitted to present its case uninterrupted, but once the staff side case was under way, the chair repeatedly intervened, especially as I was giving my evidence. We recorded nine such interruptions in one five-minute period. This at first was unsettling and had the effect of throwing me off course in the presentation of my defence, but it soon became quite intimidating. Time and again Mr Clarke objected to the chairman's unreasonable attitude but it was water off a duck's back.

When the atmosphere became intolerable we adjourned. On the third such adjournment Mr Clarke, Mr Swinnerton and I decided that if the interruptions continued we would have to withdraw from the appeal altogether. Looking back, I think we should have refused to continue, but we were in no doubt that such a move would have been ruthlessly exploited by the health authority to our disadvantage.

FOURTEEN
ABANDON HOPE

I noticed early on that our National Health Service seemed to spend inordinate time and resources in displaying in the industrial tribunals, in which I used frequently to appear, a standard and style of industrial relations which were unique in their inept insensitivity and arrogant incompetence. Multinational corporations, nationalised industries, civil service departments, local authorities, manufacturing companies, service industries, retail outlets, media consortia, even 'cowboy' builders – no class of employer seemed as impoverished in terms of 'human resource management' as the various health authorities I observed in the tribunals — **John Hendy QC**

We had arranged to present to the appeal one or two character witnesses and the first of these was Mrs H Forrest who came straight from work at the end of the second day of hearing. It was she who had sent in the petition form from the Whitelegg family. At about 4pm Mr Clarke was informed that she had arrived and went out to invite her into the room. He returned to say that she was not alone but had her husband and mother with her. Mr Higginbottom said that Mrs Forrest could come in and speak, but the other two must remain outside. Mr Clarke left again to return a moment or two later to say that Mrs Forrest would prefer to have her family around her as she spoke. Without any reference to the other members of the panel, Mr Higginbottom made it clear that he had agreed to only one person at a time entering the room and did not approve of this but would allow all three in on the clear condition that only Mrs Forrest spoke. All three now quietly entered and sat down. The chairman invited Mrs Forrest to speak but repeated that neither her mother, Mrs Whitelegg, nor Mr Forrest was to say anything.

Mrs Forrest began by saying that she had always had a good opinion of the general standard of care in the hospital and she had come to speak up for Mr Pink who had nursed her father while he was a patient on ward A14. She then went into a description of how her father had been treated during his stay. The lack of care and outright neglect they had witnessed, she said, had horrified the family. I am unable here to do justice to Mrs Forrest's most eloquent and detailed account of the 'nightmare' they had experienced, but it seemed to me that the chairman would at any moment intervene and stop her. He had, though, met his match, and so clearly impassioned was Mrs Forrest that perhaps discretion persuaded him for once to remain silent, despite the fact that she appeared not to have come in to speak about me at all.

As the account progressed, so did Mrs Forrest become more affected and upset. Mr Whitelegg, we were told, had been put into a side room and given little attention. 'When we came in to see him on Sunday, the whole bed was covered in blood. No one was caring for dad; they could not care less.' She said they had to ask for a kidney bowl to collect the blood her father was vomiting. Her mother was left to hold it. 'You wouldn't treat a stray dog that way!' No member of staff had come to explain what the diagnosis was, until she went out to ask the sister in charge. 'Well, you do know he's terminal, don't you?' the sister replied. 'I'll never forget that sister's face,' went on Mrs Forrest. 'The whole staff was utterly callous; you wouldn't believe this was possible.'

Mrs Forrest was now openly sobbing as she spoke but managed to continue. 'Dad was left in pain all evening and not until Mr Pink came on duty at night was anything done. Mr Pink was absolutely wonderful with us. He gave dad an injection and changed the bed.' The family had been requesting 'all day' that a priest be called but nothing was done. It was at this stage in her disturbing and most moving account that I recalled the event in 1988. 'Mr Pink sent for the priest and stayed with us. We'll never be able to thank him enough for what he did. As father died he sat and held his hand.'

By this time the atmosphere in that room was electric and apart from Mrs Forrest's choking words there was total silence. Everyone was transfixed by the sheer awfulness of what we were experiencing; most of us were ill at ease; some could not hold back their own tears. Even to me, who knew more than most the reputation of A14's day care, this description was shocking and I was deeply disturbed at what I was hearing. Mrs Forrest's distress had now reached the point where she was unable to continue and I am sure we all felt a sense of relief. It was not over though. Her mother now stood up and came across to comfort her. With an arm round her distraught daughter and ignoring Mr Higginbottom's prohibition, she quietly and calmly took up the impeachment of the hospital, for it was no less. Looking from appeal panel to management she said, 'You ought to be utterly ashamed of yourselves for the way you treated my dying husband. There should be a large sign above the entrance to that ward – "Abandon Hope All You Who Enter Here". I shall never forget his cries of pain. I will never forgive you for your inhuman treatment of my dear husband.'

She then turned and pointed directly at me. 'How dare you discipline this man? He was the only person on that ward to show us any kindness and compassion. He is a decent, caring person. What a pity you do not have more like him! You ought to be congratulating him, not treating him like this.' And with that, mother and daughter in each other's arms, slowly left the room.

For some time no one was able to speak or look up. Miss Farrington-Wood went out to offer comfort to the family. It had been the most unexpected and harrowing five or six minutes. After a long pause we gathered up our papers and quietly left. Outside, both Mr

Clarke and Mr Swinnerton, who like me had been visibly shaken by what had just taken place, seemed convinced that the appeal would now, surely, have to be abandoned. I did not share this belief. Mrs Forrest and Mrs Whitelegg must have opened people's eyes but, I feared, not their hearts and minds. That evening I wrote a short note to them:

> What can I say? Your appearance this afternoon was one of the most moving and profoundly disturbing experiences I have ever had. No words of mine can ease your pain or soften your sense of revulsion at what happened to Mr Whitelegg. I can only extend to you all my respect, my appreciation and my love. Your action today called for massive strength of character and great courage and there is no way that I can thank you enough.
>
> May God support and care for you all. To have helped in some small way to ease Mr Whitelegg's suffering is a privilege and an honour. My own feelings as you spoke were a mixture of shame to be associated with Stepping Hill Hospital, and humility at the kind and generous things you both said about me. Forgive me if I say no more.

It seemed self-evident that there would have be an enquiry into Mr Whitelegg's care with an explanation and apology sent by management to the family. Joe Swinnerton, Tony Clarke and I were in no doubt that this was the right and proper action, but no approach to Mrs Whitelegg or Mrs Forrest was made. That senior managers and members of the health authority could sit through what we had just witnessed and subsequently simply ignore the family defies belief. That the chief nursing officer could take no action to dismiss or establish the accusations seems incredible. Knowing, as I now do, of the very many similar incidents of relatives' concern over outright neglect, perhaps this was small fry to these managers. On behalf of us and all COHSE members in Stockport, Mr Swinnerton wrote to the family and sent flowers which I know were much appreciated.

In a letter to the family on 8th May I wrote:

> It disturbed me to learn that the hospital management has not been in touch with you. At the very least, I'd have expected some sort of enquiry to have been established by now and an apology, even if a qualified one, to have been sent. Perhaps I shouldn't be too surprised at management's apparent total unconcern, for in a letter last year I wrote: "Absolutely nothing, I fear, no matter how ghastly or indecent, touches their hearts or reason."
>
> If yours was the only case of its kind, involving what relatives see as neglect of a loved one and callousness by staff, it would be enough to warrant a most searching enquiry, preferably carried out by an outside, independent body. Yours is but one of many and all the more reason for action. Instead of hounding, suspending, discrediting and persecuting me, the attention and effort should be going into moves to ensure that never again will a patient (and relatives) have to go through the appalling treatment that you have described. As you know all my efforts these last 20 months have been directed to this one end. But sadly, and to their everlasting shame, managers just do not want to know. All that matters is to silence and be rid of me.

This family's experience illustrates failings that I may have thought at one time only Stockport permitted, but which I have since found out are common to many hospitals. There appears to be no way that a hospital can say 'sorry' to patients or relatives. Even in the best run establishments mistakes occur, and usually the patient or relatives want no more than an explanation and some expression of regret. Except perhaps in the most serious cases, they do not want compensation but only a reason given and an assurance that lessons have been learned.

Mrs Whitelegg and her family wanted to know that their experiences would lead to improved organisation and practices so that other seriously ill patients and distressed relatives in future would not have to suffer similarly. No such lessons were learned, no changes implemented in the geriatric department as a result of their experience. There is something seriously wrong with any group of people which is unable to accept its failings and learn from them.

The result of this inability by managers and nurses to accept that errors should lead to changed procedures, improved equipment and/or better trained staff can be illustrated by the tragic case of Mrs Ada Nunns, which may well have been on Mr Caldwell's mind (he was the manager ultimately responsible), as he pressed for my dismissal at the appeal. The *Stockport Express Advertiser* of 9th January 1991 reported the incident as its main news that week:

A public enquiry is being demanded into the horrific scalding of a 67-year-old woman in a hospital bath. Her distraught husband is trying to find out why the pensioner, said to be "dressed and walking around the ward" within hours of the incident, is now "poorly" in Withington Hospital burns unit. The scalding is the second in Stockport hospitals in two years. In July 1989, an elderly mentally handicapped man died in Withington burns unit after a bathtime scalding at Offerton House Hospital, Stockport.

The latest incident involves an elderly, frail mother who was found in a bath in the psychiatric unit at Stepping Hill Hospital. Bathroom doors are supposed to be locked and patients must be escorted there and supervised by staff.

Hospital chiefs have launched an internal inquiry to find out whether safety procedures were followed.

Her husband said: "When I saw her I couldn't believe my eyes. Her feet were like cooked meat and she had appalling burns down the back of her legs, across her buttocks and waist. I was told there was little hope of further treatment and any recovery could involve amputation of a leg. My wife was a regular outpatient at Stepping Hill psychiatric unit and had only been kept in hospital under observation because of a urinary infection."

COHSE and psychiatric department health and safety spokesman Joe Swinnerton said: "Staff have regularly complained that the water system was faulty. Special thermostatically controlled taps were introduced at Offerton House Hospital following the previous tragedy. Only one bathroom on the unit has a thermostatic water temperature control and that was paid for by charitable contribution."

Mrs Nunns died in the Withington Hospital. There was no public enquiry.

Another problem that jumps out of the Forrests's experience is the inability of nurse managers to weed out the incompetent, unsuitable or disturbed nurses among us. There are more of these, I suspect, than we might care to admit and they can do untold harm, as Stepping Hill so vividly illustrates. This failing I was aware of, but the extent of it has become clear to me over recent years by the correspondence from nurses throughout the country. It is inevitable that some who take up the care of the sick are unsuitable or, for a variety of reasons, become so. But it seems that such people remain in post for years on end. Only a few weeks ago at a nurses' conference, I was approached for advice by a ward-based nurse. He told me that the sister in charge of his ward had a drink problem.

This was a longstanding situation and known to all the other staff. Mr Smith (as I shall call him) was most concerned for the safety and welfare of the patients and had expressed this to colleagues. He was told he should not become involved. Nevertheless, he witnessed events with the sister that he considered unacceptable and feared that unless action was taken there would before long be a serious, maybe fatal, incident. He spoke to his manager who was unhelpful and evasive but who, it seemed, was already fully aware of the problem.

The nurse manager pointed out to Mr Smith that he was new to the hospital (although qualified many years), and he should steer clear of matters which did not concern him. When he suggested that the care of patients was his direct concern and he feared not only for the effect on patients and relatives but perhaps the reputation of the hospital, the manager became hostile, hinting that she had received less-than-satisfactory reports on his work (of which he was unaware). He felt threatened and isolated and sought my advice. By discussing his concerns with the manager he was doing exactly what his code of conduct requires. Clause 13 states that a nurse must 'report to an appropriate person or authority any circumstances in which safe and appropriate care for patients and clients cannot be provided.'

The reaction he described is all too common. Senior nurses often seem unable to face difficult but necessary decisions; at all cost they want to avoid what they see as unpleasantness. The continuing danger and stress which their indifferent approach sanctions can do untold harm to staff and patients. If such nurses are aware of their code ('...act always in such a manner as to promote and safeguard the interests and wellbeing of patients; ensure that no action or omission on your part, or within your sphere of responsibility, is detrimental to the interests, condition or safety of patients') they are prepared to disregard it.

During my appeal period a copy of a letter to Mrs Frederiks from the Norfolk & Norwich Hospitals Branch of NUPE was sent to me.

> There are a number of issues surrounding the suspension of Mr Pink that concern us. Firstly, in raising objections about staffing levels Mr Pink was doing what any dedicated nurse should have done, ie following the UKCC's code of professional conduct to the letter. He was doing his utmost to get the standards of care raised for his patients. Mr Pink went through the proper channels to try to achieve this. It was only when his correspondence with his managers failed to elicit any significant response that he allowed the press to publish this correspondence.
>
> Secondly, Mr Pink has been offered a post in the community unit. We see this sideways move as a tacit admission of guilt by the health authority. The implication is that Mr Pink is being moved to an area where it is hoped that he will not raise questions about staffing levels and standards of care.
>
> We would urge Stockport health authority to reinstate Mr Pink to his former position. He should not be penalised for trying to give his patients a better standard of care. Nurses such as Mr Pink should be heeded over calls for improved staffing levels; they are at the sharp end of delivering patient care and are the people best able to judge when the standard of care is unacceptable.

In mid-May, and while the appeal stood adjourned, I was informed by the solicitor for the English National Board for nursing that the allegations against the assistant general manager Mr Geraghty and the assistant night nurse manager Miss Carew were not to be investigated by the UKCC. But that the case against Mrs Frederiks, the chief nursing officer, was to be 'forwarded for a full hearing before the professional conduct committee' of the council. No action was to be taken against me.

When my appeal resumed on 8th July for its fifth day of hearing, the chairman announced that the panel had decided that management's case regarding the drugs charge had not been made and the charge was dismissed. Mr Clarke immediately informed the panel of the findings of the UKCC, underlining the point that the national nurses' professional body, having seen all the evidence in the case, had decided that there was no case for Mr Pink to answer on charges 2 (failure to comply with accident policy) and charge 4 (failure to comply with a legitimate instruction). This, he stated, was of the greatest importance. A completely impartial, respected and independent body, having considered the case for many months, had exonerated his member from any unprofessional behaviour on the drugs and confidentiality charge. In view of this, he submitted, there was clearly no case to answer and he invited the panel to discontinue the hearing.

To further support his argument, Mr Clarke reported that whereas Mr Pink had no case to answer before the statutory body, the most highly-placed nurse in Stockport, the chief nursing officer, had. That such a senior nurse should be required to appear before the conduct committee of the UKCC was almost unprecedented.

'It would seem,' continued Mr Clarke, 'that the investigating committee of the ENB believes that if anyone is to blame for what has happened in Stockport it is not my member but Mrs Frederiks herself.'

Needless to say this cut no ice with Mr Higginbottom. One might have expected him at least to adjourn for a few minutes to give his colleagues the opportunity to consider our submission and voice their own opinions or take the nurse panel member Mrs Farrington-Wood's advice. But without batting an eyelid, Mr Higginbottom dismissed Mr Clarke's application out of hand and the charade continued.

The outcome of the appeal was announced on 9th July.

> The panel, having carefully considered the evidence on both sides, upholds the allegations relating to (1) Breach of confidentiality, (2) Failure to comply with the accident policy and (4) Failure to comply with a legitimate instruction. It was the decision of the appeal committee that your conduct amounted to a series of breaches and omissions that justified disciplinary action and that this warranted dismissal. They therefore rejected your appeal and supported management's action that, as an alternative to dismissal, you be given a final written warning with a transfer to a night nursing post in the community nursing service. The appeal committee confirmed that a refusal to take this alternative post would result in your dismissal.

In my judgment, this was an overtly political decision and had nothing to do with the care and protection of the sick. When one realises that health authorities, and then the NHS trust boards, were packed with political appointees, accountable to the government, this is to be expected. Speaking in the House of Commons on 26th October 1994, Mrs Margaret Beckett, then shadow health secretary, denounced the heavy government bias of trust boards. 'Sixty six of the trusts,' stated Mrs Beckett, 'are chaired either by Conservatives or someone connected with a company that has made a donation to the Conservative party. The party and other Tory front organisations have been given nearly £2 million by companies whose directors were appointed by the secretary of state to now sit on NHS trusts.'

Calling health secretary Mrs Bottomley 'the Madame Mao of the health service,' Mrs Beckett continued: 'You attack the authority of medical staff. You banish or sack people who disagree with you, and Parliament and the public have to sneak information out through a system of Chinese whispers.'

The climate of NHS secrecy and intimidation being what it is, we shall never know the facts regarding the Stockport decision or whether it emanated from higher up. Writing in the *Guardian* on the day following the outcome the newspaper's medical correspondent, Chris Mihill, said:

> Graham Pink's failure to win his appeal comes at a time of growing warnings from the nursing and medical professions that their rights to speak publicly about patient care are being curtailed. The growth of the market culture within the NHS, which puts corporate loyalty before duties to the patient, and the existence of trust hospitals, which can set their own terms and conditions of service, is leading to a climate in which people censor their own criticism or face possible disciplinary action.
>
> A number of managers have privately been making no bones about the fact that they would like to muzzle doctors from publicising the ill effects of closures and cuts. One manager told a consultant that the first thing he would do when the main local hospital became a trust was to institute a ban preventing staff from speaking in public.
>
> John Chawser, head of the British Medical Association's consultants committee, said last week that the issue that most concerned senior doctors about the reforms, apart from patient care, was the right to freedom of speech. The growing number of redundancies among hospital staff are concentrating minds. Few people are willing to be a hero if it means getting the sack.
>
> Ironically, a report published yesterday, the same day as Mr Pink's hearing, looks at trade union recognition, bargaining structures, pay and conditions, and grievance and disciplinary proceedings under the new NHS, and concludes

that rights are being substantially weakened. An examination of the first 57 trust hospitals was conducted by Industrial
Relations Services, an independent employment research
company. It concludes: "Many trusts intend to abolish the
right of appeal to district or regional health authority level
for staff involved in disciplinary or grievance proceedings.
At least one trust intends to make the divulgence of information on trust matters to non trust individuals a disciplinary
offence."

In a ten-page statement, Mr Higginbottom discussed the panel's
findings. I sent a detailed response to the health authority, tackling
point by point the chairman's findings. One example will suffice. 'It
was clear,' states the document, 'that the relationship between him
and those with whom he worked was so strained by his conduct as
to have broken down altogether.' No evidence was produced which
would support this accusation. Of a total of 25 staff with whom I
regularly nursed at the bedside, three only appeared as witnesses at
the two hearings. Is it sensible or valid to make a sweeping generali-
sation based on a 12 per cent sample of the population in question?
As it happened, one of the three, staff nurse Peel, was most supportive of my position and knew of no breakdown in relationships.
In fact, she testified that her petition attracted 80 per cent support
from those on duty when approached and that 'Mr Pink's relations
with staff were excellent'.

This leaves us with two bedside staff only, one nurse and one
nursing auxiliary. Even if both had agreed with the chairman's
assertion, which they did not, the support would be down to eight
per cent. In evidence, however, neither lady mentioned a 'break
down in relations' and the nurse was one of those who had signed
the petition! So we are left with one person who expressed mildly
critical comments although she and I had always got along well

with never a hint of disapproval from her at any time. Yet Mr Higginbottom felt able to make the remark he did.

I wrote to Tony Clarke following the outcome:

> First, may I say again thank you for the unremitting support of yourself and Joe Swinnerton throughout the appeal. Your tireless and highly-skilled efforts on my behalf were outstanding and the depths of our "failure" are in reverse proportion to the heights of your professionalism and commitment.
>
> The outlook is bleak. I can see but two moves which might delay the authority from sacking me – COHSE members in Stockport making their voice heard or legal action against the SHA for conducting a grossly unfair disciplinary hearing and appeal. Is an injunction a possibility? We must move quickly or all will be lost.
>
> If ever there was a cause and need for trade union action then this is it. Joe tells me that there is massive support for my stand for improved levels of nursing care among his members. One action which might halt my sacking is the message to the authority that our members will not stand idly by and see me dismissed. You will accept that words, no matter how well intentioned, mean nothing to these people; they treat our arguments/requests with derision and scorn.
>
> You will have seen this week's *Nursing Times* leader, I'm sure. It reads: "There is an important tactical lesson which is, contrarily, that going it alone may be magnificent but it won't win the war. One wonders how different the outcome might have been had Mr Pink had the support of a union from the start." Now that I have that support, I urge you and the whole Confederation to stand up by me with pride and honour and attest to what is right, moral and just. Members have a right for their views to be heard.

Among the mass of letters reaching me at this time was one from a Mrs Regan. If lessons had been learned following the death of Mrs Forrest's father, then relatives like Mrs Regan (and many others who have contacted me), might have been spared a similarly dreadful experience.

I find her letter to management, relating to events in late 1990, not just utterly sickening but as damning an indictment of those running the geriatric wards, nursing and lay alike, as one is ever likely to find. She wrote:

> Dear sirs
> My late husband was in A14 ward in March and also in Oct. I could never understand why he had to sit in a chair in his own bowel movements although he had plenty of pyjamas it made it very hard for him, because he was such a clean man. I did mention it at the time. I was so disgusted at bringing them back on the bus I mentioned to one of the sisters.
>
> When he was taken in on October 30 to A6 surgical ward they made him very comfortable but phoned me on 31 October to say again he was taken to A14 ward. I said oh no not again!
>
> I went to see him on Wednesday pm he was on oxygen antibiotics through his nose and improved. Get a phone call Thursday am to say he had fallen out of bed and cut his head right across the back.
>
> I go up, the first thing I said was why weren't the cot sides up? They put the blame on night staff.
>
> He passed away on Thurs Nov 1 in the afternoon. I knew he was a poorly man but will always believe the fall hastened his death.

On 11th July I wrote to Mr Hector MacKenzie, the general secretary of COHSE:

As you may know, my appeal was lost on Monday and within a matter of days I am to be dismissed. May I tell you what a tower of strength Mr Clarke has been. His defence of me has been excellent. He has been unavailable during the week but I'm hoping we can meet early next week. Not that there is much we can achieve alone.

So I write directly to you to request support at the highest level from COHSE and from the TUC. If dismissed, I and many others believe it will be a massive defeat for the union movement in this country. If a member is sacked for speaking the truth, and I have done no more, then it seems to me that there is little point in having unions.

One charge "proved" against me was "failure to attend a meeting". When I requested representation, at the meeting called without notice with three senior nurse managers, it was denied point-blank. Tony protested at the appeal, but his words were ignored. The whole composition and conduct of the hearing and the appeal were a farce from start to finish. Countless nurses, patients and relatives have phoned or written expressing support and praise but this counts for nothing. Only powerful and open support from yourself and the whole Confederation can hope to save the day.

My Stockport union representative, Mr Joe Swinnerton, phoned today to say that he is finding considerable support among members for my defence and growing general concern at the level of care in some areas of Stockport's hospitals. Many members have already written to the UKCC, a fairly pointless gesture, I fear. May I request that a ballot of COHSE members in Stockport be held to: 1) object to my impending dismissal; and 2) to call for an independent enquiry into the care of the elderly at Stepping Hill. The one thing that might give the authority pause for thought is the knowledge that the

Confederation, at local and national level, will not stand by and see an innocent member 'thrown to the lions'.

I appeal to you, Mr MacKenzie, to move heaven and earth to stop my sacking. This I ask not for myself but for patients, relatives, nursing staff and all our members. As has been written: "Nursing must bend its collective will to ensure that Mr Pink survives." I shall survive, with your help and that of others, but if need be alone. My aim is simple and well worth fighting and even suffering for – as so many men and women down the centuries have done.

As Mr MacKenzie never responded to my letter, I do not know what his thoughts on the situation were. Nor was I aware of any concerted local support or representation following this letter and that to Tony Clarke (following the last day of the appeal, I heard no more from him and we never met again). If a ballot of local members had been taken, it might have demonstrated the strength of feeling of fellow trade unionists for my position though management might have taken no notice. The complete lack of organised approval for my stand from the Confederation and the wider union movement was not unexpected. Since the heyday of the unions in the 1970s, their power and influence have dramatically declined. Whereas at one time my predicament might have attracted union interest and backing, what the government did to organised labour after 1979 left unions all but powerless, as sidelined and ignored as nurses themselves. I could quite accept that my small fight for patients' and workers' rights was of little concern to a movement fighting for its own survival. Richard Shore, writing to the *Guardian* from Bristol on 13th July seemed to have similar thoughts. He wrote:

It is to be hoped that the employment secretary will look long and hard at the case and treatment of Graham Pink. The erosion of trade union rights has, in effect, eroded the rights of the protection of individuals in employment as this case so graphically shows. All Mr Pink is guilty of is exposing bad management. I know the government throughout the 1980s continually emphasised the right of managers to manage but did they really enshrine within that the right to manage badly and to dismiss the employees who rightly exposed them?

A letter appeared in the *Guardian*: from the chief executive, Mr Milnes, on 22nd July. It stated:

There is a breathtaking arrogance about the assumptions made by some of the commentators who have used your columns in recent months to air their prejudices about Mr Pink. Two letters are similarly based on a partial ignorance of the essentials of the Pink case and a total ignorance of our approach to health service management in Stockport.

For example, one letter from Bristol offers up the Pink case as an example of the effects of the erosion of trade union rights. Mr Pink only chose to exercise his right to join a union after his suspension. He was then represented by the RCN but he is now represented by COHSE. At no time did Mr Pink ever attempt to use the agreed trade union representative system to express his concerns.

What is unusual is that he should now be offered up as some kind of icon for the trade union movement. In Stockport there are over 3,000 members of trade unions and professional organisations and our managers enjoy good working relationships with virtually all of the accredited representatives. Branches of NUPE and the RCN issued press statements distancing themselves from Mr Pink's allegations and the way he had presented them. Their views were either ignored by the press or misrepresented. Stockport Health Authority has never prevented its staff from talking to the press and has no rules governing such contacts, other than those relating to confidentiality (which was where Mr Pink was found to be in breach). I can, however, see that the Authority's decision does not fit the stereotype that casts them as punitive and incompetent.

Yours faithfully,
Peter Milnes

On 19th July I wrote to Andrew Bennett MP:

On July 8th at the appeal I read from a letter written by Mr Caldwell in May this year to a Mrs Regan whose husband fell out of bed early in the morning while no one was around and died shortly afterwards in distressing and possibly avoidable circumstances late last year. Mrs Regan is convinced that her husband's death was due to neglect. In the last paragraph on page 1 the manager makes an astounding statement. He writes: ". . .when your husband was in Ward A14, he was nursed in a 4-bed area, which can be monitored closely at all times."

This is a glaring untruth and how Mr Caldwell, the most senior manager in the hospital, has the nerve knowingly to lie to a grieving relative is beyond my comprehension. He puts out deceit, deception and shameless perversions of the truth and continues in his post. I write and speak nothing but the truth and am about to be dismissed from mine!

FIFTEEN
AGAINST
IMPOSSIBLE ODDS

A man may fulfil the object of his existence
by asking a question he cannot answer,
and attempting a task he cannot achieve
— **Oliver Wendell Holmes**

The outlook now was bleak. All I had wanted to achieve was improved standards of patient care and safety with some relief for the superb but harassed staff. All I had achieved was the sack – a wretched way of ending a working lifetime of 43 years, all of it in public service. Was it time to call it a day and withdraw with whatever grace one could? This did not cross my mind. Maybe it was letters like this of 9th July from London SW19 that blunted my common sense.

> Dear Mr Pink,
> It was with great sadness that I read the results of your disciplinary appeal in today's *Guardian* newspaper. After eight years of nursing I have yet to meet a nurse who hasn't experienced the pressure you highlighted in your letters to the management printed in the *Guardian*. However, I have also yet to meet a nurse who has been prepared to stick his/her neck out to bring these conditions to the public. I am ashamed to say that as a young nurse I belong to this category. Many nurses, especially young females, are browbeaten

and intimidated into accepting these conditions without complaint and I greatly admire and respect you for the stand you made. I only wish there was more support and solidarity amongst nurses then plights such as yours would not occur.

I intend to leave nursing myself to pursue another career, but wonder how many more nurses will leave as a result of being systematically ground down by working with inadequate staffing levels, intimidation from senior nurses and doctors and a feeling of hopelessness. After your case I feel even more strongly than I did before that the UKCC code of conduct is no more than a red booklet, responsible for trapping nurses in a catch 22 situation. I would be honoured to give you any support I can.

One MP who had always been concerned and had spoken up for me was Mr Nicholas Winterton, the member for Macclesfield, who had never waivered in his support, disregarding the convention that MPs do not become involved in the problems of colleagues' constituents. On 16th July he wrote to me:

I am very sorry indeed to hear of the most disturbing outcome in your case. I can well understand how disappointing and frustrating it must be to have been treated in this manner. I am writing to the health authority once again to see if, even at this late stage, there is anything which can be done.

Meanwhile strangers continued to write letters in my support. In mid-August 1990 Mrs Jean Clark, writing to the *Guardian* from Harlow, echoed what so many others had said:

I was very moved by Mr Graham Pink's description in the *Guardian,* some months ago, of his ward experiences, and admired the selfless way in which he placed the needs of patients in his care before personal position.

He is probably speaking on behalf of thousands of other nurses and patients in acute hospitals throughout the country, as has been suggested. It raises an important question of civil liberties. Surely a nurse has a normal "citizen's right" to exercise freedom of speech and thought, even if his/her views conflict with those of "line managers"? Shouldn't the health authority welcome the fact that Mr Pink is defending patients so vigorously? Is knowledge of care in hospitals so dangerous? Apart from the general principle of encouraging some "glasnost" in the NHS, on a more pragmatic basis can the NHS lose the services of such a committed professional so readily? I urge it to withdraw the suspension in order to rectify this grave injustice.

The health authority and government's answers to Mrs Clark's last four questions are clearly 'No, No, Yes, Yes' as opposed to the general public's 'Yes, Yes, No, No'. If anyone had asked me four or five years ago whether we had freedom of speech in Britain, I would have thought the question facile. I now understand differently. What I do not understand is how those in authority get away with it. The health authority and the government must have been bombarded, privately and publicly, with representations on my behalf, yet could just ignore the lot – a symbolic two fingers to thousands of ordinary citizens.

The NHS belongs to the British people and the first duty of those who work in it is to their patients. Yet so many hospital managements (Stockport being a prime example) are tight oligarchies, accountable to no one but themselves. Years ago hospitals were run by matrons, who despite their often fierce image, were directly in touch with both patients and staff. I had been on the wards of my training hospital but one week before I knew who matron was. She visited each ward at least once a week. I had been there no more than one month before she knew who I was, for one of her prime tasks was to take a direct interest in the staff.

Maternalistic and over-regimented it may have been, but she was a hands-on nurse whose immediate concern was the welfare of patients and she knew her staff by name. Contrast that with today. In my three years on the wards at Stockport, I never once saw the chief nursing officer, Mrs Frederiks. In fact, the first time I set eyes on the lady was the day I walked into my disciplinary hearing. Only once did I see the chief nurse, Mr Geraghty, and then only because I had phoned him up at home and told him to come in. I doubt if either knew by name any of the night staff – apart from one. For any nurse trained in the 1950s, this is behaviour both inexplicable and unforgivable.

Not only are managers out of touch, but their number has escalated. In my training hospital there was one matron, one deputy-matron and one administrative sister to run all the nursing services; then you were down to ward level. That hospital today has perhaps twice as many beds so you would expect more managers, but not 60! Most of these people seem to remain remote from patients and staff. Many senior nurses I have encountered in recent years have come over as spineless commissars, defensive and inflexible, only too willing to kowtow to lay managers' orders to cut costs right, left and centre. What they do all day I have no idea. What they do not appear to do is involve ordinary nurses and nursing auxiliaries in decision making or spend time talking to patients. Like the administration of the NHS itself, hospital managements are all too often not simply unrepresentative but unashamedly anti-democratic. Where incompetent management exists, there appears no way of bringing it to light. Today's message to bedside staff is 'Keep your heads down, your eyes closed and your mouths tightly shut'.

If my case established anything, it is that there is no freedom to speak the truth in the NHS. I believe that remains true today as it did then. From former mid-Staffs nurses Helene Donnelly and nursing student Barbara Allatt to older cases such as those of Dr Helen Zeitlin (Redditch), Dr Chris Chapman (Leeds), Sister Pat Cookseley (Plymouth), Dr Helena Daly (Truro), plus many less well-publicised examples can leave no room for doubt.

In a letter to the *Guardian*, Dr Zeitlin wrote:

> My case, that of a hospital consultant who loses her job because of her persistent out-spokenness on the subject of cut-backs in the NHS, together with that of Nurse Pink's, are two demonstrations of the loss of professional credibility and freedom of speech for senior doctors and nurses, with all that this implies for our standards of health care.
>
> Graham Pink and myself have come up against the difficulties and frustrations of taking responsibility for patients without having the means to affect change.
>
> I believe that neither of these cases is unique, but that they result from dangers inherent in the structure and organisation of the present system of management in the NHS. This system, borrowed from industry, consists of a line of managers on short-term contracts, rewarded if they achieve goals, and contending with the fear of job loss if they do not.
>
> When impossible targets are combined with extreme ambition at the top, the medical advisory machinery is rendered impotent, cries of help from the ranks are ignored, protesters are silenced or removed if too vociferous, standards fall and there are simply no incentives for managers to bring the deficiencies of the service to the public's attention.

I am led to believe that so-called performance-related pay for managers at Stepping Hill came down as far as the night nurse managers. Bedside nurses found this very difficult to understand. What does 'performance' mean? In a geriatric unit, does it relate to the number of patients who are sent home, the speed with which beds are vacated, the average length of stay, how quickly/slowly patients die on the ward, how few nurses can be provided, how many patients can use one bed in a week, how much each patient costs per day? The senseless and unattractive suggestions are endless. The one thing performance does not appear to refer to is how carefully, skilfully and lovingly the patients are treated. Performance in the NHS appears to mean counting, measuring and numbers – that is quantity. How does one count recovery, alleviation of pain or distress, a quiet and dignified death? We at the bedside were more interested in quality – the quality of the staff and of the care we provided, but as we understood it, performance related plainly and simply to cash. This was the single all-important goal. To achieve this no sacrifice was too great, excluding of course, managers' 'performance related' pay ('bribery' might be a more accurate word).

Miss Carew once remarked to me that she had to save £10,000. While not against waste, there are other savings apart from cutting staff. (For example, it was normal for scores of lights to be on all day along a corridor flooded with daylight.) Who decided that £10,000 could be saved? On what basis? Any manager or financial officer who spent two or three nights on the ward with us could not possibly have justified cutting down on geriatric night staff, any manager that is with the kind of morality we espoused. On reflection, this statement is more hope than reality, because few if any managers would expect/allow their loved ones to end up on wards C5, A14 or A15.

Allowing that some way of assessing performance could be arrived at, why should staff be paid more for achieving it? Isn't top performance what all staff try to provide at all times irrespective of monetary reward? Were I in a nurse manager's position, I would neither expect nor accept additional money for doing the job to the very best of my ability. With some jobs (on an assembly line maybe), performance related pay might well be justified, but surely not in nursing. Nurses should be giving 100 per cent all the time and if the incentive of extra cash is needed to bring out the best in their work, then they are in the job for the wrong reasons entirely. If fewer nurses can be employed without reducing standards or putting staff under unnecessary stress, then fine. To pay managers additional salary to make cut backs, which is what is now happening in the health service and was, it would seem, the situation at Stepping Hill, strikes me as an unacceptably objectionable practice. Nurses who connive at such arrangements, as apparently many do, are in my book a disgrace to their calling and deserving of outright condemnation. As far as I know no nursing body, nor any other body representing staff, has spoken out against nurses accepting this tainted money, nor challenged those who do.

◆ ◆ ◆

Soon after the appeal result became known, nurse Jo Peel phoned to say how offended she was by the outcome. She had by this time left Stepping Hill and moved to another hospital and authority. She had found a very different management approach – open, understanding and caring. She told me that she had written to *Nursing Times*. This is the letter:

> I am writing to express my disgust at the treatment of Mr Graham Pink at the hands of Stockport Health Authority. Can anyone believe that his was an unbiased disciplinary hearing? Would you expect to see the family of the man you are accused of shooting on the jury at your trial. Would this situation be tolerated anywhere else?

I worked closely with Mr Pink for three years until his suspension last year. I was a staff nurse on night duty on the wards Mr Pink has so accurately described. I can vouch that everything he said was true. Staffing levels were often dangerously low with two staff to cover a 20-bed ward and three staff to cover a 26-bed ward that was structured like a maze. The patients could not always get full care despite the outstanding efforts of the too-few ward staff due to the very heavy workload. Pressure on the nurse was often dreadful but we felt we could not complain as we would then be considered inadequate. I often felt isolated and weighted down and went off duty drained and frankly upset. We all know our chosen career is not an easy one but you could not help feeling abused.

Mr Pink was unfailingly devoted to his patients and his sole aim was to improve staffing levels and thus improve the standard of care and lessen the pressure on the staff. He is a very sincere, caring man, and it soon became clear that he was not to be fobbed off in his efforts and in my opinion the powers that be just sat and waited for an opportunity to silence or get rid of him. I personally tried to start a petition to support him and soon had signatures from over 40 per cent of the staff on the three wards (80 per cent of those on duty), but when it came to my attention that I was being branded a "troublemaker", I withdrew the petition as I was not prepared to get anyone else in trouble. The support for Mr Pink was widespread but most people felt too intimidated to speak out for fear of recriminations. The health authority no doubt took this to mean that no one else agreed with him.

So Mr Pink has ended up guilty of gross misconduct, a verdict reached by two "kangaroo courts". Are nurses ever going to be able to speak up for what they believe in, what they know to be true? Luckily for me I now work in a small hospital where I am happy. I feel as though I'm treated as a valued member of the team and I have complete support and backup from my superiors and contemporaries. Some of my friends still work at Stepping Hill where unfortunately nothing has changed. I want to see Mr Pink vindicated completely; I do not want to see a colleague treated this way ever again and I would like to feel some pride in being a member of the nursing profession.

The last stage in the disciplinary process was for us to apply to the north western regional health authority in Manchester for an appeal at regional level. Mr Clarke did this on 25th July:

The confederation acts on behalf of charge nurse Graham Pink who has been the subject of formal disciplinary action by his employing authority. We make application for Regional appeal in accordance with the provisions of paragraph 10, section 40, of the General Whitley Council Handbook. The grounds for seeking a Regional appeal are:

1. The chairman's opening remarks clearly demonstrated his lack of impartiality in this matter. Before I, as the appellant's advocate, had any opportunity to make a submission, or indeed before the proceedings got under way, Mr Higginbottom entered into a hostile exchange during which he made reference to press reports and claims and counter-claims regarding Mr Pink's competence. Mr Higginbottom claimed that the documents proved that Mr Pink had received written confirmation of his previous incompetence, but when challenged on this point, he was unable to produce evidence to this effect. Later in the proceedings the staff side pressed the chairman to make

available copies of the correspondence to which he made reference, but he refused to comply with this request.

2. It was noticeable throughout the hearing that management were allowed to present their case and call evidence uninterrupted. This contrasted starkly with the position when the staff-side case was presented. During the latter, the chairman made frequent unnecessary interruptions which compromised the presentation of our case. A formal complaint was lodged at the time.

3. During the presentation of the management case it was clear that continued reference was being made to the transcript from the disciplinary hearing at which Mr Pink was represented by Mr Mullany, RCN officer. Given that COHSE was not involved at that stage, we did not have contemporaneous notes from the hearing and therefore sought copies of notes taken by officers of the authority. Given the length of the hearing and the complexity of the case, I believe it was entirely reasonable to access these notes which were a constant source of reference by the management side. My request for copies to be made available to the staff side was promptly dismissed by the chairman, and this further compromised my ability to cross-examine management witnesses.

4. During the course of presenting Mr Pink's case, I wished to make reference to the decision of the investigating committee of the ENB, which had considered the case. The chairman prevented me from so doing, insisting that such a reference could be included in my closing remarks. In my opinion, this was yet another example of high-handedness which unreasonably restricted my ability to represent Mr Pink and compromised his defence. Furthermore, I regard his advice as totally improper given that the admission of

new evidence during an advocate's summing up is both inappropriate and contrary to procedure.

From the details set out above, you will appreciate that I believe the chairman acted in a most provocative and biased manner, which served only to undermine the credibility in the appeal's procedure. Given the extent of media interest in this case, I am being pressed to publicise our views on the handling of the internal appeal, but I would prefer to deal with the matter within established procedure.

Letters continued to arrive supporting and thanking me for my stand. A group of 15 nurse tutors from Stafford wrote:

We the undersigned were astonished and disgusted at the treatment that you have been subjected to and disheartened at the outcome of the disciplinary hearing. We write in order to support you morally and feel that you have acted in the best interests of your patients and upheld the values of the nursing profession. Your action should serve as an example to others, if only all had the same courage. We feel that under a fair and just system there would have been a different outcome. Our thoughts and best wishes go with you.

Two nurses from Salford wrote:

May we say how sorry we are at the outcome of your long and drawn out battle with Stockport Health Authority. Nurses nationwide have followed the case closely, admiring your courage and the conviction with which you fought for your principles. Your dedication is admirable and an example to us all.

It is a sad reflection in this so-called enlightened age of nursing that those who dare to speak out are penalised and victimised, presumably with the intention of deterring others. In *Nursing Times* you state "At the end of two years I have achieved nothing". Not so. You have made us sit up and take stock and question the importance of our own principles and for this we thank you.

One person to contact me at this time was Mrs Mary Williams from London SE12. She was similarly supportive but wanted to make a practical contribution. She suggested the setting up of a support group to marshal assistance for me and to highlight the plight of the elderly sick in hospital. She foresaw that I was going to require legal advice and representation at an industrial tribunal and this would need to be financed. The confederation had made it clear that it would continue to represent me but was unable to do more than provide a full-time officer for a tribunal. Despite what many saw as a critical test case, independent legal advice would be too expensive and set an unwelcome precedent. This was understandable. Mrs Williams wrote to the *Guardian* inviting like-minded people to contact her and support the "Friends of Graham Pink". I accepted her kind offer though did not foresee at that stage the vital part she was to play in the continuing saga. The public's response was immediate and generous.

Stoke-on-Trent,

20 September 1991.

Dear Mrs Williams,

I am a heartfelt supporter of Graham Pink's courageous stand against inhumanity and injustice, in his championship of his profession and of helpless elderly patients. I have long wanted to write to Mr Pink but have not known how to contact him. I was, therefore, delighted to read your letter in today's *Guardian* and hope it may be possible for you to convey to him my gratitude and good wishes. I have watched my own parents and many others suffer from standard neglect on geriatric wards, due to deplorable understaffing. I have also witnessed the devotion of overworked nursing staff and their struggle to provide a humane service against impossible odds.

And the same day from London NW3:

Thank you for what you are doing to help a brave, unselfish and principled man. I should like to join you, but cannot do very much as I am a pensioner close on 80. However please call on me if there is anything you think I could do within the limits of a small pension and my age. I want to do something, however small, to help. I am writing to my MP and the health secretary.

Once the group was established, Mrs Williams wrote to the secretary of state for health, Mr William Waldegrave:

We, members of the public, are seriously concerned at the dismissal of Nurse Graham Pink by Stockport Health Authority. We believe the allegation of "gross misconduct" to be totally without foundation and think that his record shows Mr Pink to be a conscientious and competent nurse.

There are two issues at stake here: one, the question of patient care, which it appears was Nurse Pink's absolute priority, and two, the question of freedom of speech. The two are inextricably linked in this case. We understand that the UK Central Council for Nursing imposes a professional duty on nurses to speak out on behalf of patients if they feel their charges to be receiving inadequate care. This appears to have been precisely what Graham Pink did.

In addition, on page 18 of "A Manifesto for Health", recently published by the Royal College of Nursing, it states: "Often nurses take the role of advocate, helping to articulate the wishes or fears of patients who need help in expressing their views. We believe that the Departments of Health should recognise and encourage advocacy."

This describes exactly what Mr Pink was endeavouring to do. If a friend or relative dear to you were in the position of needing hospital treatment, would you want that person attended by Graham Pink or a nurse who ignored the poor standards he found? I know what my answer would be and suspect that everyone would feel the same in that situation. We therefore maintain that Graham Pink has no case to answer and would urge you, Mr Waldegrave, as a matter of common justice, to call for his reinstatement.

It was now left for me to consider my position. I would have liked to continue nursing. Work as a community (district) nurse would have suited me down to the ground and in other circumstances I would have jumped at the offer. To care for people during their last days in their homes must be a great privilege. Unlike the hurly-burly of a noisy hospital ward, the nurse is able to be close to the patient and bring comfort, support and affection (particularly where there are few or no relatives). To have been allowed to do this for the remaining years of my working life would have been a delight and honour. To have accepted the post, though, would have sanctioned management's handling of the case and this was out of the question. Additionally, the final chance to seek justice at an industrial tribunal would have been lost. Of course, I was aware that once sacked, my job was gone for ever. There can be little doubt that the management's moves to discipline me were premised on the knowledge that once dismissed, justly or otherwise, an employee has no right to return to work. This is the law of the land, and the sizeable slice of the healthcare budget that had been and was about to be spent on persecuting me had clearly been anticipated and seen as money well spent to be rid of this persistent nuisance who could not keep his mouth shut. My whole stand throughout, I suppose, had been on moral grounds and these still needed to be upheld and defended. Although I would have preferred to continue nursing, there was no hesitation in the need to see this through to the end.

The expected letter came late in the afternoon of 17th September 1991, delivered to my home by hand:

Dear Mr Pink,

I am writing to acknowledge your letter dated 11 September, 1991 which contains your refusal to take up the post of charge nurse in the community nursing service. As you know, this transfer to the new post was an alternative to your dismissal following the disciplinary interview at which I decided that you had, by your acts and omissions, committed gross misconduct. My decision was upheld by the health authority at their appeal and this also has been confirmed in writing to you.

I am, therefore, with regret, left with no alternative but to terminate your employment with immediate effect (17 September, 1991). You will receive 12 weeks' pay in lieu of notice plus any outstanding holiday pay owing to you. I am making the necessary arrangements for this money and all the documentation to be forwarded to you at the earliest opportunity.

Yours sincerely,

D Caldwell, General Manager

News of the dismissal brought in a huge volume of correspondence.
Mr Marr from Cheadle Hulme, close to Stockport, wrote to Mary
Williams c/o the Friends of Mr Pink:

> From 12th May to 25th June 1990 my 93-year-old aunt, Miss
> Elizabeth Dorothy Duffy BA, was a patient in a geriatric ward
> in Stepping Hill Hospital. She was then transferred to Cherry
> Tree Hospital, where she died on 22nd July, 1990. While she
> was in Cherry Tree, she asked me to write to the management
> of Stepping Hill praising the kindness and hard work of an
> elderly male nurse who had been on night duty in her Stepping
> Hill ward. I did so during July 1990. From subsequent news-
> paper reports I gather that the object of her praise must have
> been Mr Pink. I have never met him and I cannot express any
> opinion on current controversies but in loyalty to my dying
> aunt and as her executor and nearest relative, I felt that I must
> put on record her high regard for him.

Does it say something of management's whole approach that it did
not see fit to send me a copy of this writer's first letter? It would
have cost them so little but would have meant a great deal to me.
It has since come to my attention that many relatives wrote in to
management regarding my care of a loved one, but none of the
letters, full I now know of eloquent tributes, was shown to me. A
day or two later this letter arrived from Shrewsbury:

> Dear Mr Pink,
> I am very sorry for all the trouble you have had for exposing
> some of the horrors suffered by elderly patients. My father
> died in Stepping Hill Hospital in 1990. I wrote a letter to the
> staff nurse expressing my anger at the way the news of his
> death was relayed to us. My mother was horrified at the lack

of care my father received. If you need anyone to support your case I'm sure she would be very glad to.

On 27th September I wrote to Mr Nicholas Winterton MP:

Thank you for your kind letter. The close interest and concern which you have shown have been very much appreciated. You have done all you could, I'm sure, and far more than you need have. Now that I have been dismissed there is little more that I can do. My efforts to obtain more nurses have come to nought; my job and my livelihood have been taken from me; a proper pension, as with freedom of speech, justice and truth are denied me. There must be something dreadfully wrong with a National Health Service (and with its political masters) which allows a "concerned and truly dedicated nurse" (a patient's relative's words) to be sacked for trying to improve patient care by speaking the truth.

A report appeared in the Stockport paper on 11th October under the heading: '"Pink wrong" – minister'. It read:

A health minister defended Stockport Authority's handling of the Graham Pink affair on a visit to Manchester last week. Stephen Dorrell said the authority had been "patient almost to a fault" with Mr Pink and pointed out it had offered an alternative job before he parted company with the health service.

Mr Dorrell said the terms on which NHS staff were employed were clear. "If an employee sees something going on which doesn't seem right, it seems entirely reasonable that the first thing they should do is pursue the matter within the hospital.

In letters from Mr Duncan Nichol, Mr R Martin QC (chairman of the regional health authority) and Baroness Hooper it was made clear that responsibility for managing at the hospital lay with local managers and that it would be inappropriate for central government spokespeople to become involved. Yet the health minister, parroting Mr Milne's oft-repeated phrases, saw fit to comment directly about my dismissal. Not only that, but his disingenuous remark that 'If an employee sees something going on . . .' etc., describing precisely what I did 'all within the hospital', is most misleading. Yet Mr Dorrell has the effrontery to imply to tens of thousands of people in the north west that I did not go through the proper channels. This was, as far as I know, the minister's sole contribution to the national debate.

During October both Dr Helen Zeitlin and Dr Wendy Savage suggested that I ought to make contact with their solicitor, Mr Brian Raymond of Bindman & Partners in London, the foremost person in the field of defending those who had been treated as I had. I spoke to Dr Zeitlin and said that there was no way I could retain such a high-profile and costly solicitor. 'Ring him up,' she said. 'He wants to speak to you. Do not worry about the financial side.' So I rang him.

He asked to see all the papers, now well over 1,000 pages, and a week or two later my solicitor Brian Hamilton and I went to London for a two-hour meeting. Straight away Mr Raymond made it clear that if he took the case, no cost would fall on me personally. He said that he was most impressed at the way the matter had been handled so far, but thought that expert, legal representation was now essential to prepare for the industrial tribunal. As to fees, he suggested launching an appeal for funds. I was able to tell him about the Friends of Mr Pink group that Mary Williams had launched, but I thought that it would be most unlikely we could raise a fraction of the money needed. This seemed to be the least of his concerns.

To have the solicitor who represented Drs Savage and Zeitlin, not to mention Mr Clive Ponting (the Belgrano affair) was a singular honour and a considerable boost for the cause.

At the end of November 1991, Tony Clarke of COHSE received a short letter from the regional health authority regarding our appeal application. 'The RHA has decided that there are insufficient grounds to support a regional appeal hearing and therefore the request is rejected.' The carefully-stated grounds for the application were ignored. Why it had taken four months to come to this conclusion was not mentioned nor was any apology given for the inordinate delay. As I had been sacked two months previously, the belated letter and the decision it contained just added insult to injury.

However I was buoyed up by people like Mr Arthur Robinson who wrote in September from Marple in Cheshire:

> Dear Friends of Graham Pink,
> I spent a week in the geriatric ward, A14, at Stepping Hill Hospital, after a heart attack in March last year and was most impressed by charge nurse Graham Pink, and am disgusted by the contrived accusations which the Stockport Health Authority has attacked him with. Obviously they could not tolerate his exposure of acute understaffing. He was on his feet during long nights of 12 hours, and although this duty finished at 8am, he was frequently around at 8.30, and throughout this time there were generally more than one needing attention at once, calling out for it in loud and desperate ways. "I'm coming as fast as I can," was Nurse Pink's frequent response.
>
> I was sometimes aware of another nurse on the ward, but I'm sure Nurse Pink was mostly on his own. My brief contact with him was my best recollection of my week in Stepping Hill, and his dismissal disgusts me.

SIXTEEN
TIME DOES NOT HEAL

*Ms [Angela] Eagle [Labour MP for Wallasey]: I ask the
secretary of state what representations she has received
from employees afraid to speak publicly on NHS matters.
Mr [Gerald] Malone [health minister]: None.*
— **Hansard, October** *25th, 1994*

This book could be filled with no more than the letters written to
government ministers, MPs, the health authority, the press and
other media, to the Friends of Mr Pink group as well as directly to
me. Mr Brian Davenport of Bristol wrote to his MP Mr Waldegrave,
who also happened to be the health secretary:

> Nurse Graham Pink did no more than any good nurse should:
> he acted as the patients' advocate, and for this he has been
> suspended and may lose his job altogether. He intends to seek
> justice in an industrial tribunal hearing, but I urge you to
> make this unnecessary by persuading the health authority
> that they are wrong, so as to secure his full unconditional
> reinstatement without the need to resort to a hearing. A
> public apology from the authority would also be in order,
> I feel. I have empathy with Graham Pink on the grounds of
> social justice, and because I too am a nurse, but mostly I have
> empathy with him because what he did was right.

Mr Sean O'Donoghue from London, SW5 also wrote to the health
secretary:

The fact that the very authorities which "tried" Nurse Pink were the same ones which he publicly complained about must surely be reason enough for him to have an external hearing on his case. Would not a "not guilty" verdict have vindicated Nurse Pink's "whistleblowing" and thereby placed the very authority which found him guilty in the dock. The outcome of the disciplinary hearing was therefore predetermined in that the health authority was never likely to produce any verdict other than guilty in order to save its own skin.

Before the publication of extracts from my letters and the public interest in the affair, I do not think I was aware of this term 'whistle-blowing'. It seems an inelegant expression – to my mind 'truth telling' is more accurate and straightforward. Soon after being dismissed, I spoke at a conference in Nottingham on 'Whistleblowing in the NHS'. In a report of the day by Zelda Tomlin for the *Health Service Journal* she wrote:

> It was a small, quiet affair. It had been scheduled for the weekend because many participants – nurse managers, students and teachers – had not told their employers they were attending. The press were allowed in on condition they did not divulge the identity of those attending. "My employer doesn't know I'm here and I've paid my own fee," said one. She had good reason. Her district general manager had pulled her to one side and told her: "We're trying to establish a corporate team with a corporate loyalty, and we'd like to assure ourselves that you will sing from the same songsheet as everybody else."
>
> The conference was organised by Nottingham University's department of nursing studies. It came in the wake of the Graham Pink affair and at a time of increasing "corporate

identity" in the new NHS. "Why should anyone have to defend the right to speak the truth?" asked Geoffrey Hunt, director of the National Centre for Nursing and Midwifery Ethics. "The onus is on the organisation to prove that speaking out is wrong, that it is false or malicious." In the United States, two states had enacted laws to protect whistleblowers, Dr Hunt told the conference. In New Jersey, employers could be found guilty of criminal acts if they demoted or sacked employees who had revealed wrongdoings.

That seemed a long way away from the world of the NHS, where whistleblowers could only look forward to a Kafkaesque chain of events, said Virginia Beardshaw of the King's Fund Centre. Ms Beardshaw, who wrote a book about whistleblowing in the NHS in the early 1980s, argued that the health service had learned little in the past decade. She had found then that those who had exposed abuse in large mental institutions had gone through an "incredible mill of disbelief, victimisation and attempts to silence them". The system was based on shooting or discrediting the messenger and on character assassination. "The whole rigmarole shifts the attention away from the patient who is the subject of possible abuse, to the whistleblower."

Conference participants agreed that a national mechanism for staff to voice anxieties about the service was needed. Unless the Department of Health issued a policy statement endorsing the right to speak out about shortcomings, one nurse said, the task would be left to people like Graham Pink, a David confronting Goliath.

The practice of exposing wrongdoing in hospitals, which has a long and depressing history, has one common factor running through it – the persecution and punishment of the exposer. In her excellent *Conscientious Objectors at Work*, referred to above, Virginia Beardshaw asks: 'Are nurses able to protect their patients' interests by speaking up when they are abused?' and concludes that often they are not. 'They may be forced to stand by when individual patients are ill-treated or when poor conditions deprive them of adequate care. Their silence is enforced by feelings of impotence, and by fears of reprisals. The victimisation of some nurses who have spoken up about abuse is a vivid illustration that these fears can be well founded.' As the author said at the conference, there appears to have been no improvement in the situation in a decade. The number of employees today in trouble for exposing fraud, maladministration or poor quality of care appears to be on the increase. This report (*Independent on Sunday*, 15th September 1991) is an example:

> This weekend, Graham Pink is waiting to be sacked. The final showdown has arrived for the 61-year-old nurse, who became the most famous whistleblower in the National Health Service after speaking out about a "catalogue of shame and neglect" involving geriatric patients in Stockport. As Mr Pink waits, *The Independent on Sunday* has found that other nurses around the country face the grim reality that when they highlight poor conditions, the authorities react by attacking the whistleblower
>
> In July 1989, Paul Turner, an assistant professional nurse adviser in Kent, was given responsibility for five new wards for the elderly mentally ill at Maidstone Hospital. Spending on the wards was £90,000 a year over budget. He was told they had to break even, but after investigating with a specialist consultant he concluded that each ward needed at least eight staff a day, which still left an overspend.
>
> For a year Mr Turner was repeatedly reminded that he was still in the red and he said he was finally warned that his

career could be at risk if he did not work within budget. "I was stunned and then angry," Mr Turner said. "I told the manager I was not prepared to compromise safe practice." Mr Turner found himself wrestling with his conscience. He wrote to the Royal College of Nursing, which advised him to comply with management instructions but ensure his superiors were aware of the implications. Over the next six weeks, diaries kept by ward staff revealed that the use of the major tranquilliser promazine increased; some patients became more agitated because staff did not have time to spend with them; and between 15 and 17 patients went unobserved for long periods.

"What makes me particularly angry," says Mr Turner, "is when the UKCC demands that we uphold their code – putting ourselves at risk – and then doesn't do anything to support us."

And from the *Observer* on Sunday (19th April 1992):

Pressure can go further than threats. Nurse Jean Stapleton (not her real name) lost her job at a Buckinghamshire NHS unit a year ago, after informing the senior nursing officer in writing of her concerns about drug administration and understaffing on her ward.

Nurse Stapleton, a deputy sister, had been on six months' probation. Before she made the allegations, she had been praised for her excellent work and told that she would be recommended for a full-time job. After the letter, which she wrote on the advice of a nurse tutor and her union, she was told her contract would not be renewed because she was unable to cope with the job and must leave immediately.

"I regret it," said Miss Stapleton, a nurse for 20 years, "because I am a very honest person and I will probably have to lie about what has happened. But in terms of honesty, integrity and professionalism, it was the right thing."

These stories are typical of those told me by any number of nurses who have made contact since my case became news. Criticism is just unacceptable in the NHS today. Why is it, though, that all those threatened, victimised or dismissed are bedside staff? I have yet to read of a nurse manager losing his or her job for truth telling.

I am invariably asked at the meetings what advice I would give to staff faced with a similar situation to mine. I reply that it is not for me to tell others how they should behave when faced with unacceptable standards of care. 'Your conscience is your guide,' I say. This is, of course, a too-glib response, for I accept that down-to-earth self-preservation supersedes lofty idealism. If only nurses realised how much damage they are doing, not just immediately but in the long term by remaining silent then they might accept their duty to speak out. This was brought home to me when a journalist spoke to staff at the Grantham and Kesteven Hospital where enrolled nurse Beverly Allitt worked (she was given 13 life sentences for attacking and murdering babies and children). When it sounded as if staff had realised that perhaps there was something dreadful happening on ward four, they were asked why they had not spoken up sooner. A number of them, spoken to individually, answered: 'We didn't want to be another Graham Pink.'

When I first heard of this, I was shocked and distressed. I read Nick Davies's gripping book, *Murder On Ward Four*, and, describing the unease felt by nurses at Grantham, the author writes:

> They could hardly complain even if they did think there was something wrong. Nurses were trained to obey, to defer to the doctors. It had always been like that. Nurses could not complain. Nurses never did. They had learned that it didn't

pay. It was bad enough if you got a colleague into trouble, but the chances were that you would get yourself into hot water too. You daren't even admit your own mistakes, for fear of being disciplined. There was a staff nurse in the papers only the other day who had been disciplined for writing a letter to *Nursing Times* daring to criticise her hospital. And look at Graham Pink, the charge nurse in Manchester who had lost his job after complaining about staff shortages.

Starting in the late autumn, regular meetings were held with Mr Raymond in the Bindman & Co office near King's Cross station to prepare the case for the tribunal. Although just about everything was documented, he needed to question and research in depth as he drew up statements which, as concisely as possible, set down the salient facts of the case. He did this in a kindly and sympathetic way and I soon appreciated that he was a consummate professional, knowledgeable, intelligent and deeply committed to helping the downtrodden – an extraordinary and wonderful man. He organised a press conference for 20th January 1992 to promote public awareness and encourage people to subscribe to a fighting fund. As a past master of presentation he saw the value of publicity. He prepared a press release to be read on the day:

> Ladies and gentlemen, we live in an age of irony and paradox. While our cousins in Eastern Europe are discovering for the first time the freedom to criticise state institutions, here in Britain, where we supposedly learned these lessons centuries ago, the health service seems to be engaged in a quick march backwards down the alleys of bureaucratic orthodoxy.
>
> For you have in front of you today, a man whom any nation ought to be proud to have working in its health service – a man whose honesty, compassion and sheer commitment to

his fellow citizens has already touched the conscience of the nation. But he is here today because his reward for giving his considerable energies to the care of the sick and helpless elderly of Stockport has not been a civic citation, but the sack.

And what is his crime? What is it about him that makes Stockport health authority so anxious to rid itself of his presence on its wards? It is simply that he could not remain silent when the elderly people in his care as a night nurse, nearly all heavily dependent and many near death, were sometimes denied their dignity because the health authority failed to provide enough nurses to look after them.

The pattern of events speaks for itself. Graham Pink started writing letters to the authorities complaining about the conditions for geriatric patients in August of 1989. Eight months and 51 letters later, nothing had been done, so on 11th April 1990 he agreed to the *Guardian* printing an article complied from his letters.

Faced with revelations that the old people in the wards often endured appalling and heartrending conditions at night, the reaction of the health authority was rapid and decisive – it started disciplinary proceedings against Graham Pink on 11th July and crowned it all by suspending him from duty on 9th August. By this time, Mr Pink had written another 46 letters in addition to the first 51, but nothing had changed on ward A14; there were no more nurses than there had been on the nights that Mr Pink had described so movingly, only he was out of the way, there would be no new articles in the *Guardian* or *Daily Mirror* and the window that he had opened for a short while on the dreadful conditions that were sometimes to be found on that ward, was firmly shut.

But if it is ironic that the exercise of free speech in the public interest is being punished in Britain while whole nations are discovering its blessings in the rest of the world, there are also ironies and contradictions here at home. I do not think it has been sufficiently appreciated that the official national body which has the responsibility for maintaining professional discipline among nurses, has taken action in this matter which directly contradicts and wholly undermines the actions of the Stockport health authority. Complaints against nurses go first to a filtering body called the English National Board and are either thrown out or passed on to a higher body called the United Kingdom Central Council for Nursing, Midwifery and Health Visiting which has the power actually to strike a nurse off the register. In November 1990, the health authority, when it had found Graham Pink guilty of disciplinary charges that were later used to justify his dismissal, referred the matter to the ENB, thus putting him in jeopardy of being struck off the nursing register, as well as being sacked.

Seven months later, on 21st June 1991, the ENB made its decision. It didn't refer the case up to the UKCC (which it was bound to do if it found any validity in the charges) but threw the case out altogether, rubbishing the charges that Stockport now say justify it sacking him.

But that was not the only case before the ENB in June of last year. A year previously, in 1990, Graham Pink had himself laid a complaint before the Board, alleging that the chief nursing officer had breached her own professional obligations by failing to take action in relation to inadequate night staffing levels. In June 1991, 3 days before it threw out the complaints against Graham Pink, the ENB sent the allegations against the CNO up to the UKCC and her case currently awaits a hearing before that body. It is not without significance that the disinterested professional body has thrown out the charges that the health authority is relying on to justify Mr Pink's dismissal and has chosen to take further the charges against the chief nursing officer.

I hope that you now have some idea of why I have decided to take on Graham's case even though I have no idea of how my fees are going to be paid. I do not want to embarrass him even more than I have already, but it's people like him, the ones who speak out when the rest of us turn a blind eye and just carry on, who stop the health service bureaucrats from letting services decline while pretending that everything in the garden is lovely. That's why we link our appeal fund with a call for an NHS Whistleblowers' Charter, so that qualified staff in the health service who have a professional duty to identify poor conditions cannot be punished for doing so.

This is not just happening in isolated cases; it's going on up and down the country. Only two days ago, I was contacted by a health visitor in the north of England who is facing disciplinary action for organizing a public petition against cuts in a community clinic. At this rate the NHS will be recruiting its managers from among redundant Politburo members of the USSR and East Germany – those people at least will have no difficulty in dealing with people who believe in freedom of speech.

As it happened, there was another gathering that day to which I had been invited. In December I had received a letter that read:

I am pleased to say that the Campaign for Freedom of Information wishes to recognise the contribution you have made in speaking out about standards of patient care by an award at the 1991 Freedom of Information Awards ceremony. The awards will be presented by the leader of

the Liberal Democrats, the Rt Hon Paddy Ashdown MP on
Monday January 20th.

Reporting on the ceremony in the *Guardian*, Richard Norton Taylor
wrote:

> A Freedom of information bill, ending excessive secrecy in
> government, would be among the Liberal Democrats' imme-
> diate demands in the event of a hung parliament Paddy
> Ashdown said last night. The party would "use what power
> and influence the voters give us to press that an FoI bill should
> be in the Queen's Speech of the new Parliament," he said.
>
> He challenged John Major to back up the Conservatives'
> Citizen's Charter with freedom of information legislation. An
> act with safeguards to protect genuinely sensitive informa-
> tion would improve the scrutiny of government legislation
> and ministerial action and raise the quality of opposition, he
> said.
>
> Mr Ashdown was speaking at the annual awards of the
> Freedom of Information Campaign to those who fight against
> official secrecy. They included the sacked nurse Graham
> Pink, and Dr Helen Zeitlin, a consultant dismissed after
> drawing attention to a report critical of nursing provision at
> Alexandra hospital in Redditch, Hereford and Worcester.

Mary Williams at the Friends of Mr Pink was now receiving a steady
stream of letters and most contained a cheque. This one came from
a gentleman in Cheltenham:

> Please find enclosed my cheque. As an OAP who has recently
> seen his wife through three difficult spells in hospital I can
> claim experience of the effect on the NHS of understaffing and

reliance on untrained probationers, even auxiliaries in some cases, for care of patients. I could in fact make a catalogue of horror or near-horror stories arising from this situation.

Qualified staff with long service experience are pretty helpless to remedy the situation, caught between inexperienced juniors and hard-nosed administrators. These last annoy me most. Allowing that they themselves are under pressure because of lack of resources, they all too often refuse to acknowledge that anything is wrong in their nursing provision instead of joining the protest regarding the starvation of some sectors of the hospital service. Career prospects outweigh commitment to patients' wellbeing.

I am sending a copy of this letter to the Stockport District Health Authority to indicate to them support for Mr Pink, although my wife was in hospital elsewhere. We need more whistleblowers throughout the NHS, and rather than being punished they should be honoured.

From Poynton, near Stockport, dated 24th January 1992, came this:

Dear Graham Pink,
You have my wholehearted support. Your courage in speaking the truth about patient care in Stepping Hill Hospital is tremendous and I wish you every success in your fight to win back your job. We actually witnessed the callous, uncaring attitude of some of the staff towards those sick and helpless elderly patients who had the misfortune to be in C5 ward. Our mother died in there in February 1986. The lack of real care and the treatment meted out to her still horrifies us. She was left without food or drink for four days before she died, although we asked the doctor to put her on a feed. We visited her one day to find her head stuck between the bars

of the cot-bed. My brother-in-law managed to free her after my sister had tried and failed. When my sister went to tell a nurse that mother's head had been caught between the bars she just stared back at my sister without any comment at all. Mother had complained about the nurse that afternoon; she said she had put a catheter in and had really hurt her...

...After that her condition really deteriorated. The remorse and guilt we feel will be with us always. Time does not heal.

We always thought that anybody entering the medical and nursing professions did so because they were interested in caring for people and for saving life. We found this was not the case in Stepping Hill Ward C5.

We wrote a letter of complaint to the hospital management committee on March 3rd 1986, and did not receive a reply until ten weeks later, and only then because I persisted and wrote further letters requesting a reply...

...So we, my sisters and I, are very grateful to you for speaking out about patient care at Stepping Hill and I hope my small contribution will help. What has happened to you is a monstrous injustice.

Yours sincerely,
Wendy Peacock

Mrs Peacock was later to send me a copy of Mr Caldwell's communication to her of 14th May, an impersonal, tactless and negative letter, displaying total indifference to the family's concerns. From start to finish, there is not one word of comfort, regret or sorrow for the obvious distress the relatives had undergone. I read it with mounting disbelief and anger. Had Mr Caldwell lost his own mother under similar circumstances how different his reply just might have been?

Mary Williams found that so many letters were coming in that she could not hope to reply to them. Every five or six weeks she packaged up and posted them to me. For example in mid-February I received more than 200 letters in one batch. Some had no address; one or two requested no response. For most of the rest, I wrote a personal reply thanking each for the most supportive and kind comments that were almost invariably contained and, where appropriate (just about all) my appreciation for the donation. This ranged from a 50p piece to a £1,000 cheque. The overwhelming generosity of people to a complete stranger was staggering. The task of responding was considerable but it seemed the least I could do was express how heartened I was. There is in the British people, as I have always believed, a deep-seated sense of right, justice and decency. From Swindon, Mrs Pearson wrote:

> I have today written to my MP regarding Mr Pink. I am genuinely worried about the freedom of speech issue in this case and the pressures that that puts on people to keep their views to themselves rather than speak out...
>
> ...I feel it pays to protest as loudly as possible about the erosion of such freedoms. When the silent majority really is silent, then that's when those in power, of whatever political persuasion, feel that they can treat human beings like cattle.

Late in 1991, Mr Peter Dale, a BBC television producer, approached me. He was researching for a *40 Minutes* programme on whistle-blowing in general, not specifically in the health service. He came to visit me but made it clear that if his programme went ahead, my contribution would at most be minimal. He went away with a full copy of the correspondence to that date – a hefty package. This, it seems, he found both compelling and disturbing, with the result that, within a matter of days, he had decided to devote his film solely to the case. As Granada's *World In Action* had made a film on the affair only a year previously, this came as a surprise.

He set about his investigations by discussing with me, over two or three days, every possible aspect of what had happened. During January he visited many people throughout the country in a most detailed and painstaking enquiry. I was pleased that Stockport Health Authority agreed to co-operate as this would present a more rounded picture than had the earlier film. Mr Dale spent many days at the hospital. He did not confide in me whom exactly he had spoken to nor what others had said and I did not attempt to question him on this. The programme was transmitted on 28th April.

Because of my involvement in the film and its story, my observations are less reliable than those of viewers. Let some who wrote to me, to the BBC, to the press or to the Friends of Mr Pink campaign give their impressions. Of the hundreds of letters and cards received, these few were written from Gloucestershire, Oxford, Derby, Dundee, Canterbury and Stockport. The first was sent by a GP to the *British Medical Journal*:

> I would not disagree that Mr Pink is an individualist but he also appears to be intensely humanitarian and a dedicated professional who aspires to the highest standards. Mr Pink is not prepared to subside into the state of mute acceptance apparently adopted by his colleagues. In any conflict it is easier to eliminate your enemy if you first isolate him. The programme showed Stephen Dorrell attempting to do this in Parliament. Mr Pink was therefore tactically quite correct in gathering support nationally. It is perhaps easier for those of us who do not work alongside him to recognise the truth of his arguments. It was professionally the correct thing to do. The concerns he raised affected not just the geriatric wards or even Stepping Hill Hospital generally but the health service

as a whole. I believe that the "Pink affair" assisted the successful request for additional night staff in one NHS unit where I work. I hope that eventually the people of Stockport and the NHS as a whole will feel able to thank Graham Pink for his extraordinary effort of genius and courage.

A clinical psychologist wrote to the *Guardian*:

Anyone familiar with a ward of acutely ill old people will recognise the humiliating predicament of the incontinent patient described by Graham Pink on BBC TV's *40 Minutes*, but dismissed as "sensational and grotesque" by Stockport health authority. Old and ill patients may indeed be repeatedly incontinent, paralysed, confused, severely emaciated or grossly overweight. Some inevitably are about to die.

Other senior nurses on the BBC documentary saw no option but to struggle with inadequate resources to meet the exceptionally heavy demand such patients make. Mr Pink, with no family to support, felt it right to protest, first to the hospital management and then through the media. He refused to accept that staffing levels defended as adequate by his authority could properly meet the needs of his patients.

Mr Pink is unusual in his ability to go on being shocked, and on his insistence that nurses must be given time both to respect and respond to the feelings of patients as well as to their physical needs. He attached great importance to patients' contact with relatives dear to them, and to a nurse sitting with and comforting patients who would otherwise die alone.

Other geriatric nurses cannot be expected to expose conditions as Mr Pink has so persistently done, risking their jobs and their family's income. Responsibility rests with those

of us who visit such wards. If we fail to support Mr Pink we
may eventually find ourselves geriatric patients, whose distress nurses are reluctantly too short-staffed to relieve.

A sample of other letters included:

Dear 40 Minutes,
I have just finished watching your programme. Thank you
for televising Mr Pink's one-man campaign for better nursing
standards in the NHS. His example stood out like a shining
beacon. I am a practice sister with 16 years nursing experience
within the NHS. The views and frustrations expressed by Mr
Pink, reminded me of similar scenarios I have witnessed
during my career. Bare minimum standards of nursing are
not only distressing to patients and relatives but take their
toll on the nursing staff by way of fatigue, ill-health and disillusionment. For far too long nurses have put up and shut up.

Dear Mr Pink,
It was with great interest I watched the "40 Minutes"
programme. I was drawn firstly to it because of your name.
I attended school in Manchester where you were one of my
teachers in the late 1960s and I remember that you always
had certain high standards. These shone through in the programme and I am pleased to say that you have stood by them
in the face of adversity.

Dear Mr Pink,
I have just finished wiping the tears away from my eyes after
watching BBC 2. It was very moving. I am a senior nursing
student currently undertaking my RGN course with more
than two-and-a-half years experience behind me. You are

a remarkable man (who has my full support). In helping
to improve patient care you risked everything, all for your
patients, not yourself.

Dear Mr Pink,
I would like to express my heartfelt gratitude for your courageous fight with Stepping Hill Hospital. I am an ex-nurse. I
left nursing because of the same problems as you highlighted.
As you started to tell your story, you told my story but I never
could find the words. I thought I was the only nurse that
felt like that. I cried at times when I was watching that programme, not just for myself but the countless patients that
have been in pain, discomfort and had to lose their dignity.
You put words to my feelings that I never knew I had before.

Dear Mr Pink
I am a student nurse in my final year and after watching 40
Minutes this evening would just like to thank you and tell
you how much respect and admiration I have for your courage
and beliefs. Seeing that there are people like you in nursing
has given me a great deal of determination and enthusiasm to
finish my training and specialise in caring for the elderly. Just
over one year ago my grandmother was admitted to a care of
the elderly ward where our family watched her deteriorate and
die. This particular ward appeared to be not unlike the ward
you worked on, A14. Although the majority of staff's standard
of care was high there just weren't enough of them so inevitably
patients, including grandmother, had to suffer. I can't explain
the terrible feelings that myself and my family went through
during that time. I can only say that I would never wish what
my grandmother went through during her last days on anyone
and will do my utmost to prevent this from happening

SEVENTEEN
GUILTY NURSES

The judge is condemned when the guilty party is acquitted — **Publius Syrus**

Whatever else may in time emerge from my experiences and the publicity given to them, it is the state of care of older people that must be of greatest importance. Other issues there are – the right of nurses and others to disclose unacceptable conditions, the conflict of code and terms of employment, the corruption of power etc, but for me the matter above all else that needs addressing is our care of older people.

Before going to work in Stockport, I was blissfully unaware of what was happening. Even after a year or two there I assumed that what I was witnessing was peculiar to that one hospital. The mass of letters, phone calls and meetings I have now had with staff and relatives, leaves me in no doubt that care of older people in very many wards and hospitals in this country is poor, and in some is a disgrace.

And let me add straight away that staff shortage is by no means the only reason. There appear to be some very unsuitable people working in geriatric care. This is disturbing enough, but to make matters worse it seems that nurse managers do not know, or do not care, how low standards have sunk. If they do appreciate the situation, either they accept it or are too intimidated (or too weak-kneed) to stand up and proclaim what they know to be unacceptable.

Could it be that the unprecedented response that the *Guardian* experienced, and the continued interest the case aroused, suggest that the British people are aware that what was going on in Stepping Hill was far from a little local difficulty?

Mrs H Rourke, writing to the secretary of state for health from London SW4 on 1ˢᵗ May seemed to think so:

> Dear Mrs Bottomley,
>
> That compassionate charge nurse Graham Pink is paying a terrible price for pricking the nation's conscience about what happens to geriatric patients in hospital. The conditions he exposed are by no means unique to Stepping Hill. Nurses around the country know that he is correct in what he says about night-staffing levels but dare not speak out because of pressure on them from their unit managers not to expose the hospital, and by implication their management, to criticism.
>
> Those managers are only complying with government policy (rightly or wrongly), so the buck stops with you. My own experience as a patient at (hospital name given) in August 1991 showed me that elderly, acute patients can be decidedly labour-intensive if they are to be looked after properly. On my ward was a demented lady in her late sixties, a polio victim by now bedridden and doubly incontinent. She was in our ward following attempted skin grafts for intractable bedsores.
>
> She was a difficult patient, and often it took several nurses and a couple of doctors to restrain her gently, soothe her, and persuade her to submit to very necessary treatment. That left the rest of us to get on with matters as best we could. How a ward full of similarly disabled and demented old people could be said to be "staffed" with only one nurse on duty at night, as was the case with Mr Pink, beats me. I would like to know what steps you are taking to improve staffing on these acute geriatric wards, and whether Mr Pink is to be vindicated.

My experience at Stepping Hill now leads me to question the concept of separate geriatric wards/departments/hospitals. We do not segregate people over 75 years of age in our workplaces, on transport, in recreational and shopping areas or neighbourhoods so that they never mix with others, younger and fitter than themselves, so why do it in hospital?

The advantages of mixed-age wards might far outweigh the supposed advantages of our present system. Younger patients would be available to assist and bring a more dynamic, atmosphere than pertains on most geriatric wards. Patients well enough to move about might be only too happy to engage the elderly in conversation if not in a variety of other activities – feeding for example. There would, I'm sure, be fewer falls and other accidents to the elderly and less chance for them to be lonely. The medical and nursing attention, given sufficient staff, would I suspect be of a higher order.

On 27th July I wrote to Mrs Bottomley. Almost certainly the letter never reached her. Of all the letters written to government ministers or NHS officers, I suspect that the people addressed never saw them, a belief supported by an article in *Nursing Times* in November 1990.

Despite having sent secretary of state Mr Kenneth Clarke copies of all the correspondence, in December 1989, he felt able to say in an interview with the magazine:

> Mr Pink's description of events appears to be quite groundless. Staffing levels are better than they were and nobody else agrees with him. You just have Mr Pink making a tremendous public fuss which he is not able to substantiate.
>
> What I wish would happen in the health service is that people would not put their salvation in writing letters to the newspapers but would discuss these matters with their managers. It's one of the things wrong with the health service that people believe they can progress these basically local management issues by causing wild local controversy.

My letter said:

Dear Mrs Bottomley,

It was with interest that I read your recent statement that you wished to provide healthcare professionals with the opportunity to voice concerns should they witness inadequate standards of care. You asked managers to appreciate the fears of staff that "management reforms could compromise their ability to express genuine concerns". I applaud your initiative, for I consider this to be an absolute right and responsibility of staff. Perhaps now, my own experience of such a situation merits reinvestigation and your personal intervention.

Three years ago, I raised the issue of care of the elderly where very ill and dying patients received what I considered to be inadequate care at night. From your own commitment as a psychiatric social worker to the importance of human relationships, I am sure you will share my conviction that no patient should die without the support of close relatives or at least of a nurse.

I am speaking of a nightly predicament where I, as the one nurse, assisted by two nursing auxiliaries, carried alone the responsibility for the total care of 26 patients for 11 hours. You can well imagine that conditions frequently arise in which more than one patient at a time requires the attention of a nurse. Indeed, during the one-and-a-half hours of meal breaks each night, there was usually no nurse at all on the ward, a quite deplorable state of affairs.

While realising that the price of perfection is prohibitive, I know that one additional nurse could make the difference between patients dying alone and unnoticed, as happened so often, or being given proper nursing care in the last hours of their lives. It is with relief and hope that I welcome your initiative. When I reported my concerns to the managers, the reaction was one of denial, closing ranks and defending the status quo. No objective assessment of the situation, involving the regular bedside staff, was made.

My experience is that nurses who voice their concerns expose themselves to enormous stress and (often) open threat to their careers. I am presently preparing my case for appeal to an industrial tribunal against unfair dismissal. In fighting this appeal the health authority's costs may amount to as much as half-a-million pounds. This is a dreadful and irresponsible waste of scarce taxpayers' money. A more con-ciliatory attitude on the part of the authority could avoid this profligacy. The money saved could then be spent on caring for patients and fund for many years the extra nurses I have been seeking.

I look to you to share my profound concern over the present failure to provide enough hospital nurses to care for the very old and dying with the respect and dignity which they so richly and so rightly deserve.

One day we too are likely become geriatric patients, as in turn are our children. I ask you to do everything in your power to press for a proper staffing ratio now for the very sick and old in our geriatric wards.

The reply of 14th August – signed by 'C Pearson' – reads:

Mrs Bottomley has asked me to thank you for your letter of 27th July.

In view of the pending industrial tribunal hearing about your dismissal, I hope you will appreciate that it would not be appropriate for the secretary of state to comment on the points you raise.

Obviously the Department of Health was not going to alter its policy of disregarding anything I wrote, and some junior employee had been detailed to write this bland, empty response. The only hope remaining was that the nurses' national council might be persuaded to accept its statutory responsibilities and consider the possibility of disciplining the nurse managers.

By now this seemed unlikely, but I was not prepared to accept it could wash its hands of the matter, in the manner of Pontius Pilate, without further attempts by me to prick its leather-bound conscience.

> Dame Audrey Emerton, Chairlady,
> The United Kingdom Central Council for
> Nursing, Midwifery and Health Visiting,
> 23, Portland Place, London W1N 3AF

September 5th, 1992

Dear Madam,

May I bring to your attention, and through you to your members, my serious disquiet at the council's apparent inaction regarding possible hearings before the professional conduct committee.

I MRS J FREDERIKS

On June 28th 1990, I reported to the UKCC the chief nursing officer of Stockport health authority, Mrs J Frederiks, for consideration of possible professional misconduct. To assist the council I have provided a huge amount of evidence, statistics, reports, description of incidents, correspondence etc. What the present position regarding my reporting of the CNO is I am unaware, and this complete lack of meaningful information on progress is, it would seem, intentional. Two serious concerns emanate:

1. The chief nursing officer's continuance in post

The charges that I have brought against the CNO relate to perceived serious and blatant neglect of patients and disregard for the health and welfare of the night staff. The charges are cardinal to the direct care of hundreds of helpless and frail patients. The supporting facts (never contradicted or questioned by the CNO or health authority) are quite considerable; many who have followed the case closely would say "decisive". Yet the lady continues in post. This I find incredible, the more so when one compares it with the treatment of the bedside nurse involved in the affair.

Nothing that I was accused to have done/failed to do put patients at any risk or danger. On the contrary, my every action was designed to improve care and safety and to reduce stress for the staff. The moment the charges were put to me, I was suspended from duty, staying so for 13 months. How the UKCC would justify Mrs Frederiks remaining on duty, in view of the gravity of the accusations against her and the strength and quality of the detailed evidence, is beyond my comprehension and would, I suspect, confound the sagacity and erudition of a council of Solomons.

2. "To no man will we sell, or deny, or delay, right or justice." (Magna Carta, 1215)

Two years and two months have passed since I reported the CNO to the council, yet no proper hearing of the case has been held and, for aught I know, none is envisaged. No explanation for such a delay has been offered. Each member of the council will be aware of the wise maxim that "Justice delayed is justice denied", which does no more than validate the discerning judgment of our far-sighted forebears who set down their thoughts 777 years ago. Remember we are talking here of justice for four people: Mrs Frederiks, Miss Carew, Mr Geraghty and me.

It might be worth pointing out that these matters will be reported to, and have considerable importance for, the 600,000 plus nurses throughout this country who, to repeat Lord Hewart's dictum, will demand that justice "should manifestly and undoubtedly be seen to be done". To date the UKCC's achievement in promptly and efficiently dealing with his case has been in every respect, I believe, abysmal.

Once a nurse is reported to the council, investigations one presumes, are immediately started. Clearly this has to be done fairly and with great care. A reasonable period would perhaps be three or four months, gathering evidence while people's memories are fresh, and while documentation is still readily available. I find it very difficult to understand why after six months the work could not be completed and ready for consideration. The task surely is to establish whether there is evidential sufficiency to proceed with the charges, and try as I may, I am unable to accept that the process needs TWO YEARS. Where a nurse's reputation and very future may depend on the outcome of the enquiry, the apparent leisurely inertia ill-becomes our statutory body, leaving open the possibility (seen by many well-informed followers of the case as a distinct "probability") that the council is intention-ally dragging its feet, unable or unwilling to face up honestly to its mandated responsibilities. Short of admitting the council's gross inefficiency and/or indifference, it is difficult to see how you would rebut such an imputation.

The council's response to these suggestions is now requested. My disciplinary hearing before Mrs Frederiks and her two health authority colleagues was a disgraceful sham. Truth, impartiality and fair play were not allowed to cloud the issues. From beginning to end it was a disreputable mockery of all that British justice stands for. And Mrs Frederiks helped initiate and supported in full this pretence, this "lynch law", summary justice with a vengeance. Disillusioned as I and thousands of others have been by Mrs Frederiks' treatment of me, I would want her to have an open and just hearing – anything less would be unacceptable.

II   MR J GERAGHTY AND MISS E CAREW

On September 26th 1990, I reported to the UKCC the two above-named nurses for consideration of possible professional misconduct. The ENB informed me on June 22nd 1991 that "no action should be taken in respect of the report received". When you know the extent of both persons' behaviour – disregard of reported patient neglect and danger; abuse of individual staff by creating and defending intolerable staffing levels which nightly jeopardised safe standards of care; deception, mis-representation and false evidence disseminated to cover up incompetence; written, blatant untruths clearly designed to discredit nursing staff, to name but some, then you might be as baffled as I. That this behaviour can be seen as professional does a grave disservice to your organisation and inevitably makes one question the standards of those who come to such a decision. By allowing these nurses, in Stockport and those on your council, to continue unchallenged, nothing but dis-respect for nurses, for the Council and more importantly lack of proper care for patients can ensue.

Following new facts revealed at the disciplinary and appeal hearings, I reported Miss Carew and Mr Geraghty again to the ENB on serious charges...

... Yet to the best of my knowledge, neither nurse is to be called to account before your council. That possibility leaves me, and I'm sure every right-thinking person, let alone every nurse in this country, dumbfounded.

III   THE PERCEPTION BY NURSES OF THE ROLE OF THE UKCC

Over the last 18 months, I have spoken to/corresponded with many thousands of nurses throughout the land. What has become apparent is the complete misconception most have of the purpose and powers of your council. It is generally believed that the UKCC is a body which defends and protects nurses' and patients' interests; which provides a sort of insurance when they need support and help; which will speak up loud and clear when a nurse finds him/herself in the sort of situation I did; which will respond promptly when advice is sought; which not only says that it is concerned about professional conduct but is prepared to do something; which would act swiftly and decisively when unacceptable behaviour is reported to it; which would back foursquare any nurse upholding the code. Based on my experience, and that of many others, I am able to disabuse nurses of these misguided notions.

As I am sure you will appreciate, a great deal of forethought and bleak experience has gone into the writing of this letter. May I suggest that it be circulated to each member of the council and discussed in detail and I trust that "confidentiality and/or sub judice" will not be offered as a reason for shelving or delaying the council's detailed and substantive reply.

To assist the council I enclosed 36 documents (running to more than 110 pages). These were in addition to the many hundreds of pages which had previously been sent. Dame Audrey did not reply.

I wrote to her again in October and November but never heard anything from her. Remembering that my initial letter to the council had waited 114 days for a response, and that between August 1990 and May 1991, 16 letters to the registrar and assistant registrar were ignored, should have perhaps warned me not to hold out hope of a response. It seemed to me, however, reasonable to expect that correspondence to a person of Dame Audrey's standing and position might elicit a reply. An explanation of sorts from the council maintained that any fault lay with the ENB, which wrote to me in September to say, as it already had done regarding Mr Geraghty and Miss Carew, that there was no case for Mrs Frederiks to answer.

In view of all that had become known and my careful submission of evidence, these findings were disappointing to say the very least. It was not for me to decide that these three people were guilty of improper conduct; others, well away from the situation, should be left to make a decision. But surely, by all that's right and decent, there was a case to answer and the council had a duty to investigate. In my reports to the council and ENB I had made certain points.

1. None of the senior nurses had ever questioned or challenged the detailed evidence presented to management that nightly patients were being neglected and put in danger. Their refusal to do so was tantamount to accepting the validity of my descriptions. They knew that not only was nursing cover generally insufficient but, more alarmingly, that for long periods each night no nurse at all was present on duty.

2. Despite the Herculean efforts of staff, the environment of care was perforce regularly debased and safe practice put in jeopardy. The number of falls from bed would alone be sufficient testimony to this. Then, in February 1990, notwithstanding the desperate staff situation, managers reduced the qualified cover on the wards by 25 per cent. Yet the ENB and council must have concluded that the three nurses bore no responsibility under the code.

3. The nurse managers appeared to make no efforts to ascertain the opinions or observations of patients, relatives or bedside night staff. Between August 1987 and August 1990 I spent a total of 18 days and 392 nights on duty in the geriatric area. During these 4,848 hours Mrs Frederiks was never sighted and Mr Geraghty once only.

4. I had voiced outspoken and undisguised disapproval of the CNO's lack of action over the perceived failures. These observations, while always polite, had called into question Mrs Frederiks' competence and professionalism. Yet, despite her immediate and close association with events, she saw fit to sit as a member of the disciplinary panel. This not only flouted all accepted norms of fair play, but repudiated the authority's own procedure and the council's code. The ENB/Council must, though, have concluded that in sitting as part of management's "judge, jury and executioner" she acted correctly.

5. At the end of the disciplinary hearing the senior nurses agreed with the findings that I was incompetent and guilty on four counts of gross misconduct. With such findings it would be signally inappropriate, in fact downright dangerous, to allow me to continue caring for patients. With their approval, if not at their instigation, I was offered a community post where I would be attending to very sick and terminally ill patients in their homes, unsupervised. The national body must have considered that such action signified that nurse managers were acting in such a way "as to promote and safeguard the wellbeing and interests of patients" and that by putting a disgraced and negligent nurse into patients' homes alone they were ensuring that no action on their part was "detrimental to the condition or safety of patients".

6. Neglectful and dangerous practices by other members of staff, including very senior nurses, (which had gone on for years and been known to managers) were reported to the

board and council. These included misidentification and non-identification of patients; massive carelessness with drug administration; slack record keeping; incorrect transfusions/intravenous infusions and lack of required standards of care. Yet no other nurse was disciplined. Why were others (culpable and dishonourable as they were) not similarly treated? While the nurse management was willing to support the prejudice and cover-up involved, the UKCC must have judged that these nurses acted in the best traditions of nursing and behaved in a thoroughly honourable manner.

7. Despite the fact that my every action upheld the code of conduct to the letter, that my accounts were never doubted, that everything reported had occurred, I was dismissed with the nurse manager's approval. The council must have seen this as an example of their duty to "protect society and above all to safeguard the interests of individual patients".

To Mr Pyne I wrote:

> Over the last two-and-a-half years, I have met, spoken to and been written to by a huge number of nurses. Two themes dominate their conversations/writings: their own encounters over similar problems, especially with unacceptable standards of care and threatening/self-serving nurse managers, and their disillusionment with and often disdain for the UKCC. Until recently, I have been prepared to suspend judgment but these findings of the ENB/UKCC appear to confirm the commonly held belief that not only does the council fail to support nurses, but connives at bad practice...
>
> ...I believe that the manner in which the council and board have conducted this matter and the incredible and alarming conclusions reached must be challenged and exposed. My

treatment at the hands of the health authority is seen by countless people as unjust, devoid of all morality and decency and
a frightening abuse of power. Much the same view I must now
take of the council's/board's treatment of the case.

In January 1993 the board wrote to say that 'in view of the decision
taken by the Investigating committee this case is now closed and
the board will be unable to correspond further, on this matter.' What
the Stockport case has so vividly exposed is the unwillingness of
the nursing regulatory body to properly monitor and control staff on
the register. The powers exist to do the job but council members and
officers appear, on occasions, reluctant to do their duty to protect the
public. So many nurses have written and spoken to me with stories
of reported wrongdoing and intentional neglect by staff to which the
council has turned a blind eye. As far as I could see the UKCC was
run like some secret fiefdom, omnipotent, unaccountable and remote
from those it is meant to protect, the patients, while protecting to
the hilt much incompetent and indefensible behaviour by nurses.
Whether things have changed, I do not know.

◆   ◆   ◆

Preparations for my industrial tribunal appeared to move at a snail's
pace, but at length the starting date was fixed for 15th March 1993. I
was convinced that the authority would go to almost any length to
prevent the hearing going ahead or, if once started, back out at the first
opportunity. To date its actions had been carried out away from the
penetrating gaze of public scrutiny. Even with this cloud of secrecy,
the public condemnation had been prodigious and to have its behaviour examined by a Queen's counsel in an open forum must have
been a disturbing prospect. Any doubts about this were dispelled in
March when the solicitors acting for the authority informed Bindman

and Partners that it was their intention to apply for the tribunal to be heard in secret. Brian Raymond found this move unprecedented and resisted it. He put out a press statement on 5th March:

> The employers of Graham Pink are attempting to have his appeal to the industrial tribunal heard behind closed doors. The Stockport Health Authority will be applying for his claim for unfair dismissal to be heard in camera. Mr Pink said today:
>
> "I have nothing to hide. This will be the first time that an independent outside tribunal has heard the facts of my case and I deserve the same full public hearing that everyone is entitled to." His solicitor, Brian Raymond, said: "We shall fight this all the way. It would be a travesty of justice for the country's best-known NHS whistleblower to have to fight for his job in secret. I am amazed that the health authority should think they could get away with this – we hope the tribunal will give it very short shrift indeed."
>
> Graham Pink's moving descriptions of the plight of the elderly people under his care at night touched the heart of the nation when some of his hundreds of letters appealing to the authorities for help were published in the *Guardian*. Since then he has been the subject of a programme in the *40 Minutes* series and last month was elected to the UKCC. His nursing colleagues gave him over five times as many votes as the next successful candidate.

The elections referred to were held in January 1993. The votes in the English region put me way ahead of the field of 129 candidates for seven seats. The voting system was complicated but I was the only candidate to win a seat outright receiving 54 per cent of first-preference votes cast. As *Nursing Times* reported:

For many, no doubt the most noteworthy aspect of the recently announced election results will have been the success of the profession's best known whistleblower, Graham Pink. There is, after all, a delicious irony in the fact that the indefatigable Mr Pink, for so long the scourge of the UKCC, is now to be one of its representatives. He received 8,770 first-preference votes in total, compared with 1,637 for his nearest rival. He notched up more first-preference votes than all the winning Scots candidates together and more than all the combined first-preference votes of winners in Wales and Northern Ireland.

I was later to learn that more UK votes were cast for me than for over half the 40 elected members combined. I found it remarkable that a disgraced, sacked nurse should be so massively supported, but the letters that flooded in implied that such an overwhelming avowal for my stand demonstrated how badly were the existing leaders of nursing failing us. In a short article I wrote for the *Nursing Standard* in early February I said:

> The council's functions "are concerned with serving the public interest and protecting the vulnerable public". These words, taken from information supplied to prospective candidates in the recent UKCC election, have a fine ring to them, do not they? Sadly though, they are empty words and the ring is hollow. If my experience is anything to go by, the council is certainly serving an interest, but not that of the public. My repeated requests for a justification of the decision not to hold a hearing into the managers who so eagerly and so disgracefully supported my sacking and who blatantly accepted dreadful standards of care, open neglect and exposure of patients to serious danger, has been ignored. And tell me which members of the public are more "vulnerable" than

our geriatric patients. The watchword is "secrecy", at least where matters of professional conduct are concerned. If the council believes that its decisions are right and proper why not openly defend and justify them? What is there to hide?

One of my first aims as a council member is to open up just about everything to public scrutiny and make members accountable to you, the electorate, and that includes the 83.5 per cent of nurses who chose not to take part. If you find that number alarming and depressing, ask yourself why so few bothered to take part. Could it be that they see the council as remote, deaf to nurses' real worries, yet one more pointless and costly bureaucracy. I do, and that's what I want to change. I want to put patients first, second and third. And if I am wrong as I may be (only 14 per cent of candidates in England mentioned "patients" in their statements of intent) I want you to put me right. Members are there to concern themselves with your hopes, fears, aims and difficulties. I refuse, though, to believe that we are as spineless, impotent and unconcerned as many think my experience implies.

Were you as sickened and ashamed as I was by the Ashworth Special Hospital Report? You should have been; a place where nurses supported a "culture of denigration and devaluing of patients"; where there was such a low standard of care that the hospital "must be a prime candidate to be included as one of the establishments to be visited in the near future by the Committee for the Prevention of Torture!" Every nurse in the country shares the blame for this disgrace. Unless and until each one of us is prepared to accept our responsibility for standards, to face up to lack of care, bullying managers, intolerable stress... need I go on? we will continue to be ignored, as was I, to be hounded and treated with contempt, as was I, and we will have only ourselves to blame.

EIGHTEEN
DEFENDING THE INDEFENSIBLE

. . . if you are thinking of making a complaint, however legitimate, however appalling the situation about which you wish to complain, then you must expect to be made sick, sacked, financially ruined and at the end of the day your complaint will almost certainly not have been addressed — **Geoffrey Hunt, director of the National Centre for Nursing and Midwifery Ethics**

Five days before the industrial tribunal, the authority offered an ex-gratia payment of £11,188 (the maximum sum one could recover for unfair dismissal in a successful complaint) if I would drop the case, with the proviso that should the offer be rejected the authority would reserve the right to draw the fact 'to the attention of the tribunal at the appropriate juncture in regard to the issue of costs'. There is no legal aid for an industrial tribunal. Each side must bear its own costs and either party, more usually the successful one, can apply to have part or all its costs paid by the other side. Thus the apparent conciliatory offer on the 10th of March was in part a threat. The authority, through its solicitors, went as far as to draw up, uni-laterally, two proposed 'Statements': They read, in part:

> Mr Pink and the Health Authority consider that in view of the limited but fundamental issue between them the limited resources of the Health Authority would be better spent on

patient care than on legal proceedings, and have compromised the case by issuing this agreed statement. The tribunal was scheduled to last ten days though the lawyers consider it could have taken twice as long.

After all that had occurred, it seems incredible that Mr Milnes and his fellow managers could consider that I saw the issues in the case as 'limited'. With the best will in the world, it is difficult to see the statement as other than a cynical ruse to avoid facing open argument and additional condemnation. A less favourable interpretation is that it was proof positive, if any was needed, of management's arrogant misuse of power and its determination to silence further publication of the facts. In view of these facts, the reference to 'patient care' is wholly crass and offensive.

The advice from both Mr Raymond and Mr John Hendy QC, who had been retained to defend me, was that I really should seriously consider accepting a settlement. The authority had made it clear that the offer was a concession on their part and no improvement was to be expected.

This assertion I found unconvincing, and told Mr Hendy to expect another, no doubt improved, offer even as late as the morning of the tribunal. I did not seek or want such a pre-tribunal settlement. If I was to keep faith with the patients, my colleagues and the thousands of people who had made contact and by now raised more than £25,000 towards my legal costs, (apart from considerations of honour and probity), then the last thing that would be appropriate or acceptable was some sort of arrangement which let the authority off the hook and able to sweep their behaviour under the carpet. Having come so far, it seemed incumbent on me to stand up for openness and decency, even if that were to lead to my losing the tribunal. Compromise under duress, like silence, was not an option.

Following a meeting in London (the day after the offer) with Mr Hendy, his junior barrister, Brian Raymond and colleague, at which I was strongly advised to settle, I asked Mr Raymond to inform Stockport that I would be prepared to consider not proceeding following: (1) The withdrawal of all charges against me, (2) an offer to reinstate me in my post forthwith and (3) a public statement by the authority accepting these terms. None of us expected a positive response and, of course, the proposal was rejected. A second attempt to avoid the tribunal was then faxed to Bindman and Partners on 12th March. It was similar to that of 10th March with the addition of an offer of money to go to charity for the care of the elderly (see below). I opted to continue.

Thus it was that we assembled at the regional office of the industrial tribunals in Alexandra House, Manchester, on the morning of 15th March 1993. I arrived around 9.30 am and within 20 minutes everyone on our side was in place. Then just before 10am, one of the authority's legal team came in and spoke quietly to Mr Hendy who left the room. A moment or two later, I was called out to a side room. As I had anticipated, at 'one minute to midnight' another offer, the third, was on the table. I was disinclined even to listen to it but it had to be given an answer. The offer, in part, read:

> We are instructed to put forward terms for settlement of your client's application. Our client is willing to pay to your client the sum of £16,336 (being the maximum sum your client might recover as compensation for unfair dismissal including any additional award in the event of our client failing to comply with an order for re-engagement).
>
> In addition our client will agree to the publication of a joint statement which will, we trust, enable both parties to withdraw from these proceedings without claiming success or conceding defeat. We enclose a draft of such a statement/

media release. Our client would be willing to accept the addition of a quote to be attributed to your client which is consistent with the sentiments expressed therein.

Insofar as the monies which have been donated to your client's fighting fund will not have been applied towards the payment of legal costs and are capable of being used for such a purpose our client would be willing to contribute an equal amount to an agreed charity having as its object the care of the elderly. The statement/release can be amended to make reference to this part of the agreement if such is achieved.

The rejection by your client of the proposals referred to hereinbefore will be an indication that he seeks to ventilate issues beyond the scope of a complaint of unfair dismissal to the tribunal. The cost involved, as he has already pointed out, could be better applied to patient care. In the circumstances we have made this offer in open correspondence and it will be the authority's intention to point out to the industrial tribunal that your client's ambitions appear to be to use the industrial tribunal as a forum for a debate on the health service. We do not consider that that would be a proper purpose and we intend to say so.

There was really no need to give Messrs Raymond or Hendy my response but they were obliged to put the offer to me. As I said to them, if the amount offered had been not £16,000 (itself, I gathered, a quite exceptional figure) but £160,000, it would have made no difference to my resolve to go on. What the offer does clearly indicate, however, is that for these managers, appearance and perception are what mattered, not the substantive principles. On what evidence they hoped to demonstrate that I wished to 'ventilate issues beyond the scope of my dismissal' we never discovered but the implied threats could be seen as one more indication of their arrogance. This last stick and carrot manoeuvre had all the hallmarks of a drowning man's ultimate, desperate cry for assistance. We were soon back in the tribunal room.

I shall not attempt to detail the progress of the tribunal, the first part of which ran for ten days. Following an opening statement by Mr John Hand, QC for the authority, the tribunal adjourned until the Wednesday morning for the three members to read some 500 pages of the documents (out of the 2,000 plus) which Mr John Hand thought the tribunal needed to be familiar with before hearing the evidence. On the morning of the third day, the hospital general manager, Mr Caldwell, took the stand as the first, and principal, authority witness. In all he was giving evidence for some three-and-a-half days. It seems sensible to deal with the matters raised in his cross-examination under relevant headings.

1. PATIENT NEGLECT

Never previously had management been obliged to respond to the many patient episodes I had described. The policy had always been to ignore or very occasionally deny them. Mr Caldwell admitted, after some prevarication, that no one had challenged the truth of the incidents. Evidence was produced by Mr Hendy to establish that the first enquiry was undertaken 12 months *after* my first letter to the health authority chairman Mr Richards – that is after my suspension, and largely as a trawl for evidence to put against me.

At one point, the tribunal chairlady intervened to ask the manager if, following my first letter, he had ordered an investigation into the level of accidents and untoward incidents. 'No, I didn't at any time,' was his reply.

The unbiased listener in that room would have found it difficult not to be convinced that the duty of care that all health service employees have towards their patients was not being carried out during the period concerned, and to know where the responsibility for this lay. Addressing the tribunal, counsel suggested that the evolving evidence spoke volumes. It was 'important that all health authority employees should know that if they speak out publicly they will be dismissed,' and, directly addressing Mr Caldwell, 'The incidents didn't sicken you, but the publicity did.'

2.   MANAGERS' BEHAVIOUR

After much equivocation by the manager, Mr Hendy established that on the night immediately before my disciplinary hearing, Thursday 11th October 1990, Mr Caldwell, together with the two night nurse managers, Miss Carew and Miss O'Donnell held a two-hour meeting. By the time Counsel had finished his detailed enquiry into the purpose and timing of the meeting, few fair-minded people could have believed other than that it was held to prepare the ground for the following day; to agree the 'right' questions and answers, and to ensure that no slip-ups occurred. Mr Caldwell was to be the chairman of the hearing and the nurse managers two of the principal witnesses.

3.   MANAGERS' DRUG MALADMINISTRATION

As already established, while a minor infringement of the drugs rules by myself was deemed by the authority to constitute gross misconduct, no action was ever taken against other members of staff. Although not discussed in detail with Mr Caldwell, the subject of correct medication and management's selective treat-ment of error was brought up several times and significantly twice by the chairlady who was told by the manager that (a) the drugs check was carried out on charge nurse Pink only and (b) Mr Geraghty, the assistant general manager, had taken no action when I had reported repeated, improper drug provision by other nurses.

Thus, Mr Caldwell was obliged to accept, for the first time in public and to the panel's obvious concern, that gross carelessness with drug administration had been ignored for up to two years.

Were it not for the authority's eventual capitulation, Mrs Frederiks, Mr Geraghty and Miss Carew would have been subsequently cross-examined and the full truth exposed. But the senior managers did not have to face such disclosures as they were to throw in the towel. Rather than see an innocent nurse exonerated, these people were prepared to see a massive amount of public money squandered, then when they realised things were not going their way, they withdraw from the tribunal. What a way to run a health service!

4.   CODE OF CONDUCT

A nurse's responsibilities and obligations to patients under the code of professional conduct were discussed at length. Mr Caldwell accepted that it is a condition of employment by the health authority that a nurse must be on the UKCC register. If registration ceases for any reason, employment will be terminated. The condition is absolute. Compliance with the code is a contractual obligation and Mr Caldwell was unable to cite any circumstances when a nurse may disregard the code.

It was, though, his opinion that a breach of confidence (never established in this case) could not be in the public interest. A long exchange followed between Mr Caldwell and Mr Hendy, my QC, who slowly drew from the manager an admission that the only logical deduction one can arrive at regarding a nurse's code is that it lays on a nurse a body of obligations for her or his own practice. The nurse must act in the exercise of personal and professional accountability.

One of these actions relates to what he or she considers right if the workload jeopardises safe standards of care and it is the nurse concerned, and only that nurse, who is in a position to judge this. 'The code,' stated counsel, 'is not for employers, not for patients, not for doctors but for nurses.'

Given this assessment of my responsibility to the code and thus to the patients, Mr Caldwell was unable to refute Mr Hendy's reasoning that for a lay manager to state, as did Mr Caldwell: 'I decide what is in the public interest, not Mr Pink,' was unacceptable and improper. Nor was Mrs Frederiks correct in advising Mr Caldwell that my action was not in the public interest. By definition, only I was in a position to make that decision.

In its submission to the Department of Health on 23rd November 1992, the UKCC document, 'Freedom of Speech for NHS Staff' states: 'This council's position is that practitioners on its register must ensure that the reality of their clinical environment is made known to their managers, this being done as an expression of their personal professional accountability exercised in the public interest.'

Mr Hendy went to great lengths to establish that (a) as a nurse I owed a duty of care to those whom I was nursing, (b) in my opinion that duty of care was not being met, and (c) that having, without success, taken all reasonable steps within my domain to bring the situation to management's attention, I was entitled to take the action I did. In counsel's opinion, the code not only permitted me to speak out publicly but so *obliged* me. This Mr Caldwell would not accept, believing that where a conflict of interest between contract of employment and code exists, as it surely did here, then the former overrides the latter.

This is the intractable dilemma now faced daily by nurses and one the RCN, Unison, the council and the Department of Health need to face. When a few months later I presented the mass of fresh evidence from the industrial tribunal to Sir Duncan Nichol, he refused to consider it.

5. UNFAIR DISMISSAL

For an accused person to be given a fair, unbiased hearing, in whatever forum, it is customary in this country for those sitting in judgment to be unconnected with the defendant, the witnesses or any aspect of the case. That is one of the most precious cornerstones of our legal system. If accusers sit as judges, the system is flawed from the outset and the whole procedure is brought into disrepute.

That Stockport's Lewis Carroll 'Off with his head' scenario was seen as fair and acceptable by everyone in authority, is an indication of just how degraded is so much of our public life today. The tribunal served to underline the glaring prejudice of my disciplinary hearing and brought out the additional fact that the third member of the panel, Mr Burke, had been closely involved in the preparation and implementation of my suspension. In Mr Hendy's words management saw fit to sit as 'prosecutor, judge and witness'.

More damning evidence, however, was to be unearthed by Counsel's relentless pursuit of the truth. Mr Caldwell asserted under cross-examination that he and his fellow managers were familiar with the authority's disciplinary procedure, were bound by its rule of fairness and followed its provisions scrupulously at all times. This is no more than one would expect in so vital a matter as employment law. All senior managers would need to have a complete understanding of the relevant regulations. Yet it was to be proved that Stockport's management had not abided by its own rules in dismissing me. The procedure states that for an employee to be dismissed following gross misconduct, no 'other suitable alternative employment with the authority' should be available. In offering me the community post, management demonstrated that in my case there was such suitable alternative work. Ergo, the offences of which I was found guilty did not, as defined by regulation 9B(I), constitute 'gross misconduct leading to summary dismissal'.

6   OFFER OF A COMMUNITY POST

To propose to move a nurse who has 'difficulty in coping as he should' (Stockport chairman's words) and was found guilty on four counts of gross misconduct, to a community post shows complete lack of thought and foresight. The post would have involved one-to-one respite care of sick and dying patients in their own homes. Mr Caldwell agreed that supervision would be minimal. The proposed move of a 'discredited and incompetent' nurse amounted to an act of supreme mismanagement and displays an amazing lack of regard for patients.

So much else was unearthed at the tribunal: no warnings given that disciplinary action was being prepared; questions raised over the chief nursing officer's and nurse managers' adherence to their code of conduct; the lack of concern from managers in response to my concerns for patient welfare; the single-minded, implacable persecution of one member of staff; the tactics which managers regularly employed to discredit me; the apparent indifference to patients' and relatives' suffering and the climate of obsessive secrecy that pervaded management's attitude.

During the course of the tribunal, a local paper, *The Stockport Messenger* printed a letter it had received from a lady in Cheshire. It read:

> Today, being Mother's Day I felt it was appropriate to write in support of Nurse Graham Pink. My mother occupied a bed in the geriatric ward at Stepping Hill hospital from the end of October until December 17th 1988, when she died. The conditions in which she died have haunted me ever since and caused my 84-year-old father to have nightmares.
>
> I visited my mother most days and was horrified at the conditions. Fortunately my mother remained sane though how, I do not know, as she was surrounded by poor, senile

old men whose behaviour was very disturbing to myself and other visitors.

My mother was suffering from lymphoma which is a rapidly growing form of cancer. We did not receive this information until after they had removed her lymph gland. I tried my best to find her a place in a hospice so that she could die in the peace which she deserved. Unfortunately a bed was obtained for the Monday after her death.

When my mother was at her best she walked into the hospital. She made a special request for her little portable TV to watch her favourite *Coronation Street*. This was denied. Apart from this, her other love was a cup of tea. This was also denied.

There was one particularly upsetting incident when a cup of tea had been promised at lights out. Mum had looked forward to this all through her distressing day. When she reminded the nurse on duty she was told "Forget it", and was left to cry herself to sleep.

This was just one of the many, many upsetting episodes, which are too numerous and too distressing for me to relate, during the horrendous seven weeks my poor, unselfish, caring, loving mother had to endure in this, what my father refers to as a "hell-hole". (My father has a store of pills just in case he finds himself in the same situation as my mother.)

The reason I have not spoken out before is that I have felt too stressed to relate what happened until now. Your report on Mr Pink made me want to support and endorse what he said completely and utterly. I owe it to my mother's memory.

In mid-April the Friends of Mr Pink fighting fund set up by Mary Williams received its most generous contribution. On 19th April Mr Hector McKenzie of COHSE wrote:

> The confederation is deeply committed to Graham Pink's industrial tribunal case as has been demonstrated by the National Executive Committee's earlier donation of £1,000 to the appeal fund and by the many individual contributions by COHSE members and branches. In recognition of the continued support for Graham Pink and his campaign to support whistleblowers, the confederation agrees to make a donation of £25,000 to the fund.

Mary Williams, Brian Raymond and I each wrote with our overwhelming appreciation for the union's contribution and approbation. Unfortunately, though, the public event planned by Brian recognising the confederation's endorsement of my stand did not take place for on 22nd May an unexpected and tragic event occurred – Brian Raymond died of a heart attack. It seemed all the more dreadful because we had been speaking on the phone a few days previously. The obituary in the *Guardian* was written by Helena Kennedy QC. She rightly spoke of his work in 'confronting abuse of power, whether by the state, the professional establishments or by individual bullies. Over the last 15 years he may have been responsible for more of the news that was worth cheering than anyone in the country.'

He was a delightful person, courteous, witty and self-effacing, who devoted his enormous energies unstintingly to my case and the final outcome could never have been achieved without him. His loss to the British legal world and to the persecuted employees of this country is incalculable. I was greatly privileged to have had him as a champion and a friend.

◆ ◆ ◆

Another approach to settlement was made in mid-May when at Stockport's initiative, both leading counsel met. As a result of this, the authority stated that it was now prepared to admit that the procedure for dismissal was unfair and offered a slightly increased cash settlement of £16,500. Clearly the health authority was prepared to move heaven and earth to prevent the full facts becoming public, and I was in no doubt that the tribunal would go no further. Had Mr Hendy been allowed to cross-examine the nurse managers, the full extent of my unfair treatment at their hands would have emerged. Stockport could not possibly permit this to happen. Although advised by my legal team to very seriously consider accepting the settlement, I expressed my wish to continue with the tribunal. Stockport's fifth offer, similar to the previous one, arrived (and was rejected) in early June. This was followed a few days later by a letter from the authority's solicitors to Bindman's asking us to reconsider since 'we believe that Mr Pink should now accept the offer and so bring this matter to a conclusion, thereby preserving the substantial sums which will be required to pay the legal costs for direct expenditure on patient care.'

Many observers have commented on the way Stockport appeared prepared to spend whatever it took to avoid admitting any error, misjudgement or misconduct of any sort by its managers/officers. No one, it seems, had stepped out of line in any way at all and they were prepared to spend huge amounts of money, public money, to uphold this facade. Brian Raymond, in a letter to my constituency MP, Mr Tony Lloyd, had estimated that the authority would spend the best part of £200,000 on legal costs alone. He wrote:

> In these cash-starved times this is an extraordinary amount to be spending in order to justify the dismissal of a nurse who did no more than alert the public to the conditions in which old folk were being treated at night in a publicly-funded hospital. Graham has made it perfectly clear that he is not interested in monetary gain and that if they were to admit

dismissing him unfairly and to withdraw the charges against
him, the case could be settled tomorrow.

On 11th June, Bindman's wrote to say that the last option for the
authority was an open capitulation. 'If they throw in the towel,'
wrote Robin Lewis, who had now taken over Brian Raymond's work,
'I am assuming that the authority would admit unfairness and
submit to an order to pay the maximum award.' As they were so
obviously not prepared to proceed with the tribunal, this seemed
to be their only choice and on 14th June the expected announcement
was made. A health authority news release stated:

> We have made numerous offers to settle this case with Mr
> Pink, hoping that both parties could withdraw without
> claiming victory or conceding defeat. We also hoped that
> we were on common ground with Mr Pink in that care of
> patients should come first and that no individual case should
> consume so much public time and resources. For reasons of
> his own, he was unable to share these priorities. With 20-20
> hindsight, we were technically wrong in not issuing Mr Pink
> with a formal warning when he began his campaign in the
> media, but as a public authority we were at pains to address
> all his concerns before taking disciplinary action.

The tone of the statement was similar throughout – no admission
of fault, no regrets, no apologies to patients; the villain was solely
Mr Pink; the authority had fallen over backwards to accommo-
date him but his intransigence negated all their generous efforts.
Of course, I am open to various criticisms and must accept some
responsibility for what occurred. For my inadequacies I am ready
to hold up my hands. In contrast, though, the managers and
officers accepted no blame at all.

It is not for me to judge, but the use in the statement of such words as 'victory, defeat, patients should come first, at pains to address all his concerns' suggest that nothing was learned by management, that the conditions I had witnessed were acceptable and no changes would be initiated. Further, it has been put to me (by nurses themselves) that my actions substantially set back the cause of nursing in that no nurse in future will be prepared to put his or her head above the parapet to speak out. There may be some truth in this. Others must decide.

As I was unavailable all day on the 14th of June, sitting an examination at Liverpool University (in connection with my MSc studies), Robin Lewis put out a statement headed: 'Whistle-Blower Nurse Wins Dismissal Case':

> Graham Pink has won his battle. The health authority has admitted it acted unfairly when it dismissed him. Graham Pink's victory will bring joy to thousands of health care professionals who have supported him, and who have recently elected him with a huge vote to the UKCC. His victory represents a triumph for those whose priority is care for patients over those whose first care is for balance sheets.
>
> If Stockport Health Authority had admitted two years ago what they have admitted today, a huge amount of resources could have been saved. As it is, today's concession means not only that resources have been wasted on legal costs, but that the public has heard only half the story. Graham Pink's courage and today's outcome will remain a beacon of hope for all those who are dedicated to making the health service a success.

Had it been possible to consult me about this statement, there would have been no mention of winning, of 'battle' or 'victory' and comments regarding the case's effect on nursing and nurses would have been far more restrained. I have no evidence to suggest that what happened either has encouraged or will encourage nursing personnel to highlight poor standards of care where they exist, or that any steps have been/will be taken to improve unacceptable conditions for care of the elderly in hospital.

The final legal steps were taken on the following Monday, 15th June 1993, the day appointed by the tribunal for the resumption of the case. John Hendy and Robin Lewis caught the early shuttle from Heathrow and I met them at Manchester Airport. Over the weekend I had spoken to John to see if there was any way we could continue the hearing. He assured me that there was not. By withdrawing, the authority knew it would abruptly halt proceeding, so thwarting my hope of bringing into the open the full truth of what had happened. There was a time when I would have stared open-mouthed had anyone questioned the notion that we in Britain enjoy freedom of speech – I would have scoffed at the suggestion. Not anymore.

All that remained was for Mr Hand, the authority's QC, to make the formal withdrawal by openly admitting that I had been unfairly dismissed. I hope it will not sound too churlish to say that this gave me little satisfaction. My fate was of no significance. As he spoke, I could not but picture the helpless old ladies and gentlemen (past and future) on wards A14, A15 and C5 to whom his words brought no comfort, no solace, no hope. John Hendy read a prepared three-page statement that attempted to summarise the whole episode and lay blame where he believed it squarely rested. Part of it read:

> By submitting to an Order that Graham Pink was unfairly dismissed the Stockport Health Authority have conceded the point at issue in this case and the Tribunal will make its order that Mr Pink was unfairly dismissed. The health authority imply that the reason is that the costs of further hearing are unacceptable. It is a matter of very great regret to Mr Pink that

this concession could not have been made months ago before they had spent tens of thousands of pounds of taxpayers' money in attempting to defend the indefensible. When at the opening of the case on March 15th the authority offered in open correspondence to pay Mr Pink £16,336 and a contribution to his costs if he would drop the case, it was made clear to the authority that money was not the issue. Mr Pink sought admission of the fact that he had been unfairly dismissed. The health authority refused to concede that fact and went on to spend two weeks fighting a hopeless case.

The health authority, in conceding the maximum possible award (£11,188), has thereby conceded that no reduction should be made to reflect any blameworthiness on the part of Mr Pink. It could do nothing else

It is clear that the real reason Mr Pink was sacked was because, having failed to remedy the matter internally, he complained publicly about lack of nurses. Criticism is something the authority was not prepared to tolerate. So it sacked him. Now to avoid further damaging cross examination it has conceded unfair dismissal.

And that was that. The end of a working life of 46 years, though not exactly the way I would have chosen to finish it.

NINETEEN
I DID WHAT SEEMED RIGHT

How many times can a man turn his head
pretending he just doesn't see? — **Bob Dylan**

The chances are that in the past most health service staff have spent their employed years without giving a thought to their conditions of service. I passed 90 per cent of my nursing career unconcerned for the terms of my contract. Nor in the early years was there any code of conduct with which to be concerned (a UKCC code was first introduced in 1979). It would not have entered the heads of nurses in the 1950s, '60s and '70s that they needed a written set of rules to guide their behaviour or spell out their responsibility to patients, superiors or each other. As late as 1990, I was not entirely aware of the code's purpose or wording. When quizzed on what part, if any, it played in the case, I maintain that I did not require a set of instructions to appreciate that there was something seriously wrong with the nightly scene I was witnessing. Pressed at meetings of students or nurses, especially when asked what advice I would give others in a similar situation, I point out that everyone has his or her own inbuilt rules of behaviour – a conscience, and the nurses of the early 1950s with whom I trained would have felt offended if it had been suggested that they needed a little red booklet (the colour of the 1984 edition of the code) to spell out what was right and wrong in their daily nursing practice. While the code might at one time have been seen as a support or defence for nurses who wished to speak out, it was not needed to recognise the unacceptable face of degraded care, over-worked nurses or neglect and abuse.

Nevertheless, throughout the case I put forward the argument that the code laid on me the duty to safeguard the patients in my care and bring deficiencies in the service to my superiors' attention. Even had this not been the case, to remain silent was never an option. The action that I took was to make a clear, factual report to my managers regarding the standard of care at night in the three wards for the elderly which were my immediate responsibility. Initially this report was made verbally to the night nurse manager, followed later by a very detailed 4,700-word document with accounts of specific incidents.

Initially, there was no question of making the concerns public. In such a situation it is proper to follow set procedures, though this must at times present the conscientious employee with problems where the person or situation complained of is the person (or the direct responsibility of the person) to whom one is required to make the report. For 16 months the consequences of the Stockport understaffing were reported to managers and the health authority, but no one within the service showed any concern, or even wanted to know. I expressed admiration for all my ward colleagues. When it became clear that the hospital authorities would take no action, I sent that first letter, though without any notion that all would eventually become public.

Following the industrial tribunal, so much further evidence had emerged in the documents produced at the hearing and during the course of Mr Hendy's cross examination of Mr Caldwell (much of it previously concealed), that I thought it my duty to report the facts to the regulatory body. This I did in mid-June. The council, though, was clearly not prepared to become involved, had no interest in the reported behaviour of senior nurses and washed its hands entirely of the matter. Not only that, but it seemed

disturbed at the idea that anyone should question its omnipo-
tence. My understanding has always been that in a democratic
society everybody and every body is accountable for his or her or
its actions to some other person/authority. No one person or body
is immune from scrutiny. Accountability is a linchpin of a lawful,
just community.

The UKCC, however, as I established, was in reality accountable to no one. Its decisions may not in practice be challenged. In
discussion with its senior officers, they agreed that there was no
way in which a nurse could question its secret deliberations and
decisions, nor insist that its pronouncements be justified. Moreover,
in recent years the belief has been growing among nurses and the
public that, by its actions and failures to act, the impression is given
that nurses look after their own – a view not assuaged by two cases
of men restored to the register, who had been previously removed
following convictions for rape.

It could be argued that the statutory body is acting unethically
by insisting that nurses report their concerns of inadequate care,
or other matters seen by managers or the trust as their prerogative,
when there are no safeguards for those who act on the code's advice.
To countless observers, the behaviour of the council in my case,
reflected standards of leadership and morality not dissimilar to
those displayed by Stockport Health Authority – exhibiting delay,
denial and inertia to start with; aversion to addressing straight
questions, deflection and inability to tackle the substance of a
problem while being unduly preoccupied with appearances;
coupled with indecision, incompetence and insouciance.

An acute dilemma arises for the nurse (or other healthcare
worker who has a code to follow) when that code's explicit requirement to ensure a safe standard of care conflicts with the terms of
employment. An employee's concerns can be either discounted by
management as unfounded, or dismissed as impracticable. What is

to be done? If the only way to minimise the perceived danger is to speak out publicly, which is to take precedence, code or terms of employment? Ever more nurses are being faced with this quandary. The staff who worked alongside me might have wanted to be openly supportive but they had duties and commitments to their families that, I presume, they felt superseded any responsibilities to the patients, and who would argue with that? An ethical duty to one's family surely overrides any similar ethic to strangers.

On so many occasions now, harassed nurse managers, themselves under great pressure, are insisting that staff do their best by knuckling under, managing with whatever resources are available and above all not complaining. Until nurses can be persuaded into allowing their collective voice to be heard, the present dismal, anachronistic structure will persist.

The NMC accepts that there is a problem. Its publication *Raising and Escalating Concerns: Guidance for Nurses and Midwives* states:

> As a nurse or midwife, you have a professional duty to report any concerns from your workplace which put the safety of the people in your care or the public at risk.
> 2. The code stipulates:
> 2.1 you must act without delay if you believe that you, a colleague or anyone else may be putting someone at risk
> 2.2 you must inform someone in authority if you experience problems that prevent you working within this code or other nationally agreed standards
> 2.3 you must report your concerns in writing if problems in the environment of care are putting people at risk
> 2.4 as a professional, you are personally accountable for actions and omissions in your practice, and must always be able to justify your decisions.
> 3. Speaking up on behalf of people in your care and clients is

an everyday part of your role, and just as raising genuine concerns represents good practice, "doing nothing" and failing to report concerns is unacceptable. Nurses and midwives who raise a genuine concern, and act with the best of intentions and in accordance with the principles laid down in this guidance, will be recognised by us as upholding their professional responsibilities and adhering To the code. Failure to report concerns may bring your fitness to practice into question and endanger your registration.

In straightforward language this means that a nurse is liable to be struck off the register if she accepts poor standards. The real possibility that she may be disciplined, perhaps dismissed, if she feels obliged to publicise such standards is something that the council appears unwilling to tackle. At the hearings I stated that as my representations within the hospital, the health authority and with NHS management had achieved nothing, I felt it not just a right but a duty to bring the continuing shortage of nursing staff at night to a wider audience.

In support of this argument I cited clause 9 of the UKCC code: 'Respect confidential information obtained in the course of professional practice and refrain from disclosing such information without the consent of the patient/client, or a person entitled to act on his/her behalf, except where disclosure is required by law or by the order of a court or is necessary in the public interest'.

Having done just about everything possible to improve the situation but achieved nothing (in fact the staff-to-patient ratio deteriorated), there seemed no alternative but to go public. Using the words of my terms of employment I maintained that the people of the local community, who would in time either become patients on the geriatric wards or see their relatives admitted, had every 'right to know' what was happening. Throughout the case I made it clear that my concern was for those patients on the three wards for which I was responsible and for future patients from the local area. I was not out to make a national or political statement. I believed, and clearly stated at the disciplinary hearings, that the patient whose treatment was at the centre of the action against me, had he lived, would have approved attempts to gain more staff so that never again would a frail, very sick patient be similarly neglected and humiliated. If just one more nurse could have been provided for each geriatric ward at night, the situation would have been resolved.

I was not concerned with intentional neglect or abuse but prepared to challenge the previously accepted norms of care for the elderly. This, it turned out, was something new and unexpected. For decades care of the elderly has been generally considered adequate and non-problematic. Admittedly geriatric medicine was not the first area that keen, ambitious doctors and nurses queued up to enter. But quality of care was seen as acceptable and in places satisfactory. Nurses, apparently, saw no reason to make a fuss, although many privately admitted that standards were poor, at least in the publicly-funded health care sector. Staff who depended on their work for a living in a climate of increasingly uncertain job security, were unlikely to raise questions that could embarrass their managers.

As I have often said, my colleagues were providing the best care possible but could not afford the luxury of upsetting the accepted, if at times threadbare, staffing arrangements. Apart from personal considerations, management's assertion that Stockport was no worse in its staffing quota than other establishments across the country was, for nurses brought up never to question a senior's decision, good enough reason to accept the unacceptable. Herein lies perhaps one fundamental problem for the national body of nurses.

What constitutes acceptable, satisfactory standards of care and who decides? At one time doctors determined the treatment and nurses carried out the care. To the skilled artisans at the bedside this was the unquestioned arrangement. Once decision making and resource allocation started to pass to managers far removed (as much politically and perceptually as geographically) from the wards, clinics and surgeries, those previously in charge began to feel devalued and dispensable. The medical profession has managed to cope with this situation far better than have nurses. Nursing staff no longer feel supported and valued by their superiors; (the appreciation of patients, where it exists, is not enough). So much of what occurs today is out of the nurses' control. As I experienced, there can be regular shortages of linen and other essential items (we even had to beg/borrow shrouds); patients are packed off home, or to the mortuary, with unseemly haste; only one junior doctor, who might have been at work all day/all weekend, is left to minister to 72 elderly patients for 11 hours each night; patient numbers ever increase; too few staff are available and sickness plays havoc with the duty rosters. I do not believe these were problems unique to Stepping Hill.

Perhaps because I had no previous similar experience, I was not prepared to fall in line. The managers and lay administrators did not disagree with the presented facts. What they found they could not handle was (1) my apparent lack of respect for, and compliance with, nursing's traditional deference to authority, (2) my detailed and persistent evidence in support of the claim for more staff, and (3) the notion that the public should be informed what was going on inside the hospital.

By what right did this comparative newcomer think himself able to challenge those who had been quietly keeping the wards ticking over for years? With the financial stringency being forced on health authorities, the last thing management needed was a vocal, workplace agitator rocking the boat. Why was this uppity nurse finding conditions on the wards insupportable when others had worked there tirelessly without complaint for years on end?

♦ ♦ ♦

I was quite aware that there was a larger canvas beyond Stockport. I was told by Peter Greenwood, the editor of the local paper, a man very much with his ear to the ground, that during the exchange of letters with the authority, local MPs, the Department of Health etc, that the chief executive of the health authority was under considerable political pressure (coming right from the top) to keep a lid on things and not to concede any ground. The fact that I was requesting only a small increase in cover with three more nurses each night has, as I always appreciated, wider ramifications.

During my time on the geriatric wards, colleagues from other areas of Stepping Hill – surgery, maternity, paediatrics and psychiatry for example, had spoken approvingly, if quietly, of my efforts and had described their urgent need for improved night nursing cover. For management to admit that the claims being made on behalf of our wards were valid and to provide the staff requested, would be to open the floodgates to equally justified claims, not just from every ward in Stepping Hill Hospital, but from each of the other hospitals in the Stockport area. That in turn could vindicate demands for better provision from every hospital in the land leading to an increased staff bill of millions of pounds and all at a time when cutbacks were the order of the day.

I was aware of the pressures that our (and all) NHS managers were under in their endeavours to make ends meet. The frustrations and difficulties that their heavy responsibilities entailed were very much appreciated throughout the case, but do they not also have consciences? Why were the nurse managers and lay health committee members at Stockport, the local and regional administrators, two MPs, the ward doctors, national nurse leaders and government officials not appalled by what they were informed was happening?

If they were, they never showed or admitted it. Their inability to take action over the nightly neglect is beyond all understanding. That not one of these dozens of people involved, no doubt individually decent, hard working family members, loving towards/ concerned for their own parents and grandparents, could bring him or herself to break ranks and agree that what was reported was unacceptable or at least to initiate an independent inquiry, leaves me dumbfounded.

Possibly, the vital strings were pulled by the managers' and administrators' political bosses, remote and distant in their Leeds or Whitehall offices, but they were surely not all automatons.

The response, though, did appear automatic; disciplinary action against a whistleblower is as predictable as ice at the North Pole. Each health authority/trust has its own disciplinary procedure setting out in detail the required steps to be followed. What appears to have been happening in recent years, especially to those who highlight managements' failings or inadequacies, is that rather than use the less rigorous sanctions (such as counselling, informal warning or first written warning), the heavy-handed approach is employed at the outset with suspension the favourite ploy. No previous oral or written warning is issued. Usually this is coupled with a charge of gross misconduct which carries the penalty of summary dismissal (my situation).

This tactic enables management to remove an employee from the premises, under duress if need be, at a moment's notice without the opportunity to speak to colleagues, to hand over information/ notes or discuss patient care with those taking over his responsibilities, explain or bid farewell to patients and staff or have sight of any material that might assist his defence to the charge(s).

Suspension can be imposed often for months or years on end, on what might seem slender evidence. Dr Wendy Savage, who was suspended by Tower Hamlets Health Authority in 1985, summed up the misuse of suspension when she wrote to the *Guardian* on August 17th, 1990:

> The suspension of Graham Pink from duty will only worsen the chronic understaffing of the geriatric wards which he so eloquently and bravely brought to public attention. Like many of the doctors who have contacted me in the past four years, it seems he is being inappropriately disciplined for openly questioning the way the health service is functioning.
>
> Why do managers bury their heads in the sand when dedicated nurses, midwives and doctors bring these matters to their attention? In what way can this questioning harm patients? Suspension procedures are used arbitrarily, it seems to silence people. Many staff are prevented from coming into the hospital and seeing their colleagues. The managers appear to think that if staff are suspended on full pay, they have nothing to complain of.
>
> If health professionals become unfit to discharge their duties because of illness or addiction to drugs and will not take sick leave, or if some gross error of judgment or negligence involving patient care occurs, suspension as an emergency measure may be necessary while the facts of the matter are clarified.
>
> However the growing practice of suspending from duty those who speak out about the inadequacies of the NHS is an attack on civil liberties.
>
> Suspension was used to silence John Stalker when his inquiries became too close to the truth and uncomfortable for the establishment. I hope the public and the nursing

profession will insist that Mr Pink is reinstated immediately. Or are his managers going to argue that he is a danger to his patients?

The management's power to suspend in the NHS is not open to challenge, is not time limited, is not subject to any justification beyond a manager's say-so. In Stockport an employee was not given the opportunity to question a suspension (always imposed without warning), to see at the time any relevant evidence or discuss the arbitrary decision in any way. The conditions of employment stated that: 'Suspension should only be imposed to enable a thorough examination of the facts to be made and/or when it is clearly undesirable for the employee to remain on duty.' The necessary examination in my case could just as easily, if not more expeditiously and fairly, have been made with me still on duty. Written requests to the hospital manager to justify suspension were ignored. No case was made out to show how my remaining on duty was 'undesirable' (as far as fellow staff or patients were concerned) though it might have proved undesirable to those who were planning my downfall. It seems that an employee has no rights in the matter; all the cards are with the employer.

One accepts that there will be occasions when suspension following allegation of serious misconduct will be fully justified – for instance, where a nurse is accused of striking a patient, of being incapable on duty (from drugs or alcohol) or carelessly neglecting an essential treatment. The right of management to take immediate action without discussion with the accused is clearly necessary, for the protection of the public supersedes all else here. Such cases, though, are rare. Those occasions in recent years where suspension has taken place are all too often similar to mine, where any risk to patients comes not from the suspended nurse or doctor but from the action/inaction of management.

Unless one has experienced suspension at first-hand it must be difficult to appreciate the very serious and damaging effects it has on an employee. You are removed from the advice of those who may be supportive; you no longer have access to documentation and/or witnesses perhaps essential for the defence; you feel (and you are) isolated, powerless and alone and may find that colleagues whom one thought would rally round have in fact been ordered not to make contact – an edict seen by even experienced nurses as carrying the force of a Papal decree. After perhaps a lifetime of successful, positive and harmonious employment, it is a most debilitating experience, leaving one distressed, bewildered, embarrassed and confused. It seems incredible that trade unions and regulatory bodies appear willing to accept this absolute managerial power without question. The suspended person is filled with doubt and despondency at having been so effectively, and surely designedly, wrong-footed. From my personal experience (and discussion with many people so treated) I know the wretched feeling of helpless abandon from which many suspended employees never recover.

There is a belief among many employees that the effective long-stop to management's excesses is the industrial tribunal. Sadly this is not so. The major limitation of the system is that while the tribunal, having heard all the evidence, has the power to order the employer to reinstate the sacked employee, it has no power to see that the order is carried out and an employer may, and almost invariably does, refuse to take back the former employee despite, as with Stockport, throwing in the towel and withdrawing from the proceedings.

During the hearing, the manager was obliged to concede that the authority had knowingly disregarded its own disciplinary procedure. Had it been adhered to, I could not have been dismissed. The tribunal decision reads, in part:

> The respondents sent a letter to the tribunal...indicating that they now conceded that the applicant was unfairly dismissed... and saying that they proposed to submit that reinstatement or re-engagement were impracticable.

This situation does appear to contradict what is right and moral. No doubt some employees would not wish to return to their previous position, believing either that the atmosphere would be hostile or that they could, legally, be made redundant before too long; but the opportunity should be available for those who prove their case for unfair dismissal before a tribunal, to return to work if they so wish. The fact that less than 5 per cent of unfairly dismissed employees are reinstated illustrates the gaping injustice in the legislation.

What this case demonstrates is that an employer can set out to remove an employee in the sure knowledge that once dismissed, justly or otherwise, there in no way that he can regain his post. The sole penalty for the employer will be a financial one. The only sanction the legislation allows is the award of compensation that bears little relevance to the real losses involved. This allows an unprincipled trust or authority manager to be rid of any employee for any reason, genuine or specious, for a paltry payment of a few thousand pounds. The cost comes out of public funds and, one suspects, gains the manager concerned the thanks and approbation of his executive. I am in no doubt that, having had considerable experience in disciplining employees, Stockport Health Authority took the cynical decision to suspend and dismiss me in the sure knowledge that there was no way that I could regain my post. Once removed, the employee is without redress and the employer faces no legal restraint.

Perhaps some nurses viewed the outcome of my case as a moral victory but others, and one suspects the majority, saw it, as I did, an empty victory. What it did, as the establishment intended from the outset, was to send out a warning to other healthcare staff concerned with falling standards, or who were thinking about questioning their employers' decisions. It is no doubt comforting to be vindicated but the edge is somewhat taken off the 'victory' when you have no job, no livelihood, are massively out of pocket and know that no health authority in the country would consider offering you work.

◆ ◆ ◆

The many dilemmas and difficulties that this case has brought into the open (and which I have explored in some depth elsewhere[3]) are now beyond my influence, and were in any case, never the prime concern. My sole intention throughout was to improve the care of the elderly patients and those who were to come after. In that I failed. Whether I went about it in a clumsy, naïve manner, is open to discussion. When pressed, as so often I am, to say whether I would do the same again (in truth, an impossible question) I can give no other answer than, 'yes; I did what seemed right'. That I did not achieve my goal was most disappointing, but at least I tried. I did my best which, when it comes down to it, was all I could do.

---

3   *The Disclosure of Iniquity – Speaking Out in the Health Service.* A thesis submitted to the University of Manchester for the degree of PhD, 1998.

TWENTY
POSTSCRIPT

Hospitals are "very bad places" to care for frail, elderly patients and new ways must be found to treat them in the community. A revolution is needed in the way the health service cares for Britain's ageing population — **Sir David Nicholson, head of the NHS Commissioning Board, (The Independent, 21.01.2013)**

The NHS has been through major upheaval since the late 1980s and we have seen how badly things can go wrong if staff are not enabled to speak out about deficiencies and mistreatment – particularly when it comes to hospital care. This book has highlighted some of the many obstacles that prevent nurses raising genuine concerns.

The registered nursing workforce is a body of some 670,000 people (average age 38, predominantly female) largely committed and hard working but in my opinion conspicuously an apolitical, conforming group.

At the moment it is possible for untrained and unqualified men and women to come into the health service as nursing assistants and, within a very short time, find themselves carrying out tasks and duties that, to be properly undertaken, demand considerable knowledge and expertise.

This was the situation at Stepping Hill Hospital when untrained staff were left at night in charge on their own of a ward full of very sick, often dying, people. As former RCN general secretary Trevor Clay put it:

> It is plainly wrong from both the patients' and the staffs' point of view that people can virtually walk in off the streets to work closely with extremely sick or dependent patients in the ward setting. Yet this is often precisely what happens – with any form of training or even induction being comparatively rare (Clay, 1987, p103).

Throughout recent years nurses have appeared to be overwhelmed by the speed of change and their own inability to influence the reforms, their own situation or their patients' treatment. It is the exception for nurses to be appointed to trust executives and very few are to be found in overall charge of hospitals.

Intentionally or otherwise, a climate of avoidance (many believe fear) has developed, making free speech within the health service a risky business. A former editor of the British Medical Journal illustrated the point:

> Last year I wrote an editorial on free speech but was stopped from publishing it. Our lawyers and insurers advised against publication. Speaking up on deficiencies within a hospital was once a public duty; now it is viewed as a betrayal of the competitive interest of the NHS trust (Smith, 1994, p1644).

The NHS reforms claimed to be putting the patient first and making 'quality' of care their priority. But many nurses have become demoralised and frustrated, as the previous pages described, because their once near-impeccable standards have too often had to be jettisoned to cope with the workload.

If the health service has been reluctant to accept that there is a need for greater openness and accountability, there are signs that business, some of whose practices the health trusts have been so eager to emulate, is becoming more aware of its ethical obligations.

Codes of ethics are being adopted and employees encouraged to report malpractice, particularly in the United States. In this country, the John Lewis Partnership sets an excellent example. The company has 32 registrars who act as confidential counsellors to employees. Workers with grievances have the right to visit a registrar (at another branch if they prefer) and at the employer's expense. The company publishes a weekly paper, *The Gazette*, and anyone can write to the editor, anonymously if preferred, criticising any part of the partnership's operations or institutions, demanding explanation and correction. And the managers, from the chairman downwards, have to reply in full immediately.

The roots of so many nurses' attitude – 'ours not to reason why' – are manifold. The nature of the work and the clients' dependency, the power of the doctors, the makeup of the workforce, the public's regard for nurses (at least up until recently) plus a lack of strong leadership, have led to an overdisciplined and cowed workforce. I notice nurses' hats are making a comeback in some quarters. As one nurse once said to me: 'With our pinnies and frilly hats we have been dressed since time was as domestic servants; no wonder it is assumed we know our place.' Can we be surprised, then, that history suggests that nurses are self-abnegating, inarticulate and relatively few have emerged as whistleblowers. If nurses continue to be kept firmly in their place they will not feel able to blow the whistle on neglect or to take on the task that one or two have attempted, that of seeking to act as patients' genuine advocates, trying to raise standards of care, locally if not nationally, and exert some influence, however limited, in the management of the health service.

Of course, nurses are not alone in their reserve and reluctance to step out-of-line. The propriety of non-interference is built into both our cultural norms and our language with such sayings as 'it's nothing to do with me'; 'don't interfere'; 'mind your own business'.

So many of those involved in the Stockport case, nurses, doctors, administrators, civil servants, politicians and government spokespeople knew in detail what was happening to the elderly patients at night. But they believed, one can only presume, that it was not any of their concern; their job was to support the status quo, to plod on regardless. They did not, as far as I knew, initiate action intended to deprive patients of proper care. They just, by and large, accepted no responsibility, took no action and passed by on the other side.

If nursing wishes to change its role and image, and until very recently there has been little if any evidence that this is so, much has to be done. The problem is multifaceted but perhaps a start should be made upgrading the entrance qualifications for nurse training. There are currently no national minimum academic entry requirements into nursing courses so each higher education institution sets its own criteria. The general prerequisite is five GCSEs, plus two or sometimes three A levels or equivalent; and even this requirement, so a nurse tutor informed me some years ago, is selectively waived when applications fall. Until the starting levels are set nationally at three good 'A' levels for everyone (the required entrance standard for those entering physiotherapy training), there is limited hope of producing sufficiently intelligent, autonomous nurses ready, when the need arises, to confidently challenge the system (including their own nurse managers). Only with better educated nurses can the culture of deference and conformity be undermined and perhaps in time swept away. In the shorter term, perhaps we need to look to further legislation for relief. We may have freedom of information but, certainly in the health service, freedom of expression remains elusive.

During the 1990s a number of members of parliament attempted to introduce reform of employment legislation aimed to protect whistleblowers from harassment, victimisation or dismissal. These moves were brought to fruition with Mr Richard Shepherd's 'Public

Interest Disclosure Act 1998'. Now a number of employers have initiated internal processes to deal with employees' serious concerns though in 2010 the highly regarded charity, Public Concern At Work, found that only 38 per cent of those people surveyed worked for such companies and only 23 per cent were aware that legal protection even existed. In November 2011 Cathy James, the charity's chief executive stated that the legislation 'did not provide adequate protection to whistleblowers and should be reviewed'.

The 1988 act was a step in the right direction, but has come under some criticism as it does not force employers to have a disclosure policy nor prevent them from 'blacklisting' and refusing to hire known whistleblowers. Nor does the act alter suspension practices whereby, as the writer to his considerable detriment experienced, one is invariably given no notice of the suspension, which can continue for years, no evidence to support the reason for the action need be provided, managements' *ipse dixit* being all that is required, leaving the worker at a massive disadvantage. Speaking on the BBC programme *NHS Whistleblowers* in the *The Report* series on July 7th 2011, Ms James, stated that MPs had in the past expressed concern over the number of NHS employees being suspended, adding that 'in 2010 suspensions cost the NHS 20 million pounds'. The programme also revealed that in the same year foundation trusts alone had paid £2.5 million in pay-offs to staff.

The writer's experience, and that of other better-informed observers, is that too often nurses will not take the risk of stepping out-of-line to either tackle management, or inform patients or relatives what they know in their heart of hearts to be unacceptable. The BMA could be right when it states: 'It may be considered an offence to conceal information about a serious crime and doctors have little problem in judging whether to co-operate with police or other authorities when information clearly concerns lives being put at risk.' Over recent years, however, the evidence suggests that nursing staff have the greatest difficulty in judging when to put the risk to patients' lives above other concerns.

Most UK citizens imagine that in this country we have freedom of expression, although this is not enshrined in statute as it is with many other nations. The European Convention on Human Rights (Article 10) states: 'Everyone has the right to freedom of expression. This right shall include freedom to hold opinions and to receive and import information and ideas without interference by public authority.' It is debatable whether we in Britain truly have either freedom to express our opinions or the right to freedom of information. If a health worker discusses in public what he or she has learned during employment, perhaps believing that the public, especially local people, have a right to know what is going on behind the ward doors, the intervention by the health authority will usually be swift and severe, though neither official secrets nor patient confidentiality is involved. The iron fist of management has in recent years borne down on those 'troublemakers'. NHS managers would not, one presumes, agree with Lord Denning that:

> There are some things which are of such public concern that the newspapers, the press, and indeed everyone is entitled to make known the truth and to make fair comment on it. This is an integral part of the right of free speech and expression. It must not be whittled away. (Fraser v Evans [1969])

Britain is still a very secret society. Freedom of information may be in sight; freedom of expression is a little further away. Section 2 of the Official Secrets Act of 1911 presents a legal barrier to proper freedom of information by leaving the dissemination of information in the possession of the government to the discretion of ministers. There is only a limited legal right to know. Yet many believe that only with greater openness can people be assured that those who act on their behalf are behaving honestly and competently.

Lord Scarman (1984) had clear views:

> Ours is a free democratic society. Its freedoms and its democracy depend on certain civil rights, of which the most relevant are the citizen's right to the free expression of his own opinions; his right to participate via the secret ballot in the choice of his government; the right to criticise the government in action and to lobby Parliament. The law should recognise and enforce a right to receive as well as a right to impart information... a free democratic society requires that the law should recognise and protect the right of the individual to the information necessary to make his own choices and decisions on public and private matters, to express his own opinions, and be able to act to correct injustice to himself or his family. (Scarman, p74)

◆ ◆ ◆

The experiences on which this book was based raised for the author a number of important ethical and legal dilemmas that in the past most nurses may seldom if ever have faced in their nursing lives. They raise complex and contentious, often disturbing, questions which this brief account has not attempted to discuss. It is left to the reader to engage with the narrative provided and draw what conclusions he or she considers the evidence merits. My overarching consideration throughout, though, was to bring to the public's attention the neglect and abuse of the patients in my care. The ensuing discovery that while senior nurses obviously accepted or at least turned a blind eye to the conditions, while most bedside staff were not prepared to discuss let alone disclose the patent lack of care and dignity the elderly patients were offered, was to me an unacceptable enigma. Thus it was that these two aspects – the care of the elderly in hospital and the lack of freedom of speech for employees of the health service have dominated my concerns.

It may be apposite here to state unequivocally my belief (shared, I am sure, by the mass of British people) that the standards and practice of health care in this country are, in the main, first rate and surpassed by few other nations. Up until the disturbing events at Stafford Hospital, the NHS was held in high regard and trusted since its inception. It has always been my belief that the standards of most nurses and nursing assistants, given adequate staffing and strong, first-rate leadership by senior nurses, is of a very high order indeed. Even where staff coverage is at times below par, the best nurses/assistants do cope remarkably well, as I witnessed night after night on the Stepping Hill wards. We are fortunate indeed to be so expertly cared for, most of the time. Perhaps from a number of standpoints I am well placed to make this claim, raised as I was in a large workingclass family (five children and granny) through-out the 1930s and 1940s, well before the universal health benefits taken for granted today. With father on £5 a week or less, I recall the difficulties my mother faced juggling sickness with doctors' and dentists' bills. As Melvin Bragg commented in his film, 'The Birth of the NHS', before the birth of the service 'you either paid for health care, relied on charity or, in many cases, went without'.

Within just over a year of the inauguration of the NHS in July 1948, my training commenced and I qualified as a state registered nurse (SRN) in September 1952. My 14 years' experience as a staff nurse/charge nurse included a number of specialties in a variety of private, state and military hospitals, plus a year working in two hospitals overseas. Now in my later years I have benefited from health care in hospital and the community. Thus my view of our health facilities over the past seven decades is soundly based and leaves me in no doubt that we provide superb care for most of the people most of the time. Today the NHS treats three million people a week at a total yearly cost of £106 billion. This needs to be kept in mind as we look more closely at the fraction of situations, increasingly involving the elderly, which give cause for profound disquiet.

Following the high profile coverage by the media of the Stockport case, I was asked to speak at gatherings of nurses up and down the country. The reception was overwhelmingly supportive with staff, often it seemed for the first time, feeling able to unburden themselves of distressing and unacceptable situations in which they had been placed due to staff shortages. Once only (despite my encouraging audiences to speak their minds and be as critical of my actions as they wished) did a nurse express clear condemnation. 'By your behaviour,' she said, 'you have done untold harm to nurses throughout the land. By speaking out as you have, you have made it impossible for any nurse in this country ever again to put her head above the parapet.'

Invariably, someone would ask if I thought my stand would lead to more humane elderly care and a positive response to nurses' concerns over standards of care, to which I could only answer that the evidence did not so suggest. Rather the opposite I thought. At this observation my listeners mildly chided me for being too pessimistic and that, as one nurse put it: 'Just you wait; in ten years you'll be able to look back and see huge improvements your case and others have brought about.' Of course, the speaker had not experienced the overweening arrogance of nurse and lay managers, the total indifference of health service administrators and dismissive waffle of government spokespeople as had I, as had Drs Wendy Savage and Helen Zeitlin. Dr Savage's letter to the *Guardian* in March 1991 said it all:

> Why do managers see it as a crime when doctors like Dr Zeitlin or nurses like Graham Pink speak out about the drop in provision of nursing staff with consequent fall in

standards of care?... what has happened to honesty and openness in the NHS managerial system? Why is so much of the material classed as confidential when it has nothing to do with individual patients but is the concern of us all? It is our health service, is paid for with our taxes and we have a right to know that managers are using our money wisely. To whom are they accountable?

Time, perhaps, to see how the two major concerns set out above have fared in the two decades since I was last at the bedside. Both topics have received extensive media coverage in recent years. In fact, barely a week passes without a report on television, radio or in the press of some hospital/nursing home in trouble over poor care, relatives up in arms over the apparent neglect of their (more often than not elderly) loved ones, nurses being criticised or disciplined for speaking out about what they have witnessed, of staff shortages, deterioration of standards and so on. In fact, there seems to have been a never-ending stream of such reports.

Let us first look at the situation facing those who have dared to stand up and speak out. Whether Mr Richard Shepherd's bill giving legal protection to whistleblowers has improved the situation is far from clear, since it is only, or mainly, those cases where disputes fail to be resolved that gain media coverage. And in recent years there has been a veritable tidal wave of such cases.

The headlines of a tiny sample of the articles/reports speak for themselves:

'Nursing staff too afraid to speak out on standards of care'
'Climate of fear stops nurses speaking out'
'Whistleblowers left to stand alone'
'Why I became a whistleblower at the Care Quality Commission'
'Nurses fear to speak out as patients suffer'

'Whistleblower nurses faced daily personal insults'
'NHS bosses ignore whistleblowers' (See References)

There have been a number of high-profile cases. Margaret Haywood, a nurse of 20 years standing, was dismissed from her post at the Royal Sussex Hospital, Brighton after carrying out secret filming for the BBC's *Panorama* programme screened in July 2005. At her Nursing and Midwifery Council hearing in April 2009 it was accepted that there was a 'failure to deliver basic nursing care' to patients close to death, rendering many of their lives miserable. Having watched the film and been profoundly disturbed by what it revealed, I would say the council's skill at glaring understatement is prodigious. To the surprise, indeed horror, of the British public, Ms Haywood was struck off the register. Such was the outcry that, with the support of the Royal College of Nursing, she was reinstated within a matter of months. I would be most surprised, however, if any other hospital in the UK would offer her a nursing post.

In May 2009 the college launched a dedicated telephone line to allow members to talk in confidence about their serious worries. The RCN chief executive and general secretary, Dr Peter Carter, said:

> We've had laws protecting whistleblowers for ten years now; however they're not worth the paper they're written on if they sit in a drawer and gather dust. If trusts want to avoid another Mid-Staffs they need to make every nurse aware of the protection that the law gives when they raise concerns about patient safety.

Following the case of Ms Haywood, the RCN held a survey to seek members' experiences of raising concerns. A total of 5,428 nurses responded. The results found that 99 per cent understood it was their responsibility to raise concerns yet only 43 per cent would be confident to report them without thinking twice. Those who said that they feared being victimised or saw a negative effect on their career if they spoke out about poor practices on patient safety stood at 78 per cent, while 21 per cent had been told by their superiors not to report concerns or have been discouraged from doing so.

Mature nursing student Barbara Allatt who exposed appalling neglect of very sick and elderly patients at the Stafford Hospital in 2010 was taken off her course because, clearly, she refused to remain silent. She reported what she had witnessed to her university tutors, hospital mentors and senior nurses, but no one wanted to know. Eventually, she was left with no option but to resign. Helene Donnelly worked in the Stafford emergency department and told how she was physically threatened by colleagues after raising concerns about standards. The full story of the mid-Staffordshire hospital scandal was exposed in the first Francis Report in 2010 and further brought to public scrutiny in Mr Francis' second report in 2013.

Another disturbing case is that of Dr Kim Holt. The *Telegraph* reported on Dr Holt's predicament on December 6th 2009, in an article headed "'If Great Ormond Street had listened to me, Baby Peter would still be alive", says consultant'. Dr Holt says she and three other doctors repeatedly warned managers at the St Anne's Hospital in Haringey, run by Great Ormond Street hospital, that staff shortages and poor record keeping would lead to a tragedy. She was 'signed off with stress' in April 2006 and kept from work for four years.

Peter Connelly (known as 'Baby P') was a 17-month-old boy who died in London on August 3rd 2007 after suffering more than 50 injuries over an eight-month period. Commenting on this case in *Private Eye* Dr Phil Hammond and Andrew Bousfield observed:

So despite the public interest disclosure act, the efforts of MPs on the public accounts committee and the DoH circular, NHS managers are still hosing down bad news with taxpayers' money, silencing whistle-blowers, signing deals off with the Treasury and escaping any form of accountability.

At the launch in December 2011 of a new group, 'Patients First', set up largely by Dr Holt to support nurses, doctors and managers who have spoken out about patients safety and care, solicitor Richard Stein said: 'The NHS pays lip service to a culture that allows and encourages whistleblowers, but it rarely provides a context in which people feel able to do so.' It is worth noting that reluctance to speak up for what is right is not limited to nursing. Dr Susan Atkins, the service complaints commissioner, speaking on the BBC *Today* programme (31.1.13) ahead of that day's parliamentary debate on the military's alleged failure to deal with complaints of bullying and abuse, said that only one in ten of those who believe they have been bullied or discriminated against come forward to make a formal complaint.

A letter to *The Times* on 3rd February 2013 reads in part:

Bullying continues to be a major problem within the NHS. Some hospital trusts use subtle ways, difficult to expose in law, to make life difficult for staff who genuinely raise concerns. Unless the statutory protection for whistleblowers is strengthened we will continue to have tragedies such as those revealed by the Mid Staffs Inquiry. We request that the Government accepts that the NHS needs to be more open and accountable. There is considerable distress being caused to staff desperate to provide good care for patients.

Dr Kim Holt, founder and chair of Patients First
Professor Sir Brian Jarman, Emeritus Professor and director
Dr Foster unit, Imperial College

In the wake of all the publicity given to doctors and nurses who speak out and the attention politicians are now giving to the subject, I would like to think that in the future there will be a more positive and accepting attitude from NHS managers, both lay and nursing. In October 2011 it was announced that changes in the NHS constitution would 'protect staff who raise concerns about poor patient care'. Speaking at an 'NHS Whistleblowing summit', in May 2012 the health secretary, Andrew Lansley MP, said:

> Patient safety is our number one concern; and every member of NHS staff should feel empowered to raise any concerns, but some, too many, don't – that's why we want staff to feel comfortable to report concerns.

I am, however, less optimistic (as clearly were Mr Lansley and Helene Donnelly who says she was 'too scared to walk to her car after a shift') that nurse colleagues will follow suit. Stephen Moore's experience is so typical of colleagues' response to a fellow nurse who 'steps out of line'. Mr Moore, a mental health nurse from South Oxfordshire speaking at the 2009 RCN congress expressed his concerns that nurses who spoke up about bad practice found themselves victimised by angry fellow nurses. 'Whistleblowing,' he said, 'is often seen in a negative light, as "grassing up" or betraying colleagues, resulting in huge problems for the person' doing no more than speak the truth, adding, 'You can kiss your career goodbye.' Karen Hall, a former scrub nurse at Selly Oak Hospital in Birmingham, alleged in December 2011 that she was forced out of her job after making disclosures about malpractice in operating theatres that senior staff ignored. There is here, I suggest, a massive and urgent task of education for nursing to tackle.

This discussion of dedicated nurses prepared to stand up for better, safer care who are knocked back, or even down, could go

on for page after page after page so prolific have been the whistleblowing episodes of recent years. Hammond and Bousfield may
well be correct when they state that the 'NHS will always need
whistleblowers' since 'Healthcare is complex, rapidly changing and
dangerous; staff are fallible, variably trained and widely spaced;
and demands are huge and resources limited'. Perhaps I am over-
optimistic when I guess that it may be (a) easier and safer from
now on to speak out, and (b) just possibly less necessary to do so
as the public clamour for better patient care grows louder enabling
us to avoid, or at least lessen, the unspeakable events we have been
hearing about now for too long. And it is to this aspect of my personal quest that I now turn.

◆ ◆ ◆

When a country's senior government politician in charge of the
nation's health services, describes the treatment of some patients in
hospitals and care homes as 'shocking and tragic'; when the Patients
Association publishes a dossier describing some care as 'demean-
ing and sometimes downright cruel' with patients said to 'have
been neglected, left in pain and without food and water'; where
descriptions of 'bad care, denials of dignity, unnecessary suffering, care provided far below an acceptable standard' were given to
an inquiry; when a senior parliamentarian states that her husband
died in dreadful circumstances of neglect in a large city hospital;
and, finally, when one reads the newspaper headline: 'Neglected by
lazy: nurses, Kane Gorny, 22, dying of thirst, rang the police to beg
for water', then I for one am prepared to believe that there is something radically wrong with nursing and nurses in some hospitals.

   If the increase in episodes of whistleblowing can be characterised as a tidal wave then that regarding neglect of patients can be
described as a tsunami. Anyone not so convinced need only listen

to the disturbing accounts of relatives like Ann Clwyd. Speaking on the BBC's *The World At One* programme (05.12.12), and repeating the health secretary's words, she said she had witnessed in that hospital (the flagship teaching hospital, the University hospital of Wales in Cardiff) 'coldness, resentment, indifference and even contempt'.

She added, 'My husband died like a battery hen. He died from hospital-acquired pneumonia, and from lack of care and attention. I can't believe anybody calling themselves a nurse could actually let that happen. Nobody should have to die in the conditions like I saw my husband die.'

Speaking later Mrs Clwyd, an MP, said: 'I've had hundreds and hundreds and hundreds of letters from all over the country; the theme is the same. There are some good nurses but there are also some very bad nurses.' She quoted brief extracts from the letters. One read:

> The nursing profession is no longer the caring profession. When I sat at my husband's bedside I did wonder just why some of the so-called nurses bothered to put on their uniforms. The arrogance and indifference of some left me bewildered.

As distressing and unacceptable as this description is, the experience of a single relative alone would be most unreliable in an assessment of the quality of NHS care nationally. But, sadly, Ann Clwyd's anguish is not unique, far from it. Apart from the huge correspondence she refers to (similar to the 3,500 letters I received in the early 1990s), a mass of reported hospital neglect (not to mention that of nursing and care homes) has surfaced thick and fast in the last few years. From the countless number of cases made public, only a few – and without the graphic, heart-rending details – can be mentioned here.

A report in November 2010 from the National Confidential Enquiry into Patient Outcome and Death (NCEPOD) examined the cases of more than 700 patients over the age of 80 who died in hospital within 30 days of surgery. It concluded that two out of three elderly people suffer below-standard care in NHS hospitals. Poor nutrition leading to serious illness was 'very common', but the management of them was extremely poor. Campaigners claimed elderly patients were often condemned to an 'early death' on the wards. Dr Kathy Wilkinson, an anaesthetist, who helped compile the report, said: 'It is shocking that the survey has revealed organisational failures to respond to the suffering of elderly patients. I hope our report is a wake-up call.'

One relative commented:

> Sadly, my own father died of neglect after not being regularly watered, fed, toiletted, etc. He had had a stroke and was unable to do any of these things himself so he was left. The guilt I feel still lives with me 5 years on, and I feel ashamed that we were let down so badly by this third world care our older folks get, who deserve far more dignity than starvation.

The health service ombudsman, Ann Abraham, issued a damning report in February 2011 which found evidence that doctors and nurses denied pensioners food and drink, left them unwashed and in some cases prevented their loved ones being with them when they died. The report disclosed failures in care as well as an attitude that ignores the 'humanity and individuality' of patients and their families. In several cases the ombudsman identified 'casual indifference' of staff and their 'bewildering disregard' for people's needs. In one example, an 82-year-old woman died alone in Ealing Hospital while her husband spent three hours sitting in a nearby waiting room, because staff had forgotten about him. One family member said the maltreatment amounted to 'euthanasia'. Yet none of the trusts identified in the report said that any staff had been sacked, demoted or given warnings over their behaviour, although they insisted 'lessons had been learned' and in some cases re-training given.

That the care of the elderly in particular has a chronic problem with understaffing was emphasised in March 2012 by the Royal College of Nursing which held a survey of 1,700 nurses, 240 of whom were working on wards with older patients. The survey showed that while older people's wards only had one nurse for every nine patients on average, general wards, at 6.7 patients per nurse, and children's wards, at 4.2, were much better staffed. The college looked at the health needs of older people in hospital and identified that they are significantly more complex than the health needs of working-age adults. Yet when older people go into hospital typically they are admitted to wards that have fewer nurses and more untrained staff than other wards.

The highly respected *Guardian* columnist, Simon Jenkins, quoted further from the health ombudsman's report:

> Alfred, 69, "was left sleeping in a chair with dried blood on him... his clothes were not changed...soaked in urine...discharged when too weak to walk...had a heart attack on the way home." Mr D was so dehydrated at Bolton General Hospital "that his tongue was like a piece of dried leather." Mrs R "had no bath or shower in 13 weeks at Southampton hospital and was left for four days with an open wound on her leg."

In December 2012 the Dr Foster research group's annual hospital guide raised concerns that hospitals in England are under so much pressure that patient safety could be at risk. The guide reported that hospitals are 'full to bursting' and bed use is reaching such 'dangerous' levels and staff are struggling to maintain the safety and quality of patients' care.

'In just two years,' *Panorama* disclosed, 'investigators found 492 more deaths at Mid-Staffordshire Hospital than would normally be expected. Many experts believe the real figure could be much higher.' The latest government figures, according to the programme transmitted on 3rd December 2012, 'show that last year nearly 3,000 patients died, while more than 7,500 suffered serious harm because of unsafe care in our hospitals. It's estimated,' said the presenter, Declan Lawn, 'patient safety incidents cost the NHS a staggering £3.2bn. a year.'

A dossier on poor patient care complied by the Patients Association in November 2012 contains some harrowing stories of patients left in soiled sheets, their dignity stripped from them, and others being left for hours in pain, their cries for help ignored. And we must pay tribute to those many members of the general public who, having seen their relatives endure unacceptable conditions in NHS hospital wards, were prepared to go to great lengths to expose the scandals. One such person was Julie Bailey, whose mother was just about to be discharged from Stafford Hospital following a hernia operation in November 2007 when 'she was dropped by a healthcare assistant and her health worsened rapidly'. This it seems fairly quickly brought about her mother's death. Mrs Bailey describes the conditions on the ward where her mother lay:

> All around her were cries of agony from others who were offered little pain relief, let alone comfort or compassion. I had done what I could; emptying bowls of vomit; scrubbing blood from walls; helping a patient onto a commode; washing faeces from the hands of one elderly woman who had been left in the same soiled clothes for four days.

It was Mrs Bailey's tireless efforts that brought about the first inquiry by Mr Robert Francis in 2010. Reading his report now I am struck by the similarity of so much that I experienced and have described above:

> More often were inadequate numbers of staff on duty to deal with the challenge of a population of elderly and confused patients. The inquiry received striking evidence about the incidence of falls, some of which led to serious injury. Many, if not all, took place unobserved by staff and too many were not reported to concerned relatives for too long or only when they saw an injury for themselves. The reason for the incidence of falls and other safety concerns was probably attributable to a combination of a high dependency level among the mix of patients combined with too few staff, or staff not sufficiently qualified to cope.
>
> An atmosphere of fear of adverse repercussions in relation to a variety of events was described by a number of staff witnesses. Staff described a forceful style of management (perceived by some as bullying) which was employed on occasion. Much of management thinking during the period under review was dominated by financial pressures.
>
> It is by no means clear that the only way of finding the necessary savings was to implement a workforce reduction programme. It certainly need not have happened without the involvement of staff and the various departments. Instead, a top-down proposal was launched with departments having to identify cuts to fit the predetermined budget.

◆ ◆ ◆

One glaring question stares us in the face – why has this situation been allowed to develop and why now? In particular, why do some nursing staff appear to be lacking in care, compassion and basic decency? There are, no doubt, a multitude of possible reasons but I can only touch on a few here. But first, let me diminish, if not dismiss, the popular comment that nurses are too well qualified, that a degree (which in any case at the moment only a limited number hold) somehow makes a nurse unwilling/unable to carry out the bedside basics of continence and bladder/bowel care, personal and oral hygiene, nutrition and hydration, pressure area care and so on. This view I deem to be uninformed and naïve, lacking, to the best of my knowledge, evidential support. Once we have some in-depth research, a more enlightened, objective view might emerge. Though (a) my tentative opinion holds that perhaps better educated (not, you appreciate, better qualified) nurses might be a step in the right direction, and (b) where have all the wonderful state enrolled nurses gone? I would advise that immediate thought be seriously given to bringing them back.

The primary reason, however, for the upsurge of accounts of shocking neglect (documented particularly in care of the elderly) must be a lack of sufficient staff. During my visits to hospital wards and clinics in recent years, I have seen some areas apparently well staffed and very occasionally overstaffed. So perhaps, a more intelligent, sensible staff allocation that could ameliorate the pressure on certain wards at certain times would improve the situation slightly. But I am convinced, beyond peradventure, that the essential step that the government has to make is to increase the national nursing workforce by at least 20 per cent. Serious and immediate consideration should also be given to providing training (three months as a minimum, I suggest) for nursing assistants/support workers.

Simon Jenkins in his incisive, perspicacious article takes a close look at the NHS and sees, historic political incompetence, doctors with six-figure salaries, Britain's toughest union as the hospital consultants; a £12 billion computer system that has never worked;

every attempt to reorganise the NHS failing while doctors and management consultants 'lie on the floor, groaning with the money stuffed into their mouths; Lewis Carroll could not do justice to this story, though George Orwell might'.

As this saga draws to a close there remains but one question we must face and one which I find to be a complete mystery – why would anyone, let alone a person engaged in caring for sick, weak and/or elderly patients, appear to be uncaring, rude, negligent, unkind... you can fill in for yourself the descriptions so frequently attached to nursing staff in recent years.

I have no experience of this attitude in health care. In fact, quite the opposite. The people with whom it was my unalloyed privilege to work at the ward level in Stockport were caring, courteous and efficient to a fault, no matter how tired and stressed they might be. I never ever heard a sharp word or unfriendly comment to a patient. Note my words 'at ward level' for some (to be honest, many) nurse and lay staff in a higher, more remote position did appear, I regret to say, at least uncaring to put it no higher. Thus I am at a loss to offer any explanations for this, to me, utter enigma.

Doubtless being constantly short staffed and run off your feet can lead to some impatience, perhaps occasionally mildly unpleasant behaviour but not the sort of unacceptable attitude patient after patient, relative after relative have complained of. The popular belief is that you cannot teach people care, compassion, understanding, empathy. I am not sure this is true. Nurse training has a part to play here as have ward sisters/charge nurses. With the proper leadership such unsuitable conduct would decline, though no doubt more experienced, more up-to-date and wiser heads than mine will now be put to tackling this problem with the close, intense and immediate attention it deserves. It is time we all listen to what patients and relatives say, offering them the level of care, respect and dignity that once used to be the norm. It must be so.

With this idea in mind, I can do no better than leave the last words to one very eloquent ex-patient, the *Independent* columnist Christina Patterson. Over a period of eight years she underwent six operations in three different hospitals so she knows better than most, and certainly better than most nurses, the standard of hospital care. She explores why nursing sometimes goes wrong, and investigates what can be done to put it right. As she speaks to her fellow patients, healthcare experts, politicians, and doctors, nurses and managers across the NHS, Christina hears about everything from faulty training programmes to inadequate regulatory regimes). In her first talk, rather than berate and openly criticise, she writes in a calm, thoughtful manner, her incise and powerful critique bringing home so vividly what harm bad people can do. She discusses her own experiences of terrible nursing care. She asks why we keep making excuses for bad nursing when good care is so important, and maintains that whatever the pressures, nurses always have a choice about how they behave. I believe that all nursing staff and nursing students should read this piece, as well as anyone considering entering nurse training. Here is a brief extract:

> It was good to know that if, for example, you were still in pain you mustn't make a fuss about it. It was good to know that the nurses who seemed to have time to stand about talking to each other and didn't seem to like their jobs very much, didn't like to be disturbed and if you want to keep them happy the best thing to do was not to ask them for anything and never ever to press the buzzer.
>
> I couldn't understand how they could see people who were suffering and frightened and maybe even dying, and seemed to think they were a nuisance. I couldn't understand how nurses seemed to have time to talk to each other and didn't seem to have the time to answer the buzzer. I

couldn't understand why they didn't want to help. I couldn't understand why you'd be cruel to people if you were doing something you'd chosen to do and were being paid for.

Her parting shot, simple and candid, could not be clearer:

If you can't do it or don't want to do it, or are tired of doing it, or lost your faith in your ability to do it, then, please, for the sake of us all do something else.

GLOSSARY

Atril fibrillation	heart rate irregular both in time and force.
BM stix	blood test for sugar.
BP	blood pressure.
CCF	congestive cardiac failure.
COAD	chronic obstructive airways disease.
CVA	cerebral vascular accident (a stroke).
Dysphagia	difficulty in swallowing.
Dyspnoea	difficulty in breathing.
Emphysema	a chest condition whereby expiration is difficult.
Frequency	urine passed at frequent intervals.
GI	gastro-intestinal.
Haematoma	leakage of blood from a vessel into the tissue.
Hypertension	high blood pressure.
Hemiplegia	paralysis of cerebral origin affecting one half of body
Hypoglycaemia	inadequate level of glucose in the blood.
IVI	intravenous infusion.
LVF	left ventricular failure (heart failure).
Metastases	tumour cells spread and form malignant growths.
MI	myocardial infarction (heart attack).
NBM	nil by mouth.
Nebulizer	drug inhalation via a face mask.
Neuropathy	wasting of muscle, pain in legs and weakness of gait.
Output	urine.
Paget's disease	disease leading to progressive bone thickening and deformation
Parkinsonism	degenerative disorder of nerve cells in the brain.
prn	as necessary.
Pubic ramus	part of hip bone
Pyrexia	rise in body temperature.
Septicaemia	toxins or disease-causing bacteria in the blood.
TPR	temperature, pulse and respiration.
TIA	transient ischaemic attack – loss or diminution of blood supply.
UTI	urinary tract infection.
Warding	when staff are confined to a single ward

REFERENCES

Adams S (2010) Hospitals 'failing' on care of elderly. *The Telegraph.* November 11.

Adams S (2011) Nurses 'discouraged' from whistleblowing, says RCN. *The Telegraph.* December 12.

Adams S (2012) Hospital let Alzheimer's patient walk out to his death. *The Telegraph.* November 22.

Andrews E (2010) Neglected by 'lazy' nurses, Kane Gorny, 22, dying of thirst, rang the police to beg for water. *Daily Mirror.* March 6.

Anonymous (1993) Nursing staff too afraid to speak out on standards of care. *Nursing Times.* 89, 9, 9.

Anonymous (1993) Climate of fear stops nurses speaking out. *Nursing Times.* 89, 44, 6.

Anonymous (1993) NHS staff flood Helpline on work standards. *Nursing Times.* 3, 89, 6.

Anonymous (1997) Nurses complain to UKCC about unsafe staff levels. *Nursing Times.* 93, 6, 10.

Anonymous (2011) Whistleblowing fear grips Scottish nurses. *Nursing in Practice.* December 6.

Agnew T (1992) Doctor claims job lost over support on staffing levels. *Nursing Times.* 88, 33, 6.

Bailey J (2013) Stafford Hospital scandal: the battle by campaigner to shine a light on failings. *The Telegraph.* February 6.

BBC (2012) Ann Clwyd's campaign for compassion in nursing. *The World At One.* December 5.

BBC 2 (2013) The birth of the NHS. *The Reel History of Britain.* February 11.

BBC News (2012) Action urged over 'appalling' NHS care. November 22.

BBC News (2012) Nurses in drive for 'compassionate care'. December 4.

BBC News (2012) Alexandra hospital neglect claims: Jeremy Hunt 'disgusted'. December 23.

BBC News (2013) 17 hospitals with unsafe staffing, says Care Quality Commission. January 13.

BBC News (2013) Wards dangerously understaffed, say nurses. February 3.

Beckford M (2011) NHS shamed over callous treatment of elderly. *The Telegraph.* February 14.

Beckford M (2011) Damning report on elderly health care: the victims. *The Telegraph*. February 14.

Beckford M, Bloxham A (2011) No NHS workers disciplined over neglect of elderly. *The Telegraph*. Febuary 16.

Brindle D (1997) Moves to end NHS secrecy. *The Guardian*. September 10, p6.

Calkin S (2011) Whistleblowing Mid Staffs nurse too scared to walk to car after shift. *Nursing Times*. October 17.

Calkin S (2011) Whistleblowers call for NHS culture change. *Nursing Times*. December 16.

Calkin S (2011) Whistleblowing nurses faced daily personal insults. *Nursing Times*. November 1.

Campbell D (2012) Hunt condemns shocking NHS care exposed in report. *The Guardian*. November 22, p9.

Campbell D (2012) 'Shocking' treatment in NHS hospitals and care homes exposed in report. *The Guardian*. November 22.

Campbell D (2012) Hospitals 'full to bursting' as bed shortage hits danger level. *The Guardian*. December 2.

Campbell D (2012) Dr Foster's report reveals NHS trusts where death rates are 'worryingly high'. *The Guardian*. December 2.

Campbell D (2011) Some elderly patients were given no help to eat, or left in urine-soaked clothes, according to the health service ombudsman. *The Guardian*. February 15.

Campbell D (2012) NHS doctor's view: more admissions, fewer beds – a recipe for chaos. *The Guardian*. February 2.

Casey N (1992) Speak out at your peril. *Nursing Standard*. 6, 49, 3.

Clay T (1987) *Nurses: Power and Politics*. London, Heinemann.

Clwyd A (1997) End Secrecy before it's too late. *The Guardian* (London). May 20, p17.

Daily Record (2012) Whistleblower nurse 'vindicated' as NHS board is blasted over patient deaths in damning report. *Daily Record*. June 13.

Dayani A (2011) Whistleblowing nurse loses constructive dismissal tribunal against Birmingham hospital. *Birmingham Mail*. Decembe 31.

Department of Health (2011) NHS Constitution changes to enshrine whistle-blowing in law. London, DH, October 18.

Dreaper J (2011) NHS staff told to 'report concerns or risk investigation'. *BBC News*. July 26.

Elliott C (2012) Patient dying of thirst rang 999: inquiry hears of mother's fury at nurses who neglected son. *Mail Online*. July 2.

Francis R (2010) *Independent Inquiry into Care Provided by Mid Staffordshire NHS Foundation Trust: January 2005 – March 2009. Volume I.* p20.

Frankel M (1997) Protect the whistleblowers. *The Guardian*. May 8, p16.

Guardian (2011) Patients 'denied water for hours' report. June 16, p16.

Jenkins S (2011) The cure for an ailing, ageing NHS is to cut it down to size. *The Guardian*. February 15.

Jowit J (2013) Cases of neglect exist across the NHS, says Jeremy Hunt. *The Guardian*. January 20.

Gray R (2011) Third of nurses told they should not 'whistleblow'. *Herald Scotland*. December 5.

Hammond P, Bousfield A (2011) Shooting the messenger – how NHS whistleblowers are silenced and sacked. *Private Eye*, Special Report. June 4.

Hennessy P (2013) Seventeen NHS hospitals have dangerously low numbers of nurses. *The Telegraph*. October 12.

Hope J (2010) Neglect of the elderly who die in NHS hospitals. *Mail Online*. November 11.

Lakhani N (2011) Whistleblowers not protected from bullying, court rules. *The Independent*. October 31.

Laurance J (1997) Bullied nurses suffer in silence. *The Independent* (London). May 21, p10.

Laurance J (2009) Whistleblower nurse struck off over BBC film. *The Independent*. April 17.

Lawn D (2012) How safe is your hospital? *Panorama, BBC1*. December 3.

Linsie J (1995) I was sacked for defending parents' right to know. *The Whistle*. 3, 7, 7-8.

Lintern S (2012) NHS faces a nursing shortage, review for RCN warns. *Nursing Times*. October 22.

Macdonald V (1996) Helpline shows widespread abuse of aged. *Sunday Telegraph* [London]. June 16, p4.

Moloney M (1986) *Professionalization of Nursing.* JB Lippincott, Philadelphia PA.

Murphy K (2011) NHS Ombudsman's report: how many times do we need to hear it? *The Telegraph*. February 14.

Patterson C (2011) Care to be a nurse? BBC *Radio 4*. April 27,

Patterson C (2013) Care to be a nurse? BBC *Radio 4*. January 9.

Royal College of Nursing (2009) RCN launches phone line to support whistleblowing nurses. *RCNOnline*. May 11.

Scarman L (1984) *The Right to Know*. Granada Publishing, London.

Schlesinger F (2010) The nurse victimized for being a whistleblower: trainee thrown out after exposing abuse at shamed hospital. *Mail Online*. May 15.

Sheard S (1994) Gagging public health doctors. *British Medical Journal*. 309, 17, 1643-1644.

Sheldon K (2012) Why I became a whistleblower at the Care Quality Commission. *The Guardian*. January 24.

Smith R (1994) An unfree NHS and medical press in an unfree society. *British Medical Journal*. 309, 1644-1645.

Snell J (1993) *Whistleblowers Left To Stand Alone. Nursing Times*. 89,22, 9.

Snell J (1993) Research shows 25% want to quit nursing. *Nursing Times*. 89, 39, 6.

Telegraph (2011) Patients 'denied water for hours'. *The Telegraph*. June 16.

Triggle N (2012) Low staffing levels 'harms elderly care'. *BBC News*. March 20.

Triggle N (2012) Why can't the NHS get basic care right? *BBC News*. November 22.

Triggle N (2012) Action urged over 'appalling' NHS care. *BBC News*. November 22.

Triggle N (2013) Cameron: long way to go on NHS care. *BBC News*. January 4.

Whyte A, Waters A (2012) Speaking the truth. *Nursing Standard*. April 18.

Williams R (2012) Jeremy Hunt 'disgusted and appalled' by reports of neglect at hospital where elderly man died of starvation. *The Independent*. December 23.

Young S (1993) Nurses fear to speak out as patients suffer. *The Observer* (London). April 19, p7.